RECONCILIATION

Edited by Oliver Rafferty SJ

Reconciliation
ESSAYS IN HONOUR OF
MICHAEL HURLEY

THE COLUMBA PRESS
DUBLIN 1993

This edition, 1993, published by
THE COLUMBA PRESS
93 The Rise, Mount Merrion, Blackrock, Co. Dublin, Ireland

Cover by Bill Bolger
Origination by The Columba Press
Printed in Ireland by
Genprint Ltd., Dublin

ISBN: 1 85607 069 7

Contents

Preface

I should like to express my gratitude to my fellow contributors for their kindness and forbearance throughout the long process of preparing the articles in this Festschrift for publication.

The Irish Province of the Society of Jesus generously provided a subvention towards the cost of producing this volume, and my special thanks therefore go to Fr Philip Harnett S.J., sometime Provincial, for his encouragement in my undertaking the project.

My colleague Fr Philp Endean S.J. gave me the benefit of his incisive judgment on many points and assisted in the proof reading.

It is with great sadness that I record the death of Rev A. T. Hanson, former Professor of Theology at the University of Hull, and a close friend of Fr Hurley's over many years. Professor Hanson had undertaken to write for this collection but was unable to make much progress before his final illness. He provided me with very valuable information on Fr Hurley's early years as an ecumenist and I have incorporated some of this into the introduction.

Oliver Rafferty S.J.
Campion Hall & Christ Church
Oxford
St Patrick's Day, 1993

Introduction

The Rev Michael Hurley SJ was born in May 1923 at Ardmore Co Waterford. His early schooling was entrusted to the monks of the Cistercian Monastery of Mount Mellary. It was there that Dr Hurley was first attracted to the priesthood, and it will perhaps surprise even those who know him well to realize that he was deeply attracted to the harsh asceticism of the Trappists. However the Jesuits finally claimed his affections and he entered the Society of Jesus in September 1940.

He read classics at University College Dublin, graduating in 1945, and then proceeded to studies at the Jesuit Faculty of Philosophy in Tullamore, where he was awarded a licentiate in philosophy in 1948. He then passed three years at a boarding school in Mungret Co Limerick where he taught Greek and Latin. But in those days he was also interested in the social teaching of the Catholic Church and his instructing students in this area led to charges of Marxism being levelled against the content of his courses by some of his confrères. This was exacerbated by a one-day 'hunger strike' which some of his students undertook in protest at the general conditions they suffered in the school.

From 1951 to 1955, Michael Hurley studied theology in Louvain and was there ordained to the priesthood by Cardinal Suenens in 1954. Despite his earlier interest in social questions, which perhaps indicated a life given over to teaching at the Jesuit-run College of Industrial Relations in Dublin, Fr Hurley was appointed in 1958 to teach theology at the Jesuit theological college, Milltown Park, Dublin. He had by then embarked on research for a doctorate in theology which was awarded by the Gregorian University in Rome in 1961.

It was around this time, and as a result of accidentally being assigned to give a public lecture on Christian Unity, that Fr Hurley began to develop a serious interest in ecumenics. This grew throughout the 1960s and reached its climax by the beginning of the next decade when Fr Hurley founded the Irish School of

Ecumenics. The School was designed as an interchurch institute for research and postgraduate teaching and was opened in November 1970 by the General Secretary of the World Council of Churches, the Rev Dr Eugene Carson Blake. By then sectarian strife and political violence were once again rife in Northern Ireland, and it was one of the hopes of the school to unite christians in a common witness against the intolerance and chaos then so prevalent on the streets of northern towns and cities.

In 1971, Michael Hurley succeeded in affiliating the School of Ecumenics with the University of Hull, a partnership which was to last until 1983 when the School became associated with Trinity College, Dublin. Throughout the 1970s, under Michael Hurley's careful guidance, the School of Ecumenics attracted an international student body, and developed a diploma course and a certificate course in addition to the Master's Degree programme. The certificate course was of particular significance in that it was offered in both Belfast and Derry, and it was finally brought under the Adult Education umbrella of the University of Ulster. All these courses included interfaith issues, justice and peace concerns and fieldwork components, in addition to interchurch questions.

In the 1970s the School of Ecumenics undertook two major research projects and sponsored two international consultations, one on Mixed Marriages in 1974 and the other on Human Rights in 1979. The proceedings of both consultations were published: *Beyond Tolerance, The Challenge of Mixed Marriages* (London, 1975) and *Understanding Human Rights, An Interdisciplinary and Interfaith Study* (Dublin, 1980).

Fr Hurley's teaching, in both Milltown Park and the Irish School of Ecumenics, was supplemented by many lecturing and speaking engagements in Ireland and overseas. His travels took him to such divers places as Reykjavik and Rome, Ottawa and New Orleans, Melbourne and Minneapolis. The main Irish theological centres, Maynooth and the Presbyterian Assembly's College in Belfast, also hosted him. Owing to differences of opinion within the Presbyterian Church at the time, the latter engagement had the unfortunate consequence that both the College authorities and Fr Hurley were arraigned before the General Assembly of the Church. The motion of censure was, however, lost.

By the end of the 1970s, Fr Hurley had decided to retire from his post as the director of the School of Ecumenics, and his place was taken by an Irish Presbyterian with many years of experience in India and Australia, the Rev Dr Robin Boyd.

It was during a sabbatical year, 1980-81, in the course of which he travelled extensively in Africa and Asia, that Michael Hurley conceived the idea of establishing an interchurch residential community in Northern Ireland. On his return to Ireland he spent two years in a feasibility study exploring the possibility for such a venture and consulting widely with the main Churches in Ireland and Britain. As a result of this he founded the Columbanus Community of Reconciliation, which was formally inaugurated on the feast of St Columbanus in 1983.

The Columbanus Community aims to counteract the sectarianism, poverty and violence of Northern Ireland by a shared witness in which Anglicans, Protestants and Roman Catholics live a life of unity and simplicity in prayerful surroundings, in which cross- community contact is enabled to take place.

Fr. Hurley intends to retire from the Columbanus Community in 1993 at the age of seventy. This is a fitting occasion for the presentation of this *Festschrift* in his honour, in grateful acknowledgement of the work that he done in the cause of Christian Unity.

II

The papers in this collection are grouped into three sections, and cover the three areas that are seen to be at the heart of the ecumenical enterprise. Reconciling Churches, dealing with interchurch dialogue; Reconciling Faiths, which considers inter-faith dialogue; and Reconciling Memories, dealt with here by the inclusion of several papers on important historical topics. All these reflect the main concerns of Michael Hurley over many years of active engagement in ecumenical work.

Dr Mary Tanner's essay, which opens the collection, stresses the need for united Christian witness in situations of conflict and diversity in today's world. Such testimony is evangelical in nature, so that 'the world might believe.' The scandal of Christian disunity is exacerbated by the fact that the world as a whole is struggling to come together, and yet Christians seem almost content to live with their divisions. Dr Tanner looks at the unity statement of the 1991 General Assembly of the World Council of Churches as a way forward for Church Unity. She provides a detailed and helpful examination and critique of the Canberra Assembly's final statement 'The Unity of the Church as koinonia: Gift and Calling.'

Dr Tanner's remarks can be taken to be a reflection on the whole state of inter-church dialogue, whereas Dr Edward Yarnold confines his attention to the relationship between the Anglican and Roman Catholic Churches. His task is to offer an outline of both Anglican and Roman Catholic responses to the work of the two ARCIC commissions. Whilst concentrating in detail on the Roman Catholic response to ARCIC, he also compares this with the Roman Catholic reaction to the World Council of Churches' agreed statement on Baptism, Eucharist and Ministry.

Dr Yarnold scrutinizes the points raised by the Sacred Congregation for the Doctrine of the Faith in response to the Final Report of ARCIC I, and questions whether the criticisms offered are fair and helpful. In comparing the official Roman Catholic attitude to the Final Report and the work of ARCIC II with its response to BEM, he concludes that the Roman Catholic authorities are less critical of BEM than of ARCIC. Fr Yarnold suggests that this may reflect, ironically, the greater possibility of union on the basis of the work of ARCIC than of BEM.

For his part, Professor Geoffory Wainwright does for Methodist-Roman Catholic relations what Fr Yarnold's essay does for Anglican-Catholic dialogue. Dr Wainwright sketches the twenty-five year history of the bilateral talks and indicates where the convergence lies, and what outstanding difficulties remain. There are no prizes for guessing that the papacy is a major obstacle, but it will surprise many readers unfamiliar with the state of the Methodist-Roman Catholic talks to know in how positive a light Methodists regard the role that the papacy might have in a reunited Christendom.

One further difficulty that Professor Wainwright touches on is the question of Marian dogma in Roman Catholic theology, and the place of Mary in Catholic devotional life. This is the subject matter of Dr Christopher O' Donnell's paper. To say the least, the idea of the Virgin Mary as a helpful focus for ecumenical discourse is one that does not often capture the attention of Protestant ecumenists. Of course the Ecumenical Society of the Blessed Virgin Mary has laboured strenuously over the years to reduce tension in the ecumenical world on this sensitive and important issue.

Fr O'Donnell argues that the magisterial reformers were perhaps not as negative in their attitude to Mary, seen within the context of the communion of saints, as the second generation of reformers proved to be. Dr O'Donnell contends that it is in the area of spirituality that the way forward in this ecumenically difficult field is to be found.

There then follow three essays which form almost a sub-group within the overall theme of this section. All are concerned in one way or another with the relationship between ecumenism and the desire for justice in the world. Professor José Míguez Bonino is anxious to address the relationship between the Judeo-Christian faith and a commitment to work for human rights in the Church and in the world. Dr Gabriel Daly focuses more explicitly on how the Roman Catholic Church and the World Council of Churches have taken up the theme of justice as an integral component of the Christian message. He also takes the argument one stage further and places the ecological movement firmly within the 'oikoumene' of the theological and ecumenical enterprise. Fr Daly spends some time developing his reflections on the WCC theme of 'Justice, Peace and the Integrity of Creation'.

Dr Emilio Castro brings this section to an end by emphasising the missionary heart of the Church's vocation. Missionary activity must be linked to a solidarity with the poor, who are often, because of their poverty, the very people denied knowledge of the saving message of the good news.

But what status can now be given to evangelization in the midst of a plurality of religions? Are not individuals 'saved' in and through the faith they actually possess, be that Judaism, Buddhism or Hinduism? What is the future for Christian missionary activity in an ecumenical context which accepts and respects the religious experience of non-christians? These are some of the questions explored in the section on interfaith dialogue.

Professor Francis Sullivan's stimulating paper, on the necessity of the Church for salvation, has application for both inter-church and inter-faith dialogue, but it is placed in this section as a bridge paper between both areas. Professor Sullivan skilfully outlines Roman Catholic teaching on this matter, and sees in Vatican II not just a departure from the teaching of Robert Bellarmine and Pius XII, but he also illustrates how that council for the first time in Catholic teaching introduces a new differentiation in ecclesiological status of non-Roman Catholic Christians and people of other faiths.

Dr John May is, like Professor Sullivan, concerned with the connection between interchurch and interfaith dialogue. He questions whether the one poses obstacles for the other. Is the salvific significance of non-Christian religions underlined by the fact that in many places, in Asia for example, Christianity has made but a tiny impact? Dr May offers here an essay in fundamental ecumenics which will doubtless encourage much discussion.

Dr Robin Boyd underlines the importance of interfaith dialogue in the ecumenical process. His essay seeks to complement the World Council of Churches 1990 report, *Church and World*, which perhaps tended to neglect the centrality of inter-faith dialogue. Dr Boyd illustrates the fact that it is only by stressing our Christian heritage that we can offer anything of value to the world. He further argues that neither the communitarian nature of the triune God nor the centrality of Christ can be sacrificed for the sake of dialogue.

Professor Franklin Sherman reflects on one aspect of interfaith dialogue which is as old as Christianity itself, namely the relationship between the Church and Judaism. In recent decades Jewish scholars have been more willing to evaluate the postive contribution that Jesus as a Jew makes to Judaism. Dr Sherman demonstrates that many of the principal ideas in Christianity are also prevalent in Judaism. In focusing on the Jewishness of Jesus we are enabled to appreciate the deep kinship between the two religions. This however is not to deny the fact that in Jewish-Christian dialogue the figure of Jesus represents a profound paradox.

We now pass to the final section of the collection. It is only by an accurate assessment of the past that we can hope to understand the historic division of the Christian Church. Professor Bossy, in his article, which started life as a lecture at the Queen's University Belfast to mark the 450th anniversary of the founding of the Society of Jesus, summarizes the role of the Jesuit order in the Reformation. Although the Jesuits were subsequently to be seen as the archetypal Renaissance men, Ignatius Loyola was rather distrustful of 'evangelical humanism'. Indeed Professor Bossy regards Loyola as more a fifteenth than a sixteenth century man.

Ignatius Loyola was not an ecumenist, but Dr Bossy does point out the similarity of methods for evangelization employed by Loyola's followers and the reformers. He concludes however that such similarities as exist are probably superficial, and that the basic attitude of the Jesuits to the reformation was that they were against it.

One of the first missions undertake by the Jesuits was to Ireland in 1542. More than one hundred years latter a mission of a different sort was embarked upon by Prince William of Orange, to secure his claim to the British throne. It was by no means certain that William would succeed in his designs and his final triumph was as much a matter of luck as of diplomatic and political skill. Dr Patrick Kelly shows the importance of the Williamite campaign for the internal politics governing the relationship between Britain and Ireland, and he also demonstrates Ireland's significance as a theatre of operations for the European conflict between France and her many enemies.

The Church of Ireland has long had a prominent position in Michael Hurley's affections. Fr Oliver Rafferty offers an overview of Gladstone's disestablishment and disendowment of that Church. It was a complex affair motivated in part by ideological and religious principle on Gladstone's part, but also by considerations of political expediency. But Fr Rafferty is inclined to see the charges of inconsistency or of political opportunism, so often levelled against Gladstone, as too simplistic an explanation of the process which brought about the loss of the Church's position in Irish society.

Professor R.F.G. Holmes, in the final paper in the collection, tells the tale of the often bloody and antagonistic attitudes of Catholics and Protestants to the respective States set up as a result of the partition of Ireland. Partition created two minorities in Ireland rather than one and we still live with the consequences of the division of the country. Professor Holmes shows that the Northern State's hostility towards Catholicism was mirrored in part in the early days of the Irish Free State by its treatment of its Protestant minority population.

III

These essays are offered in recognition of the outstanding labour of Michael Hurley as an ecumenist in a working life of more than thirty-five years. They bring together scholars and administrators from very different backgrounds and interests, all of whom have had contact with Fr Hurley, either briefly or of a more sustained nature. Michael Hurley is undoubtedly Ireland's leading ecumenist and has successively encouraged and challenged the ecumenical credentials of all the Irish Churches.

It has been at times a thankless task, and clearly there were moments when Fr Hurley's must have seemed like a voice crying in the wilderness. However his dogged persistence and perseverance have produced results which are a tribute to his singleness of purpose and his ecumenical vocation. These essays are a mark of the esteem in which Fr Hurley is held by many in the Church in Ireland and overseas. It is to be hoped that in spite of his retirement he will continue to work vigourously for the unity of the Churches. To borrow a phrase coined by his close friend, the late Doreen Freer, which in turn is a play on the motto of the Irish School of Ecumenics, *floreas ne pereamus.*

PART I

Reconciling Churches

Towards Visible Unity

Mary Tanner

Recently I was in Jerusalem, the meeting place of the three great Abrahamic faiths: Judaism, Christianity and Islam. I listened to the Archbishop of Jerusalem and the Middle East talk about the intractable problems of his country: the story of a struggle for a rightful and secure home for the Palestinians, a story of violence, poverty, refugee camps. I saw for myself the soldiers, men and women, carrying guns everywhere in the old city – that city of Jerusalem, that city of peace. I saw the degrading refugee camps on the road from Jericho to Galilee as well as the blocks of smart new flats on the commanding hill-tops outside towns like Nazareth. It struck me that at the same time as there are these divisions between Palestinians and Israelis, between Jew and Moslem, between rich and poor, this is also the City where Christians from the East (Greek, Coptic, Armenian, Russian, Syrian, Assyrian, etc) and Christians from the West (Roman Catholic, Anglican, Lutheran, Baptist, Methodist etc) all jostle for a place. The Archbishop explained that what matters in the face of the devastating divisions of the world, in the face of the competing claims of other faiths, is that we Christians witness as Christians together in this place. It does matter that Christians learn to give aid, to share their gifts and their resources as Christians together. The Archbishop seemed so strikingly uninterested in being recognisably Anglican, the English Church in that place. His concern was to be authentically Christian together with other Christians in Jerusalem, preaching a gospel both relevant and at home in Middle Eastern culture.

What the Archbishop was saying seemed to make such obvious and such good sense. What is important in front of the divisions of the world, and at once attuned to particular cultures and challenging to division and brokenness in the human community, is a message that says, 'be Christians with God and each other in authentic Middle Eastern ways' not 'be Christians with God and each other in characteristic Anglican, or Orthodox, or Roman Catholic ways'. What is important is that Christians together say, 'join us as the one body of Christ, witnessing to one God, Father, Son and Holy Spirit, a God who breaks down barriers between us and wills to give the gift of unity to all people'.

As an outsider looking in, I could see in a clear way the stark contradiction between the churches that proclaim Sunday by Sunday their belief in the One, Holy, Catholic and Apostolic Church while continuing to prop up divisions between Orthodox, Catholic, Anglican and Lutheran Christians. All denominational differences in that context appear to be self-indulgent and motivated by self-interest. These continuing divisions contradict the Christian belief in the unity of God's kingdom and the hope for the unity of God's world. How could any Jew or Moslem glimpse in these churches the possibility for their own living and loving, of struggling and forgiving within a single divinely constituted and bound-together life?

I

When I returned from Jerusalem I had two reports on my desk. One was from the Bishop of Birmingham, who had attended the Synod of Roman Catholic Bishops in Europe. He had gone as a 'fraternal delegate'. A good sign, I thought, of a growing relationship between Anglicans and Roman Catholics in Europe. But his report told also the sad story of how those invited from the Russian, Romanian and other Orthodox Churches were conspicuous by their absence from Rome. They had declined a fraternal invitation. All the more sad, it seemed, because the Synod was to discuss evangelisation and mission in Europe. It seemed that just as the world was struggling to grow together in Europe the *rapprochement* between Eastern Orthodoxy and Roman Catholicism was in danger of breaking down.

The other report on my desk was from a delegation newly back from a visit to Romania and to the Czeck and Slovak Republics. This report held the key to the refusal to attend the Roman Catholic Synod of European Bishops. It told of scenes of tension and physical violence between Orthodox and Catholic Christians. Here again in countries torn by poverty, crumbling institutions, and children dying of AIDS, Christians were not simply theologically and doctrinally divided, but locked in actual violent, physical conflict. The recent history of relations between Orthodox and Catholic Christians, between Eastern and Western Christendom, is complicated and bound up with the history of the Communist regime. Under the Communist regime Western Catholic churches were taken by force by the Communists and given to the Orthodox Church. Now, with the collapse of Communism, the Latin west is demanding that the churches be returned to them. The Orthodox bishops say that the churches belong now to the faithful Orthodox who have worshipped there for more than fifty years. Force is used by one Christian group against another to settle the matter of disputed property. Accusations and counter accusations are made regarding forced conversions and proselytism. So, while Europe struggles to find a new political and economic unity, the Churches war, Catholic against Orthodox. And the Protestants in continental Europe, in fear of what they view as a Catholic re-evangelisation of Europe under a Polish Pope, set about strengthening a pan-Protestant alliance in Europe. One newspaper reporter recently wrote that the most important crisis since the schism of the 11th century is taking place in European Christianity.

As with Jerusalem and the Middle East, so with the countries of Eastern Europe, looking on as an outsider it seemed impossible to me not to be horrified by the contradiction of Christian Churches that proclaim belief in One, Holy, Catholic and Apostolic Church and their scandalous and sometimes violent divisions. And yet what I grieved over in Jerusalem, what I grieved over in those reports from Eastern Europe, was no different from the story from Northern Ireland that goes on relentlessly day by day. This is the story in which Michael Hurley's life has been bound up, and his work for reconciliation has been a beacon in that context. Is it any more contradictory than the pain of those who live within interchurch families and who week by week are deprived of the chance to share together the body and blood of Christ and thus to be united in the sacrament of unity?

II

In the face of these divisions of the Church and the open hostilities, the prayer of Jesus recorded in John 17:21 – that they may be one, Father, as we are one so that the world may believe – has an added force. It seems clearer than ever that a part of our Christian obedience must be to pray for, and work for, the unity of the Church. The unity of the Church really does matter, for God's own sake, and it really does matter for the world's sake. It matters for God's sake because we are called to be Christians together, one people worshipping one God. And we are called to offer a credible model of living and loving so that those who see us will glimpse in our lives possibilities for their own unity and reconciliation.

These stark reminders of the need for unity, and the God-given possibility of witnessing to unity, come at a time when the passion for Church Unity, at least here in England, seems to have grown cold; when the great new fact of church history, as Archbishop William Temple called it, the ecumenical movement, seems to have stopped moving. Or, as Lord Runcie, the former Archbishop of Canterbury suggested, we are living in a winter of ecumenism – even if he also expressed the hope that a spring would soon follow. Again I have heard Christians in this country say many times that all that matters is that we are nice to one another, that we learn to co-operate, that we learn to hold hands over the proper walls of our denominational structures. Many Christians seem content to continue to be Methodists, Anglicans, United Reformed, Catholic, Orthodox. Even one time passionate ecumenical leaders are heard to say that they no longer believe in the search for a visibly united church; it is after all 'a will-of-the-wisp'.

What is happening in the world, in Jerusalem, in Eastern Europe, in Ireland, surely convinces us that it does matter that we pray and work in fidelity to the prayer of Jesus that we may be one so that the world may believe. It is this world with its brokenness and divisions that gives us the urgency to pray and to work for unity. It is by looking outwards that we become convinced of the need for Christian Unity. It is God who demands our unity and it is the broken world that needs our unity. Nevertheless, we have to be more specific. It was Leslie Newbigin who once wrote that it is not possible to be committed to unity without being committed to some particular shape or vision or form of unity. But when it comes to describing that vision, most of us are strangely reticent.

It was in the summer of 1987 that Dr Emilio Castro, the General

Secretary of the World Council of Churches, challenged the Faith and Order Commission of the World Council of Churches to provide for the next Assembly of the Council what he called 'a mobilising portrait of visible unity'.[1] It was a tantalising challenge. Of course the Faith and Order Commission did not have to begin with a clean, empty canvas on which to build up its picture of visible unity. Already much work had been done since 1927 and that first Faith and Order Conference in Lausanne provided many contributions towards the portrait. The work on baptism, eucharist and ministry implied that a visibly united Church would at least be a church in which there would be a common baptism, a single eucharist, and a reconciled, interchangeable ministry. It talked also of the personal, collegial and communal structures that would hold a united Church together. The new work on *Confessing The One Faith*[2] pointed to a community of Christians confessing the apostolic faith, a faith grounded in Holy Scripture and focused in the Nicene-Constantinopolitan Creed – a faith confessed afresh in every cultural context today. The work, little known and hardly developed at all, on how the Church teaches authoritatively, and the studies on conciliarity, pointed to a community bound together by structures or councils which would help Christians to guard, interpret and teach the faith together. The wonderful studies on the renewal of the Church for the unity and renewal of the world, the studies on race, the differently-abled, the community of women and men, all told something of the quality of a community which had learnt to live as a sign in the world of the values and quality of God's kingdom.[3] It emphasised the vocation of the Church as instrument in the extension of God's kingdom in the world and as 'prophetic sign' of that kingdom.

With such riches of thinking accumulated over nearly 80 years, the Faith and Order Commission began to respond to Dr Castro's challenge to distil all of this work into a 'mobilising portrait' that would help Christians gathered together in the Assembly in Canberra to re-commit themselves to the goal of visible unity, that is after all the primary vocation of the World Council of Churches. To cut a story or many meetings, many drafts and redrafts short, the Commission gave over to the Assembly a text on visible unity which had at least the blessing of the theologians from Orthodox, Catholic, Protestant, Anglican, Lutheran, Pentecostal traditions that make up the Faith and Order Commission.[4] It was a short

statement of only two pages and was remarkable for its compre-
hensiveness. The Assembly, however, did not merely rubber
stamp what its Faith and Order Commission had brought to
Australia. It worked on that statement, that visible portrait of
unity, in the light of the Assembly's own theme 'Come Holy Spirit
Renew the Whole Creation'.

It is a fascinating exercise to compare the text given to the Assembly
by the Commission with the text which eventually emerged,
endorsed by the Assembly in Canberra. The text revised at Canberra is permeated with references to the work of the Holy Spirit,
reflecting the Spirit theme of the Assembly. So the Holy Spirit is
the power by which all are brought into communion with God
and by which the Church is enabled to live as sign of the reign of
God. The movement of divided Christians towards one another is
the work of the Spirit, the same Spirit who gives a diversity of gifts
to the Church. Secondly, the notion of *koinonia* plays a much more
central and unifying theme in the Canberra Text. *Koinonia* is seen
here as the fundamental, underlying reality of the Church, not
simply as one model among many. It is this fundamental *koinonia*
that belongs to God's own divine life and into which Christians
enter through baptism, as they die with Christ and rise to new life
in him. This new life of communion with God and with all the
baptised has to be made visible before the world. The division of
Christians contradicts the unity and communion they share in the
trinitarian life of God. A 'certain degree of communion' is already
recognisable between the Churches but the Churches are called to
make *koinonia* ever more visible and recognisable. The dominance
of the theme of *koinonia* is in line with the insights of many of the
bilateral dialogues and the growing understanding of Christian
World Communions.[5] Two further new emphases in the Canberra version of the statement are the expansion of the section on
diversity in unity and the list of sharp challenges to the churches
to act in taking steps now towards visible unity.

III

The Statement adopted on the last day of the Canberra Assembly
is called *The Unity of the Church as Koinonia: Gift and Calling*.[6] It is
amazing how much of the essential work done by the ecumenical

movement this century is encapsulated in these few paragraphs . It expresses not only the results of theological dialogue but also the experience of ecumenical living. It may not be quite the mobi- lizing vision that Dr Castro had hoped for, but it is nevertheless a prophetic document, and it is quite remarkable that an Assembly produced it.

The Statement is in three parts. The first section is foundational, exploring the inner nature of the Church's life; the second section explores the visible characteristics of the Church and the third section offers a series of challenges to the Churches to move to- wards visible unity. The Statement ends with a short but beautiful doxology echoing the Assembly's theme of the Holy Spirit.

> In the process of praying, working and struggling for unity, the Holy Spirit comforts us in pain, disturbs us when we are satisfied to remain in our divisions, leads us to repentance and grants us joy when our communion flourishes.

The text opens not with the Church but with the whole of creation. God's purpose is first of all for the whole universe. God's purpose is 'to gather the whole creation under the Lordship of Christ'. Although the Assembly accepted this opening claim there were voices raised in opposition. The claim for some was too much, damaging the integrity and witness, so it was claimed, of those of other faiths. Feminist voices found the whole notion of lordship alien to their understanding of God's way with humanity. The Assembly listened to these challenges but resisted them.

Only after stating the purpose of God for the whole of creation is the Church brought into view. The ordering of our priorities must be God's Kingdom, God's world and God's Church. The Church is the place where communion with God and with one another ex- ists. It is the place where we experience, indeed where we are drawn into the very life and love of God, Father, Son and Holy Spirit. This experience of being in the orbit of God's own life en- ables the Church to be the sign and servant of reconciliation for the world. The Church, bound in God's own life, is 'the world ahead of itself'. It is the place where divisions of all sorts, whether based on race, colour, gender or age are healed. The text is realistic enough to own up to the difference between what is indeed ours, given in Christ through the power of the Holy Spirit, and the brokenness of our life brought about by human sin. The text holds together the 'ideal', or rather what is ours by virtue of being in Christ, and what we mar by our human sinfulness. Christians are painfully divided among themselves: 'Their scandalous divisions damage the credibility of their witness to the world in worship and service. Moreover, they contradict not only the Church's witness but also its very nature.'

The first section ends with a welcome recognition that the Churches are beginning, through the ecumenical movement, to recognise that they do indeed already share a certain degree of communion. We can no longer say starkly 'we are out of communion with one another'.

The central section then paints a portrait of what a Church would be like which visibly manifests the inner nature and being of *koinonia*. The life locked together in God's own life is visibly manifested first of all in the common confession of the apostolic faith. It is a pity that the Canberra Statement says so little about the common confession of the apostolic faith. It makes no reference to the faith grounded in Holy Scripture attested in the Ecumenical Creeds, which faith is to be confessed afresh in each generation and in each place. But the Faith and Order Study *Confessing The One Faith* lies behind this single phrase.[7] This study makes quite clear that the common confession of the apostolic faith is a confession not simply born in the recitation of words but carried in the day to day lives of witness and confession of Christians: for what we say and what we do must be all of a single piece, a single confession.

The second mark of a visibly united Church is the shared sacramental life entered by baptism and nurtured and celebrated in the one eucharistic fellowship. There will be no refusals in a visibly united Church either to give or to receive the eucharist, nor will there be only partial eucharistic hospitality. A visibly united Church will be joined together around one common table where all are welcome, and where all belong, and from which all are sent out to care and serve.

The third characteristic is that it will be a common life in which members and ministries (the two belong integrally together) are not simply mutually recognised but reconciled into a single community and a single interchangeable ministry. No longer will one group say to another, 'we recognise your ministry as fruitful but your ministry is not our ministry', but they will learn to say, 'we are together united by a single common ministry'. Visible unity will be reached when the local churches, 'the all in each place', can recognise in one another the One, Holy, Catholic and Apostolic Church in its fullness, as indeed it believes the fullness of that Church to be in its own life. These local churches will be bonded together at every level, locally, regionally, internationally, by conciliar forms of life and action. This is tantalisingly brief. It is important, vitally important, because it does point us to the firm conviction that a visibly united Church will not be a loose federation, but will be held together by appropriate structures. Structures are God-given channels of communication through which God's grace can flow to all. The fact that structures have often, and still do, limit and restrict and are given to structural violence, must not blind us to their potentiality for unity.

Then comes a most significant conclusion to the portrait of visible unity contained in the second section. In case any should fear that the vision is of rigid uniformity, the Statement is clear that diversities of all sorts will characterise a visibly united Church and flourish within it. There will be different theological traditions, different doctrinal traditions: there will be differences which spring from God-given cultural diversity, and ethnic differences. The emphasis on diversity was there in the text which the Faith and Order Commission brought to Canberra. 'Difference and diversity are integral to the nature of communion; yet there are limits to difference and diversity'. The Assembly was faced in a dramatic way with just what those limits might be in the presentation of a young Korean woman theologian, Professor Chung Hyun Kyung.[8] The electrifying presentation began with Aboriginal dance to a strong, threatening drum beat. From the midst of the dancers emerged the small figure of Professor Chung who began with a litany of those from the Bible and throughout history who had died untimely and violent deaths. Professor Chung called on all of their spirits. She turned then to the spirits of Korea, the 'Han-ridden spirits'. She argued that without attending to the cries of these spirits we cannot hear the voice of the Holy Spirit. She seemed to be equating these spirits with the Holy Spirit. Professor Chung called for repentance, *metanoia*, a turning from the 'political economy of death' with its search for greater and greater material wealth to the 'political economy of life', and for the gift of the Holy Spirit. The image of the *metanoia* she offered was from what she identified as 'my gut feeling deep in my people's collective consciousness':

> For me the Holy Spirit comes from the image of *Kwan In*. She is venerated as Goddess of compassion and wisdom by East Asian women's popular religiosity. She is a *boddhisatra*, enlightening being. She can go into Nirvana any time she wants to, but refuses to go into Nirvana herself ... She waits and waits until the whole universe, people, trees, birds, mountains, air, water, become enlightened. They can go to Nirvana together where they can live collectively in eternal wisdom and compassion. Perhaps this might also be a feminine image of the Christ who is the first born among us, one who goes before and brings others with her?

It is difficult to imagine a more startlingly dramatic presentation or one that would have posed the question of inculturation of the Gospel more dramatically. Was Professor Chung's interpretation of the Christian message about the Holy Spirit, in thought forms influenced by her Korean culture and by North American feminism, damaging the Christian gospel? Was this presentation of faith in the Holy Spirit exceeding the bounds of legitimate diversity?

The debate is only just beginning. At Canberra it led to threats from some churches of withdrawal from an ecumenical community pressing such questions. The Statement on unity was challenged to include something in response about the tolerable limits of diversity. The formulation in response to the challenge is minimalist:

> Diversity is illegitimate when, for instance, it makes impossible the common confession of Jesus Christ as God and Saviour the same yesterday, today and forever (Hebrews 13:8); and diversity is illegitimate when, for instance, it makes impossible the common confession of salvation and the final destiny of humanity as proclaimed in Holy Scripture and preached by the apostolic community.

Even this very minimalist statement on legitimate diversity was seen by some as too much, too restrictive. What was clear was the need for a much more extensive and rigorous exploration of diversity in the future. The statement of Leonardo Boff made when he left the Fransiscan Order is relevant here[9]:

> I wish to involve myself through my intellectual work in the building of an Indo-Afro-American Christianity incultured in the bodies, skins, dances, sufferings, joys and the languages of our peoples in answer to God's Gospel; an answer which has not been fully given despite 500 years of Christian presence in our continent.

A truly world-wide, united Church would surely provide the best community of interpretation in which the insights of one cultural or ethnic group could be brought together and tested out. There must be limits to diversity but these are perhaps not as many as we sometimes thought. The constant searching and exchange in the widest community of faith can take place in the confident assurance of the promise of Christ to lead into all truth. We must continue to tell the Gospel story and recite the Creeds. But we must never forget that these stories and texts invite interpretation and no two interpretations will be identical, for to talk of God is to talk of a mystery which cannot be exhaustively encapsulated in any human words. The words of Scripture, and the dogmatic decrees of every ecumenical council have always provoked discussion, even dispute. Christians need each other in exploring and revealing the truth in all its richness. Then diversity will properly be viewed not so much as a problem but rather as an aspect of God's goodness. The Assembly and the Canberra Statement thus hint at an important agenda for the ecumenical movement in the last decade of this century.

The final section, before the doxology, acknowledges with gratitude the achievements of the ecumenical movement so far, the convergence of theological dialogues, the steps some have taken in ecumenical living, together with the formation of local ecumenical projects and covenants etc. It goes on to set out some carefully worded challenges to all the churches:

- to recognise each other's baptism on the basis of the BEM document;
- to move towards the recognition of the apostolic faith as expressed through the Nicene-Constantinopolitan Creed in the life and witness of one another;

- on the basis of convergence in faith in baptism, eucharist and ministry to consider, wherever appropriate, forms of eucharistic hospitality; we gladly acknowledge that some who do not observe these rites share in the spiritual experience of life in Christ.

It is important to note how carefully this challenge on eucharistic hospitality is in fact worded. It is suggested that eucharistic hospitality is offered on the basis of the recognition of a convergence in faith as set out in the Lima Text, *Baptism, Eucharist and Ministry*.[10] It also suggests that such eucharistic hospitality should be offered wherever appropriate. It is a very carefully worded challenge to encourage the Roman Catholic Church and the Orthodox Churches to go on searching both for that necessary agreement in faith and to consider those times and places where eucharistic hospitality might even now be appropriate on the basis of emerging theological convergence. The Statement also looks in the other direction. In an attempt not to be exclusive it says 'we gladly acknowledge that some who do not observe these rites share in the spiritual experience of life in Christ'. This was an insertion made in Canberra in response to those groups, like the Salvation Army and the Society of Friends, which bear witness to the sacramentality of all life without celebrating the particular sacraments of baptism and eucharist. The Statement continues with three further challenges:

- to move towards a mutual recognition of ministries;
- to endeavour in word and deed to give common witness to the Gospel as a whole;

- to recommit themselves to work for justice, peace and the integrity of creation, linking more closely the search for the sacramental communion of the Church with the struggles for justice and peace.

In case anyone might think that all of these challenges are for the Churches at regional, national or international level, the final challenge makes clear that the involvement of the local Church is vital for the growth to visible unity. Hence each local Church is challenged to move and grow and be reconciled with other Christians in the place where it is.

These three sections culminate in the final doxological passage which picks up and echoes the trinitarian beginning:

The Holy Spirit as the promoter of *koinonia* (2 Corinthians 13:13) gives to those who are still divided the thirst and hunger for full communion. We remain restless until we grow together according to the wish and prayer of Christ that those who believe in him may be one (John 17:21).

IV

There is so much ecumenical thinking and ecumenical work and experience which is caught up in this tightly packed Canberra Statement, perhaps not quite the `mobilising portrait' which Dr Castro called for but at least a summary of where we are and where we are going in the last decade of the ecumenical century. We need to take encouragement from the fact that an Assembly of the World Council, bringing together more than a thousand Christians from so many traditions and so many different cultural backgrounds, agreed to adopt this Statement. Perhaps the most exciting thing about it is that a portrait does emerge which gives space for diversity, a diversity born not out of different denominational traditions but born out of making the Gospel relevant within each different cultural context. A visibly united Church will indeed be one which, as the Archbishop of Jerusalem pointed to, is one in which Christians have learnt to be Christians together in the Middle East, in Africa, in India, in Asia, in Europe, offering a credible model of living and loving to those around; where the Gospel is thoroughly at home in the cultural context and can be heard and understood. It will be a Church in which Christians have learnt to live together with difference, to accept the tensions, the conflicts and even the pain which belongs to a Church struggling to incarnate the Gospel, but who know that to hold together with difference, to bear the pain and the cost of difference, even to enter one another's pain, is the mark of a Church which has learnt to live with the cross at its centre. It will be a Church in which Christians never again say to one another 'I have no need of you', but in which Christians believe in the promise of Christ that the Church will be led into all truth and can risk staying together in a single community seeking truth. Only then will Christians together offer that credible model of unity to the world which takes account both of human sin and frailty and which puts its confidence in the strength and promise and grace of God.

Notes

1   E. Castro, *Reflections* in *Faith & Renewal* (ed). T. Best, Faith and
        Order Paper No. 131, (Geneva, 1985).

2   *Confessing The One Faith*, Faith and Order Paper No. 153, (Geneva,
        1991).

3.   C. Parvey (ed.) *The Community of Women and Men in The Church:
        the Sheffield Report*, (Geneva, 1983). T. Best (ed.) *Church & World*,
        Faith and Order Paper No. 151, (Geneva, 1990).

4.   *The Unity Statement* in Minutes of the Meeting of the Faith and
        Order Standing Commission, Rome, 1991, Faith and Order Paper
        No. 157, (Geneva, 1992).

5.   *Church as Communion*: An agreed Statement by the Second
        Anglican-Roman Catholic International Commission, ARCIC II,
        (CHP/CTS, 1991), also *Communion-Koinonia*: A Study by the
        Institute for Ecumenical Research, (Strasbourg, 1990).

6.   M. Kinnamon (ed.) *Signs of the Spirit: Official Report of the Seventh
        Assembly*, (Geneva, 1991), p.172 ff.

7.   see above 1.

8.   M. Kinnamon (ed.) *Signs of the Spirit: Official Report of the Seventh
        Assembly*, (Geneva, 1991), p.37 ff.

9.   L. Boff, 'To my companions on the journey of hope', *The Tablet*, 11
        July 1992, p 882 ff.

10.   *Baptism, Eucharist and Ministry*, Faith and Order Paper No. 111,
        (Geneva, 1982).

Roman Catholic Responses to ARCIC I and II

Edward Yarnold

Rome has now made three responses to the work of the two Anglican-Roman Catholic International Commissions. In 1982 the Congregation of the Doctrine of the Faith (CDF) published its *Observations on the Final Report of ARCIC I*. Six years later the CDF produced a new set of *Observations* on ARCIC II's *Agreed Statement Salvation and the Church*. Finally in 1991, after a nine-year process in which all bishops' conferences throughout the world were consulted, the same Congregation was responsible for the definitive *Roman Catholic Response to ARCIC I's Final Report*.

The aim of this article is to compare (1) the claims made by these three responses concerning their own status, (2) the extent to which they refuse to endorse ARCIC's claims to have reached substantial agreement, (3) the criticisms they make of particular expressions of doctrine made by the two commissions, and (4) the hopes they hold out for the future.

In 1987 Rome passed judgment on another ecumenical agreement, the Faith and Order Commission's document *Baptism, Eucharist and Ministry* (BEM), which was published in 1982, a few months after ARCIC's *Final Report*. Since the subject-matter of the two reports partially coincides – both seek agreement over Eucharist and Ministry – it may be illuminating to compare the responses made to ARCIC with those made to BEM. However, their scope differs in two important respects. First, while ARCIC was a bilateral dialogue, Faith and Order includes all the mainstream churches; secondly, while ARCIC sought to articulate an existing 'substantial agreement' of the two Churches, BEM had the more modest aim of inviting the member Churches to explore certain lines of 'convergence'.[1]

Finally, I do not wish this article to be no more than an analysis of certain Roman documents. I shall end therefore with a consideration of the implications of our investigation for future relations between the Roman Catholic Church and the Anglican Communion.

I

The *Observations* of 1982 begin with a note stating that they were formulated by the CDF 'at the request of the Holy Father'. The Congregation speaks in its own name (e.g. 'The Congregation finally has to note that …'); there is no claim that it is the Church's definite judgment which is being expressed. As Cardinal Ratzinger explained in a letter to the Catholic Co-chairman of ARCIC, Bishop Alan Clark, the *Observations* were intended as the CDF's 'contribution to the continuation of this dialogue'.

The corresponding *Observations* on the ARCIC II statement on salvation carry a higher degree of authority. Although, as with the previous document, the aim is said to be 'the furthering of the dialogue', it is now made clear that what is offered is not suggestions, but 'an authoritative doctrinal judgment', which carries 'the authority of a text approved by the Holy Father'. Evidently these second *Observations* constitute an act of the magisterium.

The 1991 *Response to the Final Report* is a document of still higher authority. Although not actually signed by Pope John Paul, it constitutes the Roman Catholic Church's formal judgment. The communication of the Roman Catholic bishops of England and Wales refers to it as 'the Response of the Holy See'. The Archbishop of Canterbury described it as the response of the Roman Catholic Church. The key section of the *Response* is a short 'General Evaluation' of four paragraphs, which explains its own authority as that of 'the Catholic Church's … definitive response to the results achieved by ARCIC I'. It is followed by an 'Explanatory Note' some ten pages long, which is described as 'the fruit of close collaboration between the Congregation of the Doctrine of the Faith and the Pontifical Council for Promoting Christian Unity'. This note puts forward the reasons which underlie the *Response*, without itself possessing the same definitive authority.

The BEM document was not judged to require a response of comparable authority. The response made no claims to provide a 'definitive judgment', being merely headed 'An Appraisal'. It was the work of the Secretariat (now the Council) for promoting Christian Unity (CPCU). Instead of using such phrases as 'the Catholic Church judges', it is content more modestly to use expressions like 'we think', 'we believe', with the exception of statements of general encouragement, such as 'The Catholic Church sees in BEM a significant result of the ecumenical movement'.

II

ARCIC I's claim that 'substantial agreement' had been reached over the Eucharist and ordination, and was possible even over authority, caused much perplexity in Rome. The 1982 *Observations* made particularly heavy weather of the phrase, wondering whether 'substantial' was a synonym for 'real' or 'genuine', or whether it indicated 'a fundamental agreement about points which are truly essential'. If the latter, the CDF indicated that it was still not clear whether ARCIC judges that remaining differences concern only 'secondary points (for example, the structure of liturgical rites, theological opinion, ecclesiastical discipline, spirituality), or whether these are points which truly pertain to the faith'.

In reality ARCIC I attempted several times to explain the term 'substantial agreement'. The most explicit definition is given in the *Elucidation* to the Eucharist: 'unanimous agreement 'on essential matters where it [the Commission] considers that doctrine admits no divergence' (Ministry, para.17) (*Elucidation*, para.2). A somewhat different understanding of substantial agreement can be inferred from Eucharist para.12:

> We believe that we have reached substantial agreement on the doctrine of the eucharist. Although we are all conditioned by the traditional ways in which we have expressed and practised our eucharistic faith, we are convinced that if there are any remaining points of disagreement they can be resolved on the principles here established ... It is our hope that, in view of the agreement which we have reached on eucharistic faith, this doctrine will no longer constitute an obstacle to the unity we seek.

Substantial agreement therefore seems to imply that remaining points can be settled on the basis of the agreement reached and ought no longer to provide a reason for the Churches to remain disunited.

It is still true, however, that ARCIC did not provide an answer to the CDF's question regarding the status of the secondary points over which agreement was not achieved. In discussing the objections which some Evangelicals feel against any form of adoration paid to the reserved sacrament, the *Elucidation* on the Eucharist indicates that such 'divergence in matters of practice and in theological judgements relating to them, without destroying a common eucharistic faith' exemplifies the meaning of substantial agreement (*Elucidation*, para.9). It appears then that the remaining differences are not thought to relate to essential matters of faith. The earlier discussion of the question in the eucharistic statement, however, is not so clear (Eucharist, para.12). Reference is made to 'a variety of theological approaches', but it is not stated whether all differences are of this kind. It is implied that agreement is substantial provided points of disagreement 'can be resolved on the principles here established', in which event 'this doctrine will no longer be an obstacle to the unity we seek'; but again it is not explained whether these points of disagreement may include matters of faith or only matters of practice or opinion. The 1991 *Response* clearly implies that the difference concerning reservation is one of faith: 'one remains with the conviction that this is an area in which real consensus between Anglicans and Roman Catholics is lacking' (para.23).

The Secretariat (now Council) for Christian Unity worked out the following definition of substantial agreement for its own purposes in 1977:

> This relates to a basic nucleus without which the message of salvation is not transmitted in its integrity, while accepting that neither doctrinal elaborations nor practice correspond entirely among the partner churches. The essentials are assured, and there is the same shared intention of faith.[2]

In fact the distinction between matters of faith on the one hand, and expressions of doctrine and theological opinions on the other, is not free from difficulty. Even theological opinions are attempts to express the implications of the faith. The bottom limit of substantial agreement is easy to define: if one Church condemns another's doctrines as incompatible with Christian faith, there is no substantial agreement. More difficult to decide is the situation (the question of eucharistic adoration is a case in point) where one Church is unable to endorse the doctrines of another Church without however condemning them as heretical.

It would have been fair to ask ARCIC how it knew that remaining difficulties concerning the Eucharist and Ministry could be resolved on the grounds of the fundamental agreement that had been reached. One answer, which would be partly true, would be based on what Newman called a convergence of probabilities: an indefinable network of factors, arising from protracted discussion and the growth of intimate friendship, had enabled the participants to recognise their partners' faith as so close to their own that, as far as the doctrine in question was concerned, there no longer seemed any justification in their Churches remaining apart. But in addition the essential areas of belief had long been identified; ARCIC judged these points to be truly fundamental, so that other connected issues must, almost by definition, be soluble on the agreed basis. Thirdly, there could be (as in Eucharist, para.12) an appeal to the virtue of hope: the Holy Spirit that had taken them so far in agreement must be able to lead them on to solve remaining problems.

When the *Final Report* was sent to the two Churches, each Church was asked whether it was in agreement with the contents of the report. The question however was asked not in terms of substantial agreement but of consonance: each Church was asked whether the *Final Report* was 'consonant in substance with (its) faith'. As is well known, the answers which the two Churches gave are very different in tone.

On the Anglican side, each of the twenty-seven autonomous Churches gave its answer to the question, before an answer was given for the whole Anglican Communion at the Lambeth Conference of 1988. A booklet entitled *Towards a Church of England Response to BEM and ARCIC* was compiled by the Faith and Order Advisory Group (FOAG) of the Church of England to provide material on which the Church of England's response was based.[3] It was explained that:

> Minor discrepancies are of no hindrance, and it may be presupposed that the language of the ARCIC statements is not simply identical with the language of the Anglican tradition itself ... To express an opinion on whether the statements are 'consonant in substance with the faith of Anglicans' is to make a judgement, in the matters of which the statements treat, about whether they are compatible

not with any formulary of the past but with the living faith of Anglicans.[4]

On the Eucharist the verdict was: 'We believe that we can say with the Commission "this is the Christian faith of the Eucharist". Moreover we believe the Final Report on the Eucharist to be "consonant in substance with the faith of Anglicans"'.[5]

The judgment passed on ministry was similar, although it was admitted that the question of the ordination of women was a matter of 'fundamental ... doctrine': 'We agree that we can recognise our own faith in the text; it is consonant with the faith of Anglicans'.[6]

The eventual judgment of the Church of England followed the guidance of the FOAG booklet. In similar terms the Lambeth Conference, representing the whole Anglican Communion, resolved that the *Agreed Statements on Eucharist and Ministry* were 'consonant in substance with the faith of Anglicans', even though an Explanatory Note indicates that this verdict was not unqualified:

> The Provinces gave a clear 'yes' to the statement on Eucharistic Doctrine ... Some Provinces asked for clarification about the meaning of anamnesis and bread and wine 'becoming' the body and blood of Christ. But no Province rejected the Statement and many were extremely positive ... While we respect continuing anxieties of some Anglicans in the area of 'sacrifice' and 'presence', they do not appear to reflect the common mind of the Provincial responses ... Both are areas of 'mystery' which ultimately defy definition. But the *Agreed Statement on the Eucharist* sufficiently expresses Anglican understanding ...'[7]

The provinces had given a similar 'yes' to the Statement on ministry, though problems concerning, for example, language and style, and the meaning of priesthood are acknowledged. It is admitted that 'an ambivalent reply came from one Province which has traditionally experienced a difficult relationship with the Roman Catholic Church'. The note recognises that such difficulties may be due to non-theological reasons: 'this seems to reflect the need for developing deeper links of trust and friendship as ecumenical dialogue goes forward'.[8] It is evident then that the Lambeth Conference, like the Church of England's FOAG, did not believe consonance required identity of language or even compatibility with past formulas.

It seems in fact that there is a whole range of possible understandings of consonance. At the lowest end of the scale one would place compatibility or non-contradiction: in this sense one could say that the proposition that the moon is made of green cheese is consonant (i.e. compatible) with the faith of Anglicans (or Roman Catholics). At the other extreme one would find identity of meaning, even if not of verbal expression. The Anglican understanding of consonance evidently falls somewhere between these two extremes. This is especially evident in the FOAG booklet, which rejects the use of past formularies as a standard (even of compatibility!) and speaks instead of 'the living faith of Anglicans'. The CPCU's understanding of substantial agreement, quoted above, which speaks of 'the same shared intention of faith' with the preservation of essentials, also seems to fall into the middle of the range.

The 1991 Roman Response, however, comes close to the upper limit of the scale. It is, of course, inevitable that the Catholic understanding of consonance should be more rigorous than the Anglican, for the simple reason that Anglicans do not grant such normative status to post-patristic classical formulas of belief as Catholics do.

Although the creeds and the definitions of the first four (or seven) councils do constitute for Anglicans binding statements of faith, the same cannot be said of later formulas. This is evident in the Declaration of Assent and its Preface in the rite for the ordination of a bishop in the Church of England's *Alternative Service Book* of 1980, in which the Archbishop is to state that the Church of England

> professes the faith uniquely revealed in the holy Scriptures and set forth in the catholic creeds, which faith the Church is called upon to proclaim afresh in each generation. Led by the Holy Spirit, it has borne witness to Christian truth in its historic formularies, the Thirty-nine Articles of Religion, the Book of Common Prayer, and the Ordering of Bishops, Priests, and Deacons.

In reply the bishop-elect affirms his 'belief in the faith which is revealed in the holy Scriptures and set forth in the catholic creeds and to which the historic formularies of the Church of England bear witness.'

In other words, the 'historic formularies' of the Church of England do not have the same authority as the scriptures and the creeds. Scripture and creeds are the unique vehicles or expressions of revelation; the other formularies are witnesses to that revelation, and are therefore normative only in so far as their witness is accurate. Consequently what Anglicans will require of ecumenical documents is that they be faithful to the revelation contained in scripture and set forth in creeds; a document will not necessarily be deficient if it is not consonant with everything contained in the witnesses to revelation.

For Catholics, on the other hand, the definitions of all the ecumenical councils and papal *ex-cathedra* pronouncements are normative. The *ARCIC Report* will have to pass the test of consonance with them. But what does such consonance involve? Although neither the *Observations* of 1982 nor those of 1988 speak expressly of 'consonance', the *Response* of 1991 makes its understanding of the term very clear.

> … the Roman Catholic Church was asked to give a clear answer to the question: are the agreements contained in this Report consonant with the faith of the Catholic Church? What was asked for was not a simple evaluation of an ecumenical study, but an official response as to the *identity* [italics mine] of the various statements with the faith of the Church.

In the light of this understanding of consonance as equivalent to identity, the *Response* states that certain doctrines need 'greater clarification from the Catholic point of view', that 'the faith of the Catholic Church would be even more clearly reflected' if certain further points were made, that certain statements need 'further clarification *from the Catholic perspective*' [italics mine].

Now neither the *Response* nor the earlier *Observations* demand that agreed formulas should be verbally identical with those of the Roman Catholic Church. Such a demand would have been inconsistent with Pope John Paul II's address to ARCIC I in 1980, in which he seemed to commend the commission's method.

> Your method has been to go behind the habit of thought
> and expression born and nourished in enmity and contro-
> versy, to scrutinise together the great common treasure, to
> clothe it in a language at once traditional and expressive of
> the insights of an age which no longer glories in strife but
> seeks to come together in listening to the quiet voice of the
> Spirit.

The 1988 *Observations* give the clearest statement of what is wanted, though without using the term 'consonance'.

> Without disavowing anything in a method which has pro-
> duced incontestable results, one could still ask if it would
> not be opportune to perfect the procedure in such a way as
> to permit a more precise determination of the doctrinal
> content of the formulas employed to express a common
> faith.

The CDF characterises the language of the ARCIC agreement on
salvation as 'symbolic', and would perhaps pass the same judgment on the language of the *Final Report*. The danger it sees in such
a method is that it makes it difficult to construct a 'truly univocal
agreement'. What is wanted is 'more rigorous doctrinal formulations', which would permit 'a rigorous comparison between the
respective positions'. Such formulations need not be 'scholastic
ones': the CDF does not disapprove in principle of ARCIC's attempt to find a new language untainted with polemical associations.[9]

If, then, the identity that Rome is requiring between the ARCIC
statements and Roman Catholic faith is not a verbal identity, what
is it? What it seems to envisage is an agreement which, in rigorous
language which is incapable of misinterpretation, expresses the
Roman Catholic faith with the full precision and the full detail in
which it has been officially defined. Thus it is not sufficient to affirm the sacrificial nature of the Eucharist: one must also state that
'the Church ... makes present the sacrifice of Calvary', and that
the eucharistic sacrifice has a 'propitiatory nature ... which can be
applied also to the deceased' (Response, para.21). It is not sufficient to affirm that the Eucharist is Christ's gift of himself to the
Church in which the bread and wine become the body and blood
of Christ: one must also state that Christ 'makes himself present

sacramentally and substantially when under the species of bread and wine these earthly realities are changed into the reality of his Body and Blood, Soul and Divinity' (para.22).[10]

Commentators on the *Response* have wondered whether this demand for identity contradicts some very high level directives which ARCIC had been given. In 1966 Pope Paul VI and Archbishop Michael Ramsey, in their Common Declaration which led to the setting up of ARCIC, announced their intention of setting up a 'serious dialogue ... founded on the Gospels and on the ancient common traditions' which would lead to 'unity in truth'. Pope John Paul II's 1980 address to ARCIC I developed this idea:

> We have a common treasure, which we must recover and in the fullness of which we must share, not losing certain characteristic qualities and gifts which have been ours even in our divided state.

If the dialogue was to be based on the ancient common traditions, the *Report* could not be required to include agreement about all post-reformation developments of the basic common faith. Unless the Church was deficient in its faith for fifteen hundred years, the ancient traditions up to the reformation must include all that is essential.

Once more we are back with the question of substantial agreement. Can one separate the essentials of a doctrine which must be included in the common tradition and treasure, and which any genuine agreement must contain, from the more elaborate conceptions of the doctrine (the 'characteristic qualitites' of which Pope John Paul spoke), which have taken time to develop, but are still expressions of the same essential faith? An affirmative answer can claim the support of the Vatican II 'hierarchy of truths', according to which doctrines 'vary in their connection with the foundation of the Christian faith'.[11] The 1982 *Observations* expressly excludes the appeal to this concept, but does not justify its attitude.[12]

There is another side to the *Response's* insistence on identity, namely the requirement that all possible ambiguity must be removed. This demand is already explicit in the first set of *Observations*:

Certain formulations in the Report are not sufficiently explicit and hence can lend themselves to a twofold interpretation, in which both parties can find unchanged the expression of their own position… In effect, if a formulation which has received the agreement of the experts can be diversely interpreted, how could it serve as a basis for reconciliation on the level of church life and practice?[13]

The 1988 *Observations* quote this passage *in extenso*; it is in this context that they raise their doubts about the capacity of 'symbolic' language to express a 'truly univocal agreement'. So too the *Response* 'looks for certain clarifications which will assure that these [common] affirmations are understood in a way that conforms to Catholic doctrine'.[14]

The Secretariat for Unity also found BEM to be insufficiently unambiguous at certain points. Thus what BEM says about the Eucharist as the 'sacrament of the unique sacrifice of Christ' is criticised for not saying 'unambiguously that the eucharist is in itself a real sacrifice, the memorial of the sacrifice of Christ on the cross'.[15]

I have written elsewhere in connection with the 1991 *Response* that 'the search for perfectly unambiguous formulas as a prelude to reunion is a wild-goose chase'.[16] This is true for at least two reasons. First, the truth about God and his gracious dealings with the human race is too vast to be captured in any single theological formula or system. Consequently there needs to be a diversity of expressions of the faith if our conceptions are not to be impoverished. It also follows that any statement about God that is not trivial is likely to be capable of more than one interpretation. Secondly, since terms acquire new associations when they are used in new cultural contexts and translated into different languages, it will be impossible to ensure that ideas from one theological tradition are grasped in the identical sense by another tradition. A certain ambiguity is therefore of the nature of ecumenical agreements. It is harmful only if it conceals fundamental differences; it is benign if it allows each side to bring its characteristic religious experience to the interpretation of the same fundamental faith.

But how can one tell that there is the same fundamental faith? The criterion is not to be found in verbal formulas alone. As I wrote in the article quoted in the last paragraph:

Subscription to common dogmatic formulas is only one of many strands that bind the members of a Church together in a common faith. Common scriptures, a mutually acceptable standard of Christian life, shared worship, particularly shared holy Communion, a common ministry, and a single universal primacy are other bonds of faith ... If reunion is to be achieved it will come only at the end of a courtship during which the two Churches have grown together in faith, life, worship and mission.

III

The Final Remarks in the 1982 *Observations* set out five points summarising the CDF's reasons for judging that ARCIC had not reached substantial agreement: (1) ARCIC itself had acknowledged that some Catholic dogmas (such as infallibility, adoration of the reserved blessed sacrament and the Marian dogmas) were not held by Anglicans; (2) other Catholic dogmas (such as papal primacy) were only held by Anglicans 'in part'; (3) 'certain formulations ... are not explicit enough to ensure that they exclude interpretations not in harmony with the Catholic faith'; (4) certain formulations (such those concerning reception, the competence of general councils, and the relationship between primacy and the structure of the Church) are 'inexact'; (5) ARCIC has not considered some aspects of Catholic teaching (such as moral teaching) (D (1)). Our concern here is with the third point, which concerns possible ambiguities. The CDF directs this criticism against four sections of the *Final Report*.

The first point at which the CDF finds an unacceptable ambiguity concerns the sacrifice of the Mass. ARCIC had explained that in the Eucharist 'the Church enters into the movement of [Christ's] self-offering', and that 'the atoning work of Christ on the cross is proclaimed and made effective in the life of the Church' (Eucharist, para. 5). The CDF wishes these statements clarified 'in order to permit Catholics to see their faith *fully* [my italics] expressed on this point'. The desired clarification would make the 'propitiatory' nature of the Eucharist explicit, and would state that

this real presence of the sacrifice of Christ, accomplished

by the sacramental words, that is to say by the ministry of
the priest saying *in persona Christi* the words of the Lord, includes a participation of the Church, the Body of Christ, in
the sacrificial act of her Lord, so that she offers sacramentally in him and with him his sacrifice (B.I.(1)).

But can either partner in ecumenical dialogue reasonably require
to see their faith 'fully' expressed at every point? Is it not enough if
each can see their faith 'essentially' expressed? We are back with
the problem of substantial agreement and the hierarchy of truths.
Moreover the explicit statement of Catholic faith which the CDF
desires is in fact a particular interpretation of Catholic dogma.
The great Tridentine statement on the sacrifice of the Mass speaks
of it as the 'representation' of the sacrifice of Calvary, and a different decree twelve years earlier speaks of Christ's real presence;
but the 'real presence of the sacrifice' is only one of several possible interpretations of the Latin *repraesentaretur*.[17] It is, after all, the
risen Lord who is present on the altar.

The second subject on which the *Observations* call for greater care
in eliminating ambiguities concerns the real presence. While ap-
proving of ARCIC's affirmations that the bread and wine 'become' Christ's body and blood, the CDF desires a clearer affirmation of what is implied by transubstantiation (the use of the term
itself is not insisted upon), and a more explicit rejection of the
view that 'the bread and wine remain such in their ontological
substance, even while becoming the sacramental mediation of the
body and blood of Christ' (B.I.(2)).

Priesthood is the subject of the third criticism. 'The sense of
Catholic doctrine' requires it to be said that through the priest 'the
Church offers sacramentally the sacrifice of Christ'; the lack of so
clear a statement formed the subject of the CDF's first criticism.
Moreover ARCIC's affirmation of the sacramentality of ordination is said to need the clarification of a statement to the effect that
the sacrament of holy order was 'instituted by Christ'. The
Observations acknowledge that there are 'possible difficulties of
an historical proof', but no reference is made to various interpretations of dominical institution in modern Catholic theology according to which there need not necessarily have been a particular moment in Christ's life when the sacrament was instituted
(B.II (1) and (2)). A similar point is made in connection with

Christ's institution of the universal primacy (B.III (2)). The view of ARCIC (*Ministry Elucidation*, 5) that disagreement over the ordination of women to the priesthood did not affect 'the principles upon which its doctrinal agreement rests' is rejected (B.II (3)).

In its fourth point, which centres on apostolic succession, the CDF does not amplify its reason for questioning ARCIC's claim that agreement has been reached on the subject, referring merely to the need for further study. In two places in these four criticisms the document raises the question of the 'authentic interpretation' of Scripture: 'it is not possible for the Church to adopt as the effective norm for reading the Scriptures only what historical criticism maintains' (B.III (1); cf B.II (2)).

Although in examining these objections I have once or twice ventured on a brief reply, my principal aim has been to state them clearly and then to compare them with similar criticisms made in the 1991 *Response*. The 1982 *Observations*, as we have noted, summarised its objections under five heads; the 1991 document arranges its criticisms under two: the matters (such as infallibility, the Marian dogmas and reception) on which ARCIC itself acknowledged that substantial agreement had not been reached, and questions on which, though 'greater progress has been made', there is need of 'greater clarification from the Catholic point of view'. In comparing the two documents I shall concentrate on the second class of criticism.

With regard to the Eucharist, the *Response* judges that ARCIC would have reflected the faith of the Catholic Church 'even more clearly' if it had said that Christ's sacrifice on Calvary is 'made present with all its effects, thus affirming the propitiatory nature of the eucharistic sacrifice'. 'To remove all ambiguity' it should be said that the real presence is due to a 'substantial change in the elements', so that the 'earthly realities are changed into the reality of his body and blood, soul and divinity'. The treatment of eucharistic reservation 'creates concern from the Roman Catholic point of view' (paras. 21-23). These points are briefer restatements of points made by the 1982 *Observations* and summarised above.

The 1982 criticisms of the document on the ministry receive sharper focus in 1991 (paras. 24-27). It is now judged necessary to state explicitly that only a 'validly ordained' priest can celebrate.

He not only presides, but 'brings into being the sacrament of the Eucharist'. His role is not only that of reciting the narrative, but of 'pronouncing the words of consecration'; not only of invoking the Holy Spirit upon the gifts, but of 'imploring the Father to send the Holy Spirit to effect through them [the words of consecration] the transformation of the gifts'. In so doing the priest 'offers sacramentally the redemptive sacrifice of Christ'. The concern expressed by the *Observations* about Christ's institution of the sacrament of order is again evident here. A new point is added about the need to take account of the 'character' conferred by priestly ordination, 'which implies a configuration to the priesthood of Christ' and is 'central' to the Catholic understanding of the difference between ordained priesthood and the common priesthood of the baptized. The point about apostolic succession, which the CDF had made only summarily in 1982, now receives much fuller treatment. Disagreement on whether women can be ordained to the priesthood is again said to concern the nature of ordination. The point the *Observations* made about the insufficiency of historical-critical interpretation of scripture is made again (paras. 28-29).

It is evident that not much has changed. Despite nine years of consultation, during which the *Final Report* was sent for comment to every bishops' conference in the world (some of whom arrived at more favourable verdicts than that given by the CDF), while theologians submitted both the ARCIC and the CDF documents to close scrutiny, and detailed discussion was held between the CDF and the CPCU, the 1991 *Response* adds little to the *Observations* and subtracts little from them. The question must be asked how seriously this lengthy and complicated process of consultation was taken.

It is illuminating to compare the *Observations* and the 1991 *Response* to ARCIC with the earlier *Appraisal of BEM* which was drafted, not by the CDF but by the CPCU. This document also complains of ambiguity. BEM, it is said, 'does not say unambiguously that the eucharist is in itself a real sacrifice, the memorial of the sacrifice of Christ on the cross'; 'the content of the word "transubstantiation" ought to be expressed without ambiguity' (131.1).[18] 'The notion of intercession is used in a way that could seem insufficient to explain the sacrificial nature of the eucharist in the

Catholic sense' (130.1). 'Catholics would ask' if BEM's attempt to explain the propitiatory nature of the Eucharist in terms of intercession is 'sufficient' (130.2). 'Further explanation is needed from the Catholic point of view' to make it clear that the eucharistic change is not just an 'extrinsic' 'change of meaning' (131.2). 'It would have been useful' to indicate the ecclesiological and eschatological grounds for the reservation of the blessed sacrament (132.1). BEM's description of ordination 'does not express clearly the Catholic conviction that ordination is indeed a sacrament' (137.1). 'Further qualification' needs to be given to the explanation of the priest's representative role to make it clear that the priest acts *in persona Christi* (134.2). Clarification of the distinction between the ordained and the common priesthoods is desired so as to indicate that the difference is of kind and not of degree (135.1). It is regretted that BEM, in describing episcopal succession as a sign of apostolicity, discarded the phrase 'effective sign' which had appeared in an earlier draft (136.2); the absence of the same phrase is regretted in the explanation of ordination (137.1). The account of ordination, while containing elements which 'take up Catholic concerns', 'does not express clearly the Catholic conviction that ordination is indeed a sacrament'; similarly the question of the competent minister of ordination 'is not treated in a way that is sufficiently according to the Catholic faith' (137.1). The treatment of the mutual recognition of ministries (a subject which ARCIC had not discussed in detail in the *Final Report)* is described, with uncharacteristic lack of nuance, as 'unsatisfactory' (137.2); 'for us it is not only agreement on the question of the apostolic succession, but also being situated within it, that is necessary for recognition of ordination' (139.1). It will be seen that the CPCU's response to BEM has much in common with the CDF's *Observations* on ARCIC and the *Response* of 1991. Not only is the same request made for unambiguous explanations, but many of the topics on which further clarification is required are the same.

The Catholic Church would not be taking ecumenical agreements seriously if it did not pore over them through a microscope to discover the extent to which they correspond with official Catholic teaching. Where the documents differ however is in their tone. On reading the *Appraisal of BEM* one is left with the impression of a demanding, but fundamentally affirmative reaction. The assessments of ARCIC do not leave so clear an impression. The difference is due, I believe, to two reasons. The first is one of arrangement: the *Appraisal of BEM*, section by section and point by point, commends what it finds to commend before passing on to aspects that need 'clarification from the Catholic point of view'; the documents on ARCIC, though not without commendatory passages (especially the 1991 *Response*), generally arrange their exposition so that large blocks of negative criticism seem to predominate. The second reason, I suspect, is strategic: in responding to ARCIC there is more need to show that much more work needs to be done before reunion can be achieved than there is in the case of BEM, which, as a multilateral document aiming at convergence rather than consensus, is several stages less advanced along the road to unity.

IV

Commentators on the 1991 *Response* have generally concentrated their attention on the critical aspect of the document. In two articles in *The Tablet* I have maintained that this is a misreading of the *Response*, which begins by describing the *Final Report* as 'a significant milestone not only in relations between the Catholic Church and the Anglican Communion but in the ecumenical movement as a whole', and ends with a quotation from the 1989 Common Declaration of Pope John Paul and Archbishop Robert Runcie in which they solemnly recommitted themselves and their Churches to 'the restoration of visible unity and full ecclesial communion'. I believe in fact that the most important difference between the *Observations* and the *Response* is the latter's markedly more encouraging tone.

The *Observations* had also begun by giving 'full recognition to the positive aspects of the work accomplished by ARCIC', and in particular 'the quality of the doctrinal rapprochement achieved, in a serious attempt at a converging interpretation of the values considered fundamental by both sides'. But almost all the rest of the document is devoted to what are called 'negative aspects'. Whenever a particular passage is given a nod of approval ('One notes with satisfaction that several formulations clearly affirm the real presence'), a qualification follows ('Certain other formulations … do not seem to indicate adequately what the Church understands
    In the light of these observations, therefore, it seems necessary

to say that the substantial agreement which ARCIC so carefully intended to present should receive even further clarification.')

The *Response* strikes a much more even balance between commendation and criticism. The Explanatory Note devotes its first five paragraphs to indicating the 'notable progress' which ARCIC has achieved, and to the 'very consoling areas of agreement or convergence on questions that are of great importance for the faith of the Catholic Church' (paras. 5, 10). The ensuing twenty paragraphs of detailed criticism are followed by a Conclusion intended to offer reassurance:

> The above observations are not intended in any way to diminish appreciation for the important work done by ARCIC I … The quite remarkable progress which has been made in respect of Authority in the Church indicates just how essential this question is for the future of the Anglican-Roman Catholic dialogue (paras. 30-31).

The document is so anxious not to leave an inquisitorial impression that it puts to itself the objection that it has not sufficiently followed 'the ecumenical method, by which agreement is sought step by step, rather than full agreement at the first attempt'. Its excuse is that it has attempted to answer the question put to it, whether the *Final Report* is consonant with the Catholic faith (para. 33). This concern for the impression the document leaves prompted one cynical reader to describe it as a bomb in gift-wrapping. But, as I wrote in *The Tablet,* in this case the gift-wrapping itself is the most important part of the message.[19]

What future work will ARCIC II have to undertake to meet the demands made by the *Response*? Presumably after completing its current work on morals, the commission will have to try to provide the clarifications that are asked for. However, as I suggested earlier in this article, it is doubtful whether the univocal precision that the *Response* demands is either possible or desirable. So ARCIC will perhaps have to enter into dialogue with the CDF in order to determine the respective places of pluriformity and univocity in ecumenical agreements.

A passage from Pope John Paul's recent address to a group of English bishops shows that he does not regard the *Response* to be damaging to the relationship between the two churches, as the use of the words 'progressive' and 'furtherance' shows:

A number of recent events, including the publication of the
Official Response to the ARCIC I *Final Report*, have shown
that it is possible to go to the heart of the serious differences
between divided Christians and still persevere in a fraternal and progressive dialogue. The significance of the
Response lies not only in its furtherance of the theological
dialogue, important though this is, but especially in the fact
that the Catholic Church and the Anglican Communion
are speaking to each other at the level of what may be called
a truly ecclesial dialogue.

The Pope means, I think, that the dialogue is now being carried
on, not only by an official commission, but at the highest level of
authority in the two churches: 'It is precisely at this level that,
eventually and with God's grace, substantial moves towards
unity and faith and visible ecclesial unity will take place'.[20]

However the initiative does not all lie with ARCIC, and that for
two reasons. First, relationships, even formal relationships, between the Catholic Church and the Anglican Communion are not
all determined by Rome and Lambeth. The Anglican Communion is not centrally structured like the Catholic Church; the binding decisions are those taken not by Lambeth Conferences but by
the provinces. It is therefore possible (within limits which need to
be explored) for the two Churches in different regions to be formally related in different degrees of (not yet perfect) communion.
In addition the practice, already existing in places, of making
covenants between the Churches at diocesan and local levels, can
be extended. Secondly, it is not only, or perhaps not principally,
theological dialogue that leads separated Churches to recognise
the authenticity of one another's faith. As Pope John Paul said in
his address to the English bishops: 'Ecumenism is not solely a
matter for the highest Church authorities. It also involves a dialogue of life at the level of exchanges and cooperation between believers at every level.'[21]

There must take place a slow development of mutual knowledge,
respect and affection – a development that needs to be nourished
by common prayer. The members of one Church need to feel in-
stinctively that the Lord loves a Christian from another Church
just as much as he loves them. There needs to take place a process
which has been described by the Anglican Co-chairman of

ARCIC II as the 'reconciliation of memories', and by Pope John
Paul II and Patriarch Dimitrios of Constantinople as 'the purifica-
tion of the collective memory'.[22] It is not principally at the centre
that this process will take place, but, more importantly, in every
local community and in each Christian's heart.

Notes

1   These documents have been published in many forms. For the
       two sets of *Observations* I shall be referring to the editions pub-
       lished by the Catholic Truth Society, London 1982 and 1988
       respectively; for the *Response* to ARCIC I I shall refer to the text in
       Catholic International 3/3, 1-14 Feb 1991, pp. 125-30, with its para-
       graph numbers; for the *Appraisal* of BEM, to the edition in
       Information Services, Secretariat for Christian Unity, 65 (1988), pp.
       121-39.

2   Quoted in Y. Congar, *Diversity and Communion*, (London, 1984), p.
       140.

3   The judgment of the other provinces of the Anglican Communion
       are summarised in *The Emmaus Report: A Report of the Anglican
       Ecumenical Consultation of 1987*, (London, 1987).

4   *Towards a Church of England Response to BEM and ARCIC*,(London,
       1985), p.67.

5   ibid., p. 74.

6   ibid., pp. 79-80.

7   *The Truth Shall Make You Free*. The Lambeth Conference 1988,
       (London, 1988), pp. 210-11.

8   ibid., p. 212.

9   *Observations* (1988), p. 16.

10   This statement of the *Response* has been criticised as an inaccurate
       account of the Tridentine doctrine of transubstantiation accord
       ing to which, through the consecration, there takes place 'the con
       version of the whole substance of the bread into the substance of
       the body of Christ our Lord, and of the whole substance of the
       wine into the substance of his blood' (H. Joseph D. Denzinger,
       Enchiridon Symbolorum, hereafter DS, 1642). His soul is present
       through 'concomitance', his divinity through the hypostatic
       union (DS 1640).

11   *Unitatis Redintegratio*, 11.

12   *Observations* (1982), A.2 (ii).

13   ibid., A.2 (iii).

14   *Response*, Expl. Note.
15   *Response to BEM*, III.B.2.
16   'Response to the response: 1', *The Tablet*, 7 Dec. 1991, p. 1525.
17   *DS* 1651, 1740.
18   The references in brackets refer to pages and columns in the
      SCU's Information Service; see note 1.
19   *The Tablet*, 18 Jan. 1992, p. 63.
20   The text is given in *Catholic International* 3/10, 15-31 May 1992,
      pp. 452-5. The quotation is on p. 455.
21   ibid. p. 455.
22   M. Santer, 'The Reconciliation of Memories', *Their Lord and Ours*,
      ed. by M. Santer, (London, 1982), pp. 149-160. Pope John Paul II
      and Patriarch Dimitrios, Joint Declaration of 1979, quoted in *They
      are in Earnest*, (ed.) E.J. Yarnold, (Slough, 1982), p. 179.

Roman Catholic-Methodist Dialogue: A Silver Jubilee

Geoffrey Wainwright

It is tempting to date the beginnings of dialogue between Methodists and Roman Catholics, not from the start of conversations after the Second Vatican Council, but rather from John Wesley's *Letter to a Roman Catholic*. Then we should be celebrating, not the mere twenty-five years since the first meeting of the Joint Commission between the Roman Catholic Church and the World Methodist Council at Ariccia in 1967, but rather the almost two hundred and fifty years that have elapsed since Wesley penned his irenic open epistle at Dublin on 18 July 1749. In all honesty, however, we should then have to admit that those two and a half centuries contained long periods of silence on account of mutual ignorance as well as some sharp bursts of express mutual dismissal and polemics. A word about Wesley's generous letter may nevertheless not be out of place at the outset of these reflections on the contemporary dialogue.

Albert C. Outler, a Methodist observer at Vatican II and then a member of the first three series of the Joint Commission, took the initiative of including what he called Wesley's 'olive branch to the Romans' in his widely used anthology of *John Wesley* in the Library of Protestant Thought published by Oxford University Press, New York (1964). It was left to Michael Hurley, a member on the Catholic side for the first ten years of the Joint Commission, to republish John Wesley's *Letter to a Roman Catholic* in monographic form. After recruiting prefaces from Bishop Odo Hagen, the current President of the World Methodist Council, and Augustin Cardinal Bea, Hurley's fellow Jesuit and at that time President of the Vatican Secretariat for Christian Unity, Hurley himself furnished an informative and perceptive introduction to the volume.[1]

Calling for an end to mutual bitterness and barbarities, Wesley in his *Letter* grounded an appropriate mutual regard between Catholics

53

and Protestants in the fact that both were created by the same
God and redeemed by his Son. Even more, they shared to a large
degree a common faith and a common ethic. Wesley sets out the
belief of 'a true Protestant' in terms of an expansion upon the
Nicene Creed[2] and describes how a true Protestant serves God
and loves his neighbour in ways that Wesley is convinced must
meet with a good Catholic's approval. This is sufficient, Wesley
judges, for Catholic and Protestant 'to provoke one another to
love and to good works', loving one another and endeavouring
'to help each other on in whatever we are agreed leads to the
Kingdom'.

This was not all that Wesley had to say to or about Roman
Catholics. At the doctrinal level, he could be polemical as well as
irenical, as is shown in the fiercely critical 'A Roman Catechism
faithfully drawn out of the allowed writings of the Church of
Rome, with a Reply thereto'.[3] At times, Wesley could view the
Roman Catholic Church as at least 'a part' of 'the Church'[4] – and
this not withstanding the presence in it of 'unscriptural doctrines'
and 'superstitious modes of worship'.[5] Yet at other times it seems
rather that he valued individual Roman Catholics as Christians
practically in spite of their institutional allegiance.[6]

As late as the World Methodist Council's agreement in 1966 to
enter upon a dialogue with the Roman Catholic Church, Michael
Hurley could note an admission by Arthur Worrall that many
Methodists 'still believe that the Roman Catholic Church is not
part of the Christian body but is an insidious conspiracy of the
devil'.[7] By its most recent report in 1991, the Joint Commission
found it possible and necessary to acknowledge that 'while
Wesley and the early Methodists could recognise the presence of
Christian faith in the lives of individual Roman Catholics, it is
only more recently that Methodists have become more willing to
recognize the Roman Catholic Church as an institution for the divine good of its members'.[8] Not dissimilarly, the Roman Catholic
Church has in modern times moved from an exclusivist understanding of 'no salvation outside the Church' through a more af-
fectionate recognition of 'separated brothers and sisters' to an as
yet inchoate attribution of some ecclesial status to Protestant
communities. Thus again the Joint Commission in 1991: 'For its
part, the Roman Catholic Church since Vatican II certainly in-

cludes Methodists among those who, by baptism and faith in Christ, enjoy 'a certain though imperfect communion with the Catholic Church'; and it envisages Methodism among those ecclesial communities which are 'not devoid of meaning and importance in the mystery of salvation' (*Unitatis redintegratio* 3).[9] At stake is what the chairmen's preface to the 1991 report calls 'the ecclesiological self-understanding' of Catholics and Methodists respectively and the place that gives to recognition of the other. It is thus a matter of the concrete location of the Church which both Catholics and Methodists confess. That is the fundamental issue whose opening first made the contemporary dialogue possible, and to whose exploration the contemporary dialogue in turn has in one way or another devoted itself.

Let us then retrace the work of the Joint Commission over the past twenty-five years and celebrate the measure of its achievement on the occasion of its silver jubilee.[10] Five rounds of dialogue have been spread over five years each, with a report being prepared each time for presentation to the Vatican and to the World Methodist Council at the latter's quinquennial gathering. The reports have become popularly known by the place and date of the WMC meeting to which they were presented: Denver 1971, Dublin 1976, Honolulu 1981, Nairobi 1986, and Singapore 1991.[11] While the chronological sequence will set the frame-work of this essay, threads will be allowed to crisscross where the substantive discussion demands it.[12]

I

The work of the Joint Commission was marked in its first ten years by three features: first, it sought to identify certain traits of ethos and style that were characteristics of Catholism and Methodism respectively and would undoubtedly affect any bilateral dialogue between them; second, it treated certain general themes that were of common interest at the time to the broad body of Christians, such as 'Christianity and the Contemporary World' (showing the same obsession with 'secularization' as marked the 1968 Uppsala assembly of the World Council of Churches), 'Common Witness and Salvation Today' (again in tandem with the WCC conference on mission and evangelism at Bangkok 1973), and 'Spirituality'; third, the Joint Commission tackled a number of subjects – eucharist, ministry, authority – that were also occupying other international bilateral dialogues in which the Roman Catholic Church was engaged, notably with the Anglicans and with the Lutherans.[13]

The most far-sighted work was that which attempted to pinpoint the characteristic relationship between Catholics and Methodists, for these considerations have arisen time and time again in the subsequent labours of the Commission. Thus Denver noted, first, that this dialogue had 'a singular advantage: there is no history of formal separating between the two Churches, none of the historical, emotional problems consequent on a history of schism' (6). Informally put, the relationship may sometimes be easier between a grandmother and her grandchildren than between a child and its parent (as would be the case between Anglicans and Rome, or between Methodists and Canterbury). At this point, it may also be remarked that even those (American) Methodist Churches which have episcopal government are 'not claiming apostolic succession in the sense of the Roman Catholic Church' (Nairobi 1986, 33). Happily, the trauma focused on *Apostolicae Curae* does not affect relationships between Methodists and Roman Catholics. Singapore 1991 declared that 'the mutual recognition of ministry will be achieved not only by Methodists and Catholics having reached doctrinal consensus, but it will also depend upon a fresh creative act of reconciliation which acknowledges the manifold yet unified activity of the Holy Spirit throughout the ages. It will involve a joint act of obedience to the sovereign Word of God.' (94)

Next Denver noted a number of positive affinities between Catholics and Methodists. At the head stood 'the central place held in both traditions by the ideal of personal sanctification, growth in holiness through daily life in Christ' (7). If Methodists have seen 'the cultivation of "scriptural holiness" and its spread as a common task, making the church a fellowship rather than a hierarchy', they can now welcome 'the universal call to holiness' found in Vatican II's *Lumen Gentium*; and throughout the dialogue, the Catholic members have endeavoured to make clear that the 'hierarchy' that attracts Methodist suspicion is in fact at the service of the whole body for its sanctification (as recognised by Singapore 1991 in its entire second half, *Ministry and Ministries: Serving within the Apostolic Tradition*). The concern for Christian holiness was taken up by the statements of Honolulu 1981 on the work of the Holy Spirit in justification, regeneration, sanctification and the making of moral decisions; and the theme of sanctified discipleship persisted into the important section of Singapore 1991 on *The Pattern of Christian Life*. (39-48)

Denver noted, too, that 'the disciplined life of the early Methodists, aimed at renewing a lax Church, set standards for the whole of Methodism which have found Roman Catholic parallels more often in the early life of religious foundations such as the Jesuits' (8). Here emerges, at least obliquely, a way of viewing Methodism that may have some ecclesiological significance. In exploring 'ways of being one Church', Nairobi 1986 offered the following among elements for a model of organic unity:

> From one perspective the history of John Wesley has suggested an analogy between his movement and the religious orders within the one Church. Figures such as Benedict of Nursia and Francis of Assisi, whose divine calling was similar to a spiritual reform, gave rise to religious orders, characterized by special forms of life and prayer, work, evangelization, and their own internal organization. The different religious orders in the Roman Catholic Church, while fully in communion with the Pope and the bishops, relate in different ways to the authority of Pope and bishops. Such relative autonomy has a recognized place within the unity of the Church. (24)[14]

Denver implied a doxological affinity between Methodism and Catholicism when it spoke of 'a theology that can be sung'(9). It was noted that the hymns of Charles Wesley, and particularly the eucharistic hymns, find echoes and recognition among Catholics. Yet this was a point at which Methodists needed to face the more general question of 'how far the Wesleys remain a decisive influence in contemporary Methodism'. Interestingly, the Catholic theologian Francis Frost, who was later to become a member of the Joint Commission, observed in a major article written about this time that Methodism retained a fundamental unity in the spiritual heritage upon which Wesley so firmly placed his stamp;[15]

but Wesleyan theologians know what a struggle it is to keep
Wesleyan impulses to the fore. Thereby is raised a basic methodological principle in all ecumenical dialogue: is a particular ecclesial tradition to be represented in its 'ideal', its 'classical', or its
'empirical' form?[16]

Finally, Denver registered a shared concern between Roman
Catholics and Methodists for a 'common mission' (10). Evangelization has remained a recurrent theme in the dialogue. Thus
Nairobi 1986 included "mission' in its concise formulation of
what 'full communion' would entail (20) and gave a soteriologi-
cal grounding to the need and provision of 'authoritative teaching: Because God wills the salvation of all men and women, he
enables the Church, by the Holy Spirit, so to declare the truth of
the divine Revelation in Jesus Christ that his people may know
the way of salvation' (63). And, in a statement which Singapore
1991 took up from Nairobi as its own epigraph: 'Because God so
loved the World, he sent his Son and the Holy Spirit to draw us
into communion with himself. The sharing in God's life, which
resulted from the mission of the Son and the Holy Spirit, found
expression in a visible *koinonia* [communion, community] of Christ's
disciples, the Church'.

But from the outset, Denver was not blind to the kinds of issues
that made dialogue between Roman Catholics and Methodists
not only possible but necessary. In regard to three issues in particular (paragraphs 12-13), the first Joint Commission presaged
its own work together with the themes that would continue in
Dublin 1976 and even beyond. Firstly, Catholics who spoke
warmly of the Wesleys' eucharistic hymns nevertheless observed that 'few Methodists would hold the doctrine of the Real
Presence in any sense akin to the Catholic meaning'. Secondly,
interest was shown in 'recent Roman Catholic writings on ministry, in which reflection on ordinary and extraordinary ministries seems to have many points of contact with the original
Methodist situation'. Thirdly, it was noted that 'Methodists found
unacceptable 'the dogmas concerning the papacy'. Thus were set
as themes for dialogue the eucharist, ministry and authority.

As to the eucharist, Denver set out a concise list of 'points of
agreement' (83) and 'points of disagreement' (84), concentrating
on the presence of Christ, the sacrificial dimension of the rite, and

conditions of admission to communion. These were then developed -- with the help of the English Roman Catholic/Methodist Commission and in light of the Anglican/Roman Catholic International Commission or ARCIC's Windsor *Statement on the Eucharist* of 1971 -- in the second round of the dialogue that led to Dublin 1976 (paras. 47-74). According to Denver, both Methodists and Roman Catholics 'affirm as the primary fact the presence of Christ in the Eucharist, the Mass, or the Lord's Supper', 'a reality that does not depend on the experience of the communicant', although 'it is only by faith that we become aware of the presence of Christ in the eucharist'. This is 'a distinctive mode or manifestation of the presence of Christ', although 'the presence in the Eucharist for the Methodists is not fundamentally different from the presence of Christ in other means of grace, e.g. preaching' (Denver 83-84). Dublin clarifies the last point by saying that 'we both affirm that wherever Christ is present he is present in his fullness' (56), and that 'Roman Catholics, like Methodists, affirm the presence of Christ in the proclamation of the gospel and the other sacraments'(57). Both Denver (83) and Dublin (54) record agreement between Methodists and Catholics that the eucharistic bread and wine are 'efficacious signs of the body and blood of Christ', although the two parties differ over the 'transformation' of the elements, which is for Catholic teaching a change in their 'inner reality' whereas Methodist understanding goes in terms of their acquiring 'an additional significance' (Dublin 59-60).

While both sides agree that the sacrificial language of the eucharistic celebration refers to 'the sacrifice of Christ once-for-all', to 'our pleading of that sacrifice here and now', to 'our offering of the sacrifice of praise and thanksgiving', and to 'our sacrifice of ourselves in union with Christ who offered himself to the Father', Catholics 'are also accustomed to speak of the sacrifice of the Mass as something which the Church offers in all ages of her history' (Dublin 65-66). Catholics explain that this does not 'add to' or 'repeat' Christ's sacrifice but 'makes present in a sacramental way the same sacrifice' (66). 'For some Methodists', however, 'such language would imply that Christ is still being sacrificed. Methodists prefer to say that Christ has offered one sacrifice for sins and now lives to make intercession for us, so that we in union with him can offer ourselves to the Father, making his sacrificial death our only plea' (ibid.). All agree that the eucharistic memorial (*anamnesis*) is 'not a mere calling to mind of a past event or of its significance, but the Church's effectual proclamation of God's mighty acts' (Dublin, 63). While Denver had specified, in an ostensibly agreed way, that the eucharist memorial 'is a re-enactment of Christ's triumphant sacrifice and makes available for us its benefits' (83), Dublin more chastely declares that 'some' (and probably not only, we may surmise, among the Methodists) would wish to link this dynamic view not with 'a re-enactment of Christ's triumphant sacrifice, but with Christ's being present and bringing with him all the benefits of his once-for-all sacrifice for us' (63).

Liturgically speaking, Dublin notes among Roman Catholics 'a renewal in the theology and practice of the ministry of the word' and among Methodists, at least 'in many places' (71), 'a notable recovery of eucharistic faith and practice' – 'a remarkable convergence, so that at no other time has the worshipping life of Methodists and Roman Catholics had so much in common' (51). Canonically, the Roman Catholic Church admits other Christians to eucharistic communion only in cases of urgent pastoral necessity and with firm doctrinal safeguards; Catholics in similar circumstances are expected not to ask for the sacrament 'except from a minister who has been validly ordained in the eyes of the Roman Catholic Church' (Dublin 69-70). Methodists in some places often issue a generous – or lax, depending on one's point of view -- 'open invitation' to the Lord's Table; but the prevalent historic practice has been to offer, in a more disciplined way, hospitality to 'baptized communicant members of other communions who desire to come', while not thinking it fitting for Christians to receive communion in any denomination at random, for communion with Christ is linked with membership of a local church' (Dublin, 68). Here arises very concretely the basic ecclesiological question of the identification of the Church.

Denver recorded a fundamental agreement on 'Jesus Christ as the One through whom the ministry, whether sacramental or otherwise, is both identified and ultimately authorized. The minister participates' -- 'by the power of the Holy Spirit' (92) -- 'in Christ's ministry, acts in Christ's name' (89). Methodists asked Catholics (a) how to understand the 'difference in kind and not merely in degree' (Vatican II) between the ordained ministry and the laity, (b) what stood in the way of Roman Catholic recognition of Methodist ministry as 'authentic', and (c) what were the 'guiding principles for understanding the meaning of orders' as well as the 'pragmatic factors' in their development.

In its 'joint statement' on ministry, Dublin 1976 was again helped by the English Roman Catholic/Methodist Commission, working this time in light of ARCIC's Canterbury *Statement on Ministry and Ordination* (1973). Christ's earthly and continuing ministry is reaffirmed as 'the fundamental ministry', in which those who are called and ordained to 'special ministry' within the whole people of God are given a share by the Spirit so that they may 'represent' Christ (77-81). It is agreed that 'the Church's apostolicity involves continuous faithfulness in doctrine, ministry, sacrament and life to the teaching of the New Testament', and that 'in considering the ordained ministry of another church we use this faithfulness as our criterion'(84). Yet Catholics and Methodists 'differ in the account we give of apostolic succession' (ibid.). For Roman Catholics, 'the graded threefold ministry is derived from the teaching of the New Testament through the living tradition of the Church. True succession in ministry is guaranteed only by episcopal laying-on of hands in historical succession and authentic transmission of the faith within the apostolic college' (85). Methodists hold that 'the New Testament does not lay down any one form of ministry as binding for all times and places' (86), but they 'can regard a succession of ordination from the earliest times as a valuable symbol of the church's continuity with the church of the New Testament, though they would not use it as a criterion' (87). The question of apostolicity will recur in Nairobi 1986 and, above all, in Singapore 1991.

According to Dublin 1976, both Catholics and Methodists 'see the central act of the ordained ministry as presiding at the eucharist in which the ministry of word, sacrament and pastoral care is perfected' (97). That vision doubtless illuminates a rather remarkable 'agreement' concerning the 'difference' and 'interrelationship' between the ordained ministry and the 'common priesthood of the faithful':

> Roman Catholics and Methodists agree that by ordination a new and permanent relationship with Christ and his

church is established. The ordained minister is called and enabled by the Holy Spirit to be the representative person who focuses in his ministry the manifold ministries of the whole church. He is a sign of the gospel and of the oneness of Christ's church, both to the church and to the world; an ambassador of Christ who bids men to be reconciled to God and declares to them the forgiveness of sins; a priest who embodies the priesthood of all believers in which he shares, and by his ministry serves and sustains it'. (98)

It is a pity that that paragraph has not attracted wider ecumenical attention as a candidate for expressing necessary and sufficient agreement on this matter.

Denver 1971 noted that problems of authority had cropped up throughout discussions of explicitly treated themes and were 'implicit in some of the deep "crevasses" between us', namely 'the Mariological dogmas and the doctrines of the Infallibility or Indefectibility of the Church' on the one hand, and on the other 'the whole question of the origin and development of Methodism as a work of the Spirit, of an extraordinary and prophetic character, [which] has at some point to be related to the Catholic view of Church order and of its understanding of the authority of Christ in his Church' (100). There followed a discursive mini-essay that bears all the marks of Albert Outler's hand, proposing a concrete survey of the instances of authority in each Church and forecasting that they would differ chiefly in their relative importance and sequence of operation (101-118). Questions of authority came to be more formally addressed by Honolulu 1981, Nairobi 1986, and (in an interesting reversion to Outler's 'traditionary' approach) Singapore 1991.

II

The third round of the dialogue was marked by a change in method and aim that would continue up to the present. The attempts to cover whole waterfronts are now given up, and the work of each quinquennium is concentrated much more on a specific theme. Each quinquennial report now moves 'towards'– with due modesty -- 'an agreed statement' on the chosen topic, so that common and differentiated declarations no longer have to be dug out from a mass of reportage on mere discussions within the Joint Commission.

Honolulu 1981 is entitled *Towards an Agreed Statement on the Holy Spirit*. The subject was chosen because 'Methodists and Catholics repeatedly discover a notable rapport when they speak of spirituality', which is of course properly a pneumatological reality, 'the life of the Spirit' (7). Moreover, the Commission wagered that 'the doctrine of the Holy Spirit underlies much of the "ecumenical agenda" still to be considered by our Churches' (ibid.).

Since 'the doctrine of the Person of the Holy Spirit has never been a point of dispute between us', Honolulu found it sufficient to begin with a brief, orthodox statement on 'the Holy Spirit in the Godhead' (8-11). Then the work of the Spirit is seen to begin with creation and the disclosure of its meaning, always in relation to the Word (12). The Holy Spirit operated at every stage of the Word's incarnation in Jesus, at his conception, at his baptism, and during his entire public ministry (13). After Christ's death and resurrection, his work came to consummation in the gift of the Holy Spirit, by which the Church was founded and created as the community of the New Covenant (13; 19). Endowed with a variety of spiritual gifts (20), this community is guided by the Paraclete, who recalls the words of Jesus and enables the Church's missionary witness (17; 21), thus working towards the final glorious transformation of all who love God (21-22).

Close agreement is found between Catholics and Methodists on justification, regeneration and sanctification, matters on which many Protestants have historically been at odds with Rome: 'The Holy Spirit is present and active within us throughout the entire experience of conversion which begins with an awareness of God's goodness and an experience of shame and guilt, proceeds to sorrow and repentance, and ends in gratitude for the possession of a new life given us through God's mercy in Jesus Christ. Justification is not an isolated forensic episode, but is part of a process which finds its consummation in regeneration and sanctification, the participation of human life in the divine' (13). John Wesley and the Council of Trent concur in their emphasis on the prevenience of grace: 'Always it is the Spirit's special office to maintain the divine initiative that precedes all human action and reaction ... In the restoration [of the sinner to a right relationship with God through the atoning work of Christ], both the initiative, the agency and the consummation is the ministry of the Holy Spirit as he brings Christ to us and leads us to him. When a sinner is led to Christ and receives him, he is re-born and given the power to turn away from a life curved back upon itself towards a "new life", opened out to love of God and neighbour' (14-15, cf. 18).

Still under the rubric of the Holy Spirit, further attention is given by Honolulu to the 'Christian experience' of believers and to 'authority in the Church'. By 'the Spirit of adoption' the children of God are able to call with confidence on the merciful Father (16), and by the same Spirit the faithful are guided to a knowledge of the truth and to an obedience in which the fruit of the Spirit is manifested(24). 'Holiness in heart and life' represents a convergence between John Wesley and 'the mainstream of Catholic spirituality' which could have significant implications 'for the future of the cause of Christian unity' (26, cf. 30, 32).

To those gathered in Christ as the Church, 'Christ's authority is mediated through the Spirit, who is Love, and hence all authority that flows from this source is part of God's good gift. Whether it be the personal authority of holiness or the charism of *episcope* conferred by the Spirit on the ordained ministry, whether it be teaching or disciplinary, authority implies that what is propounded, commanded or recommended ought to be accepted on the ground that it comes from this source' (33). Boldly, Honolulu goes on to declare that 'the papal authority, no less than any other within the Church, is a manifestation of the continuing presence of the Spirit of Love in the Church or it is nothing. Indeed it should, in its exercise, be pre-eminently such a manifestation. It was declared at Vatican I to be "for the building up and not the casting down of the Church" -- whether of the local Church or the communion of local Churches' (35). That is the pneumatological perspective set by Honolulu for the emotional and theological clarification of the delicate issues of authority in the Church, and particularly the contentious matter of the papacy.

Ecclesiology, in fact, came to the fore in the fourth and fifth rounds of the Roman Catholic-Methodist dialogue, as it did in other bilateral dialogues in the 1980s[17] and as tended to happen on the multilateral scene also when the Churches looked for the assumptions and implications contained in the convergences regarding 'baptism, eucharist and ministry' in the Lima text of the WCC Faith and Order Commission.[18]

III

The Nairobi report was entitled *Towards an Agreed Statement on the Church*. For half its length it dealt rather broadly with a general vision of the Church and its unity, with a gentle narrowing of focus to 'structures of ministry'. The second half of the report then concentrated quite sharply on 'the Petrine office', as had become the favoured ecumenical term for matters relating to the papacy.

The Church is seen as a community and communion resulting from God's mission of the Son and the Spirit (1-3) and participating already in the life of the Triune God as 'sign, sacrament and harbinger of the Kingdom of God in the time between the times' (8). While there is some avowed reticence among Methodists about the direct application of the term 'sacrament' to the Church, yet the origination of the Church in the 'mystery of the Word made flesh' as well as the presence of the dominical sacraments in the Church allow the Church to be spoken of at least in a 'sacramental perspective' (9-16).

Nairobi notes that the word 'church' is used in the New Testament for 'Christians meeting together in a house or living in the same city' as well as 'in a more universal way for the body of Christ ... the communion of the saints on earth and in heaven' (18). Later application of the term also recognized 'diversities of language or rite, such as Syrian Church, Coptic Church or Latin Church' (19). But when the usage results from 'fundamental differences in doctrine, faith or ecclesial policy, such as Lutheran Church, Methodist Church, or Roman Catholic Church', then 'Methodists and Roman Catholics ... recognize that the divisions underlying this last usage are contrary to the unity Christ wills for his Church' (20). 'Obedience to Him who will bring about this unity' entails, says the Joint Commission, commitment to 'a vision that includes the goal of full communion in faith, mission and sacramental life' (ibid.). The full communion at which Methodists and Catholics aim must be expressed visibly, without thereby suppressing the gifts with which God has graced the separate communities (21).

Recognizing that an ecclesiology shaped in a time of division cannot be expected to be entirely satisfactory, the Joint Commission then sets about exploring 'ways of being one Church' as a means of helping Methodists and Catholics to give proper recognition to each other's ecclesial character and to overcome the present state of division between them (22). Various ecumenically current visions or realities are said to offer 'elements for a model of organic unity in the *koinonia* of the one Body of Christ' (24): (a) the notion of *typoi* (associated with the name of Cardinal Willebrands), whereby 'within one Church in which there is basic agreement in faith, doctrine and structure essential for mission, there is room for various "ecclesial traditions", each characterized by a particular style of theology, worship, spirituality and discipline'; (b) the analogy of 'religious orders' within a single Church, already mentioned above; (c) the idea of 'sister churches', which might perhaps be broadened from its predominantly geographical sense so as to 'envisage reunion among divided traditions as a family reconciliation'; (d) the example of the relations between 'Churches of the Roman (Latin) rite and those of various oriental rites in communion with the Bishop of Rome'. The Joint Commission broached the question, whether the pastoral care of such traditions would require separate, possibly overlapping jurisdictions, or whether it could be provided by a single exercise of *episcope* in each place (27).

Attention is then turned more precisely to 'structures of ministry'. A historical concomitance is recognized between the establishment of the scriptural canon, the formation of the classical creeds, and the clear emergence of a threefold ministry of bishop, presbyter and deacon; but the Joint Commission notes that Methodists and Catholics 'are not agreed on how far this development of the ministry is now unchangeable and how far loyalty to the Holy Spirit requires us to recognize other forms of oversight and leadership that have developed, often at times of crisis or new opportunity in Christian history' (29). The question is sharpened by Catholic belief in the primacy of the Bishop of Rome, which Vatican II rests on the affirmation that 'to ensure the indivisible unity of the episcopate, [Jesus Christ] set St Peter over the other apostles (*Lumen Gentium* 18)' (36). Since Catholics judge this to be 'a fundamental principle of unity of faith and communion', Methodists and Catholics are bound to consider questions of the Petrine office and the primacy of the Bishop of Rome in their search for 'full unity in faith, mission and sacramental life'.

Paragraphs 39-75 do indeed begin a treatment of these matters. Under the exegetical guidance of Raymond E. Brown, then a member of the Joint Commission, an agreed picture of 'Peter in the New Testament' is provided (41-47). This is followed by a historical account (51-54) of the early centuries in which the see of Rome, claiming Peter as its first bishop and finding that other churches also 'applied' Petrine texts to the apostle's successor in that see, exercised an outstanding role in testimony to the apostolic tradition, so that eventually the bishops assembled at Chalcedon in 451 could declare 'Peter has spoken through Leo'. This 'primacy of love', however, from the fourth and fifth centuries onwards took a 'more juridical turn', so that 'increasingly developed formulation and application of the Roman claims and more vigorous resistance to them alike contributed to the origin and continuation of divisions in Christianity, first in the East and eventually in the West' (54).

The historical role and claims of the Roman see may also be set in the sociological context of the 'desirability' or 'need' in the whole Church for 'a leader to exercise ... a unifying role in service to the worldwide *koinonia*' (48-50). That more pragmatic approach might prove more acceptable to Methodists, who 'accept that whatever is properly required for the unity of the whole of Christ's Church must by that very fact be God's will for his Church. A universal primacy might well serve as focus of and ministry for the unity of the whole Church' (58). Thus it is 'not inconceivable', says the Joint Commission in adopting the curial style of the double negative, 'that at some future date in a restored unity, Roman Catholic and Methodist bishops might be linked in one episcopal college and that the whole body would recognize some kind of effective leadership and primacy in the bishop of Rome. In that case Methodists might justify such an acceptance on different grounds from those that now prevail in the Roman Catholic Church' (62). In the matter of jurisdiction, Roman Catholics in any case 'recognize that theological exploration of the relation between the authority of the Pope and that of the local bishop remains unfinished' (61).

Nairobi finally turns to the question of papal infallibility in the larger context of 'authoritative teaching' (63-75). It is agreed that 'God … enables the Church, by the Holy Spirit, so to declare the truth of the divine Revelation that his people may know the way of salvation' (63); that 'the Scriptures bear permanent witness to the divine revelation in Christ and are normative for all subsequent tradition' (64); that 'properly understood, the decisions of the ecumenical councils which met in the first centuries command assent throughout the whole Church, and there is no reason to think that at the end of the patristic era God stopped enabling this Church to speak in such a way' (65). The difficulty arises when Catholics claim that 'in carefully defined and limited circumstances, the Pope exercises the capacity [of the Church to formulate the faith in a manner that is beyond doubt] in and for the whole Church' (69). Indeed, in the concrete cases of Mary's immaculate conception and assumption, Methodists hold that these papally proclaimed dogmas 'lack assent and reception by all Christian people', which is 'the final judge' of what is in clear 'agreement with the Scriptures' (72-73).[19] Clearly, 'further study' is needed, and the Joint Commission suggested that Methodists might approach the question of infallibility from the perspective of their own doctrine of 'assurance':

> Starting from Wesley's claim that the evidence for what God has done and is doing for our salvation can be 'heightened to exclude all doubt', Methodists might ask whether the Church, like individuals, might by the working of the Holy Spirit receive as a gift from God in its living, teaching, preaching and mission, an assurance concerning its grasp of the fundamental doctrines of the faith such as to exclude all doubt, and whether the teaching ministry of the Church has a special and divinely guided part to play in this. In any case Catholics and Methodists are agreed on the need for an authoritative way of being sure, beyond doubt, concerning God's action insofar as it is crucial for our salvation. (75)[20]

The Vatican's publication of the Nairobi report was accompanied by an invited commentary from the veteran Ottawa ecumenist, J. M. R. Tillard.[21] Recognizing that the report 'issues from honest and lucid research together into the points of convergence and points of divergence that emerged in each group's conception of the profound nature and of the structure of the Church of God', Tillard esteems it 'a significant document' that will be of interest beyond its immediate Catholic-Methodist context. For it allows one both to take stock of 'the emergence of a shared "given"' and to 'identify the major obstacles'. He places 'among the most beautiful definitions of the Church' the opening description of the Church as a visible *koinonia* resulting from the missions of the Son and the Spirit and embodying participation in the life of the Triune God. According to Tillard, the Joint Commission was right in its judgement, as he reformulates it, that '*koinonia* must not be considered as one model of unity. Rather it is the fundamental reality which any model must make possible and actualise' (cf. 23f.). Proposing to develop further the 'sacramentality' of the Church as not only the 'manifestation of God's grace' but an 'effective help' in God's hand, Tillard calls the Church 'the reality which, evangelized by God, evangelizes for God, and reconciled with God, reconciles with God, and drawn together by God, draws together for God'. Some movement in this direction was in fact to be made in the ensuing Singapore report of 1991. That was the case also with Tillard's complaint that, in admitting that 'there was no shared understanding of the nature and meaning of apostolic succession', the report did not go beyond diagnosis.

IV

With hindsight, the Joint Commission itself recognizes that a gap existed in the Nairobi report between the agreed historical description of the Church in the New Testament period and the early centuries, on the one hand, and the theological discussion, on the other, of issues such as ministerial structures, authoritative teaching, and above all 'the Petrine office'. These latter must be settled if comtemporary endeavours towards church unity are to succeed. The filling of that gap required, the Joint Commission saw, a historico-theological treatment of the theme and reality of 'The Apostolic Tradition'. George Tavard, when the Commission met at Lisbon in 1988, provided the working motto for this fifth series of the dialogue: the continuance of the apostolic tradition was to be viewed as '*koinonia* in time'.[22]

The aim, as the chairmen's preface to the Singapore 1991 report states it, was to develop historical and theological perspectives - 'consistent with the doctrinal positions of both churches' – in which it would become possible to start reconsidering controversial matters in ways that allowed convergences to be discerned and then further developed. In particular, it was hoped, as the report itself puts it, that an approach by way of 'the teaching, transmission and reception of the apostolic faith' might 'set the difficult problem of ministry in a new light, since this topic has hitherto been predominantly considered in its relationship to the administrative and sacramental life of the Church rather than in relation to its teaching' (4). This did not mean that the sacraments and ecclesial structures themselves would be neglected in the report, but rather that they would be treated in relation to the apostolic tradition which they and their ministers respectively embody, enable and serve.

In broad perspective, 'Tradition' is defined by Singapore as 'the living transmission of the Gospel of Christ, by manifold means, for the constant renewal of every generation' (5). The Church itself is first the result of the Gospel: it was born and lives from the gracious purpose of the Father as carried out by the Son and the Spirit, the Son founding the Church by his act of redemption and the Spirit sustaining the Church as its principle of sanctification (7). Then the Church is 'the place where the Word of God is spoken, heard, responded to, and confessed' (15) and where 'the Spirit abides'(29). Finally the Church is the instrument 'through' which the mission of the Triune God 'continues' as the Church proclaims the Gospel to the world (1).

The 'manifold means' by which the apostolic Gospel is transmitted in and through the Church are all governed by the Word and enlivened by the Spirit. Analogously to the coinherence of person, speech and deed in the Word incarnate (9; 17), 'every possible human resource is employed: linguistic, ritual, artistic, social and constitutional' (16). Thereby 'the risen Christ speaks to us today', provided preachers and hearers have learned 'his language' (6); since 'Christ was content to speak with other audiences and with later generations through those who became his first disciples' (15), 'the written word of Scripture' that contains the apostolic testimony remains the 'permanent norm' of the 'un-

broken process of communication between God and human beings' (16). Since Christ 'sends the Spirit to us to open our understanding and to guide our words and actions' (6), each generation is enabled to hear, speak and act for itself (18). To be assured
of the 'continued hearing and assimilation of the Word of God',
'we maintain communion with those who have heard and
obeyed the Word before us' (ibid.).

In light of this belief in a communion of the saints, the Joint
Commission next proposes as common a reading as it can between Methodists and Catholics of the historical and theological
constants in the confession of Christ, Christian experience, and
ecclesial identity. In 'the pattern of Christian faith' (33-38), a special place is given to the Nicene Creed as the work of 'those theologians who provided the earliest elucidations of the faith' and a
comprehensive and authoritative statement' that is 'common to
Catholics and Methodists and a factor in the degree of communion that Catholics and Methodists already share'. In the pattern
of Christian life' (39-48), a strongly Pauline account of faithful existence confirms the agreement of justification, regeneration, sanctification and spirituality that earlier rounds in the dialogue had
registered. In 'the pattern of Christian community' (49-52), it is
argued from the New Testament that a true hearing of the Word
of God always entails an obedient shaping of the Church's life
(50), and that 'the actions that allow the Church to grow in
strength and ordered life – the setting apart of new ministers, or
corporate decisions and teaching, for example – are always accompanied by the action of the Holy Spirit, who makes it possible for us to live in communion and harmony with one another
(Acts 13:2; 15:28; 16:6-7; 2 Tim. 1:14)' (52). It is precisely here,
however, that a common reading of subsequent Christian history
becomes difficult for Catholics and Methodists, divided as they
are on matters of ordination, decision-making and teaching authority. In such contexts the differences are both cause and effect
of the divisions between them.

That is why the Singapore report, in its second half, must then
turn from 'the apostolic faith: its teaching, transmission and reception' to the more specific question of 'ministry and ministries:
serving within the apostolic tradition'. In principle, it is agreed
that ministry stands in 'service of the Word' (54-57) and is made

possible by 'gifts of the Spirit' (58-61). For the sake of the ministry of all Christians, there is a 'specific charism received by those who are called to the ordained ministry' and which is 'directed toward the ordering and harmony which must prevail in the exercise of all the gifts' (60). The ordained ministry is 'a gift to the Church for leadership in its corporate and worshipping life, for the maintenance and deepening of its order and structure, for the organisation of its missionary witness, and for discernment in understanding and applying the Gospel' (61).[23]

According to the Joint Commission, 'Catholics and Methodists are at one in seeing in a divinely empowered ministry the guidance of the Holy Spirit and are moving in the direction of greater shared understanding of the nature of ordination and of the structure of the ministry in regard to the responsibility to teach and to formulate the faith'(77). Subsequent paragraphs indeed show a large measure of agreement on the call and commission to ministry, on the rite of ordination as the laying on of hands with prayer, and on the regular duties of the ordained. Nor is the gap a wide one between the 'sacramentality' of the Catholic ordination and the Methodist view of ordination as 'an effective sign by which the grace of God is given to the recipient for the ministry of word and sacrament (88). The crunch comes with regard to the existence and role of bishops in the matters of both 'succession and oversight'(94).

It is part of 'the Catholic understanding and practice of apostolic succession' that 'bishops', in the historic line, through the act of ordination share ministerially the high priesthood of Christ, in one degree or another, with other ministers (bishops, presbyters and deacons), who are their fellow workers in carrying out the apostolic duties entrusted to them (cf. Vatican II, *Presbyterorum ordinis*, 2; and Dublin, 85; Nairobi, 31). On the Methodist side, even those (American) Methodist churches which are episcopally ordered do not claim such a succession, even while holding to the orderly transmission of ministry (cf. Dublin 87; Nairobi, 31, 33). Methodist churches on the British model have no order superior to presbyter (cf. Dublin 91; Nairobi, 33), though they have in several cases shown themselves willing to accept the episcopal office for the sake of unity with Anglicans who have an episcopacy which, to boot, claims the historic succession (cf. Dublin 86;

Nairobi, 29, 33, 35). Again, on the Catholic side, oversight clearly resides with the bishops (cf. Dublin, 89; Nairobi, 32). On the Methodist side, supreme oversight on the British model clearly resides with the Conference (cf. Dublin, 91; Nairobi, 33), which for over a century has included laypersons, while the American model involves a delicate 'separation of powers' between bishops and variously composed Conferences (cf. Dublin, 90). Catholics and Methodists can agree that 'central to the exercise of *episcope* is the task of maintaining unity in the truth' and that 'teaching is', therefore, 'the principal part of the exercise of *episcope* (93). For Catholics, the form of this is quite precise: 'The teaching of a common faith by the college of bishops in union with the successor of Peter ensures unity in the Truth. The succession of bishops through the generations serves the continued unity of the Church in the faith handed on from the apostles' (93). Some Methodist responses to the WCC Faith and Order text on *Baptism, Eucharist and Ministry* allow us to surmise that Methodist churches might accept a historic episcopal succession as, in the Lima phrase, 'a sign, though not a guarantee, of the continuity and unity of the Church'; but the Roman Catholic response to BEM judges this to be inadequate.[24]

V

In the conclusion to Singapore 1991, the Joint Commission offers its own brief retrospect and prospect. Retrospectively, the dialogue since its inception a quarter-century ago 'has contributed to the degree of mutual recognition which now exists'. It has done so by the clarification of Methodist and Catholic positions and traditions, especially as these impinge on each other. A large measure of common faith has been brought to light, so that the increase in shared life that has begun may confidently be expected to continue' (101). Frankly it should be admitted that 'measuring' the current achievement remains difficult because much depends on the 'reception' of the Commision's work at the various levels of ecclesial life in Roman Catholicism and Methodism.[25]

Prospectively, 'the need now is to consolidate the measure of agreement so far attained and to press forward with work on those areas in which agreement is still lacking. Continuing doctrinal progress should both encourage and reflect the growth in mutual recognition and in sharing in the life of the Triune God' (101).

In March 1992, conversations took place in Rome between the current chairman of the World Methodist Council's executive committee (Donald English), the general secretary of the WMC and co-secretary of the Commission (Joe Hale), the Methodist co-chairman of the Commission (Geoffrey Wainwright), the cardinal president of the Pontifical Council for Christian Unity (Edward Cassidy), the Council's episcopal secretary (Pierre Duprey), the Joint Commission's Catholic co-secretary (Kevin McDonald) and Jared Wicks of the Gregorian University, the author of the Vatican's invited commentary on Singapore 1991.[26] It was generally agreed that the mission of the Triune God in the history of revelation and redemption provided a satisfactory theological perspective. Consolidation and development of existing achievements could take place by their explicit integration into that perspective. That was the perspective, too, in which Bishop Duprey urged that the Joint Commission should return to the difficult question of episcopacy, both diachronically as 'succession' and synchronically as 'oversight', establishing (Catholics would add) communion.[27] My own bet is that the Joint Commission will sooner or later need also to grasp more firmly the nettle of baptism and its relation to faith and ecclesial belonging.[28]

The greatest need of all, perhaps, is that local Churches become aware of the work of the international Joint Commission and, by their joint study and practical cooperation in the spirit of John Wesley's *Letter to a Roman Catholic*, both benefit from and contribute to its labours. If that task is performed faithfully and effectively over the next twenty-five years, it may not take quite two hundred and fifty years before Methodists and Roman Catholics enter a 'full communion in faith, mission and sacramental life' such as Wesley could scarcely have envisaged.

Notes

1   John Wesley's *Letter to a Roman Catholic* (ed.), Michael
       Hurley, S. J. (London and Dublin, 1968). Hurley developed a part-
       icular theme in Wesley's thought in 'Salvation Today and Wesley
       Today', in *The Place of Wesley in the Christian Tradition: Essays
       delivered at Drew University in celebration of the commencement of the
       publication of the Oxford Edition of the Works of John Wesley*, edited
       by Kenneth E. Rowe (New Jersey, 1976), pp. 94-116

2   Here Wesley anticipated the method of the ongoing WCC Faith
       and Order study, *Towards the Common Expression of the
       Apostolic Faith Today*. See G. Wainwright, 'Methodism and the
       Apostolic Faith', in *What Should Methodists Teach?* ed by M.
       Douglas Meeks, (Nashville, 1990), pp. 101-17

3   *The Works of the Rev. John Wesley, A.M.*, (ed.), Thomas Jackson,
       London, 1829-31; (reprint Grand Rapids, 1984), vol. X, pp 86-128.
       See also 'Popery calmly considered', ibid., pp. 140-158

4   Thus, in his *Journal* for 25 March 1743, in reply to Bishop Richard
       Challoner's *The Grounds of the Old Religion* Wesley notes: 'In the
       first thirty pages the author heaps up scriptures concerning priv-
       ileges of the Church. But all this is beating the air till he proves the
       Romanists to be the Church, that is, that a part is the whole' cf. *The
       Works of John Wesley*, vol 19 [*Journals and Diaries II: 1738-1743,*]
       (ed.), W.R. Ward and R.P. Heitzenrater, (Nashville, 1990), p. 319f

5   See Sermon 74. 'Of the Church' (1786), in *The Works of John Wesley*,
       vol 3 (Sermons III: 71-114), (ed.), A.C. Outler, (Nashville, 1986), p. 52

6   Thus again to Bishop Challoner, in a letter of 17 February 1761 to
       the Editor of the 'London Chronicle', Wesley countered:
       '*Whatever may be the case of some particular souls*, it must be said, if
       your own marks be true, the Roman Catholics in general are not
       "the people of God"'. *The Letters of the Rev. John Wesley*, A.M. (ed.),
       John Telford, (London 1931), vol 4, p. 138.

7   *John Wesley's Letter ...* p. 7, citing *The Methodist Recorder*, 1 Sept
       1966.

8.   *The Apostolic Tradition: Report of the Joint Commission between the
       Roman Catholic Church and the World Methodist Council, Fifth Series
       1986-1991,* paragraph 100. Published in *Proceedings of the Sixteenth*

World Methodist Conference, Singapore 1991, (ed.), Joe Hale, Lake Junaluska (North Carolina), World Methodist Council, 1992, pp. 287-310

9   *The Apostolic Tradition* (as in note 8), paragraph 100.

10   In addition to the international dialogue, bilateral dialogues have taken place in New Zealand, in Great Britain (where, for instance, studies were devoted to the eucharist, to ministry, to authority, to justification, and to the Blessed Virgin Mary), and in the United States (where reports have been issued on *Holiness and Spirituality of the Ordained Ministry*, 1976, *Eucharist Celebration: Converging Theology, Divergent Practice*, 1981, and *Holy Living and Holy Dying*, 1989).

11   The first three reports can be conveniently located in *Growth in Agreement: Reports and Agreements of Ecumenical Conversations on a World Level*, (ed.), H. Meyer and L. Vischer, Ramsey (New Jersey, and Geneva, 1984). Initial publications respectively in *Proceedings of the Twelfth World Methodist Conference. Denver, Colorado, 1971*, (ed.), Lee F. Tuttle, (Nashville, 1972), pp. 39-68 in *Proceedings of the Thirteenth World Methodist Conference, Dublin, Ireland, 1976*, (ed.), Joe Hale, Lake Junaluska, World Methodist Council, 1977, pp. 254-270, and in *Proceedings of the Fourteenth World Methodist Council, Honolulu, Hawii, 1982*, (ed.), Joe Hale, Lake Junaluska, World Methodist Council, 1981, pp. 264-277; and in the Secretariat for Promoting Christian Unity's *Information Service*, no 21 (1973/3), pp. 22-38, no 34 (1977/2), pp. 8-20, and no 46 (1981/2), pp 84-96. The Singapore 1991 report has been identified in note 8. The Nairobi 1986 report, *Towards a Statement on the Church*, was analogously published in *Proceedings of the Fifteenth World Methodist Conference*, (ed.), Joe Hale, Lake Junaluska, World Methodist Council, 1987, pp 360-72 and as a separate brochure; the Secretariat for Promoting Christian Unity's *Information Service*, no 62 (1986/4), pp. 206-16; and *One in Christ* 22 (1986), pp. 241-59. In view of the different editions, references will be given by paragraph number rather than by page.

12   I should perhaps declare my own hand and reveal that I have been a member of the Joint Commission since 1983 and its Methodist co-chairman since 1986.

13   Mention should also be made of attempts to deal with matters of
      moral theology that have been little treated in other international
      bilateral dialogues but figured between Catholics and
      Methodists: 'Christian Home and Family', 'Euthanasia'...

14   Albert Outler once described Wesley as 'rather like the superior
      general of the evangelical order within a regional division of the
      church catholic', and he extended the idea into ecclesiological
      significance for Methodism: 'We need a catholic church within
      which to function as a proper evangelical order of witness and
      worship, discipline and nurture.' These ideas are developed
      within the context of a broader discussion in my own essay on
      Methodism's 'ecclesial location and ecumenical vocation' cf G.
      Wainwright, *The Ecumenical Moment: Crisis and Opportunity for
      the Church*, (Grand Rapids, 1983), pp. 189-221

15   F. Frost, 'Méthodisme' in *Catholicisme, hier, aujourd'hui, demain*,
      (ed.), G. Jacquemet, Paris, Letouzet et Ane, 1948ff, vol IX, cols. 48-71

16   In the Roman Catholic-Methodist dialogue, the matter is made
      very complex by the long and varied tradition which Catholicism
      claims for itself, whereas Methodists tend to see themselves as
      starting in the eighteenth century. In another perspective, I
      would want to maintain that Catholics and Methodists share a
      common tradition at least until the sixteenth century. See G.
      Wainwright, *The Ecumenical Moment* (as in note 14), in particular
      (teasingly) p. 189

17   For instance: *Salvation and the Church* (1987) and *Church as
      Communion* (1991), both by the Second Anglican-Roman Catholic
      International Commission (ARCIC II); *The Church: Community of
      Grace* (1984), by the Joint Commission between the Lutheran
      World Federation and the World Methodist Council; *Together in
      God's Grace* (1987), between the World Methodist Council and the
      World Alliance of Reformed Churches.

18   See *Baptism, Eucharist and Ministry 1982-1990: Report on the Process
      and Responses*, (Geneva), especially pp. 147-51

19   In one of his celebrated *bons mots*, Raymond George, a member of
      the Joint Commission for its second, third and fourth rounds,
      launched the thought that 'the Pope has spoken infallibly on only
      two occasions, and each time he was wrong'.

20   See G. Wainwright, 'The assurance of faith: a Methodist approach to the question raised by the Roman Catholic doctrine of infallibility' in *One in Christ* 22 (1986), pp 44-61

21   J.M.R. Tillard, 'Commentary on "Towards a Statement on the Church"', in the Secretariat for Promoting Christian Unity's *Information Service*, no 62 (1986/4), pp 216-19, and in *One in Christ* 22 (1986), pp. 259-66

22   G. Tavard, 'Tradition as *koinonia* in historical perspective', *One in Christ* 24 (1988), pp. 97-111

23   So far, the Joint Commission has done no more than register the recent divergence over the ordination of women (Dublin 1976, 102; Singapore 1991, 96-7).

24   For the response of the Methodist Church of Great Britain on this matter, see *Churches Respond to BEM*, vol, 2, (ed.), Max Thurian, (Geneva, 1986), pp. 226-7; for the Roman Catholic response, see vol. 6, 1988, pp. 32-3

25   The practice of the World Methodist Council has been to give, without detailed discussion, a general welcome to the Commission's reports and extend it mandate; only at one point (Honolulu 1981) did the WMC express its 'opinion', a propos of paragraph 19 of the report presented to it, that 'baptism might more satisfactorily be stated to be *an* outward sign and means of grace and faith rather than *the* outward sign'. At the Vatican, the customary procedure has been for the Secretariat (now Council) for Christian Unity to make a brief epistolary response to the co-chairmen, sometimes incorporating observations from the Congregation for the Doctrine of the Faith and offering suggestions for future work.

26   For Wicks's commentary, see *One in Christ* 28 (1992), pp. 74-81, or *Catholic International*, vol 3, no 3 (1-14 February 1992), pp. 120-24.

27   See already Dublin 1976, 81-91, 104; Nairobi, 27, 29-38; Singapore, 92-4. Even in Singapore 1991, the treatment specifically of episcopacy remains, in Tillard's earlier phrase, largely 'diagnostic'. For a broad discussion from a Wesleyan and Methodist view point, see G. Wainwright, 'The end of all ecclesiastical order', *One in Christ* 27 (1991), pp. 34-48.

28   See already Honolulu, 19; Nairobi, 2, 11-16, 17; Singapore, 16, 26,
      40-1, 46, 59-60, 63-6. Notice the late emergence of the theme.
      Nairobi spoke quite strongly of baptism and eucharist *together* as
      dominical sacraments and 'effective signs of grace': 'By the
      power of the Holy spirit they bring into our lives the life-giving
      action and even the self-giving of Christ himself. It is Christ's
      action that is embodied and made manifest in the Church's
      actions which, responded to in faith, amount to a real encounter
      with the risen Jesus' (16). Of baptism in particular it was said that
      'neither of us believes that a non-baptized person is by that very
      fact excluded from salvation, nor that baptism automatically
      ensures perseverance unto salvation' (12, footnote 2). Yet that
      very footnote acknowledged that 'we must still examine and
      resolve persisting differences concerning the efficacy of baptism,
      particularly of infants'. I remember just how gingerly the
      Commission had to tread in formulating paragraphs 63-6 of
      Singapore 1991. The chief problem resides in the mixed heritage
      that Methodists received from Wesley and to which both 'sacra-
      mentalists' and 'experientialists' can appeal. On the one hand,
      Wesley endorsed a 'high' view of baptism in republishing his
      father's treatise on the subject, and he never quite abandoned
      belief in the baptismal regeneration of infants, although he
      appears gradually to have phased away the mention of it. On the
      other hand, his standard sermons clearly show his opinion that
      one can 'sin away' one's baptismal status and need to be 'born
      again' - again! Wesley distinguished between water baptism, as
      the 'outward and visible sign', and 'the new birth' as the inner
      reality, but he failed to give a clear and consistent account of how
      the two were related. See Bernard G. Holland, *Baptism in Early
      Methodism*, (London, 1970), and O.E. Borgen, *John Wesley on the
      Sacraments*, (Nashville, 1972). In turn, it seems fair that Methodists
      should press with Catholics the question of the ecclesiological
      status of the many baptised who never come to faith and practice
      or lapse from them.

Mary and Ecumenism: Paths Ahead

Christopher O'Donnell

The Mother of Jesus has been a figure of some contradiction between Christians. Though not apparently central to the concerns of the Reformation, the role of Mary inevitably became questioned as the implications of the reformers' insights were gradually applied to all areas of theology. Centuries of polemic followed: Catholic were often carried away by enthusiasm; not a few evangelical Protestants showed some antipathy towards the Mother of God, as they repeated *Christus solus, scriptura sola, gratia sola*. It was not a time for dialogue. There is a sense in which the Virgin gave rise to *ressentiment* with latent hostility, anger and indignation on the part of Protestants. The Roman Catholic response was often disdainful, disregarding deeply felt criticisms that were not without some genuine foundations.

The dispute between Roman Catholics and Protestants on issues of mariology was to a very notable degree operating on an affective level, a crucial fact to which neither side often adverted. Protestants saw mariology as a threat to the lordship of Jesus and hence to a central tenet of faith attested in the most primitive creeds (1 Cor 12:3; Rom 10:9). Lutherans in particular saw in many aspects of mariology a threat to the assurance of faith (*certitudo*) which lies in Christ alone.[1] Catholics saw one whom they loved ignored or even disdained.

This affective antagonism is much more significant than has been previously realized; questions of mariology are not marginal to theology. Karl Barth in the 1930s saw mariology as *the* heresy of the Catholic Church, in a sense encompassing all the others.[2] By contrast, Hans Urs von Balthasar saw the Marian dimension as a key to the understanding of the Church and of the Christian response to the divine initiative.[3] If mariology is seen by these two major 20th century theologians as being far from peripheral, indeed even a pivotal, then advances in ecumenical agreement about Mary might make a considerable contribution to the whole cause of Christian unity.[4] Such indeed is the conviction of the Ecumenical Society of the Blessed Virgin Mary, which from 1967 has contributed much to ecumenical understanding.[5]

I

In recent years there has been a significant number of studies on Mary from an ecumenical viewpoint. They can be divided into a few convenient categories. From the 1960s there have been notable attempts on the part of Catholics to study the writings of the reformers.[6] It has become clear that the reformers themselves were more open to Marian doctrine and devotion – especially liturgical celebrations – than their successors, with whom the principle *scriptura sola* led to progressive hardening of positions. Trust in Christ alone, *sola gratia* was responsible for the widespread rejection of the cult of saints and of Mary.[7] Again the Marian and mariological congresses of the past few decades produced statements agreed by at least some of their participants at meetings in Santo Domingo (1965), Lisbon (1967), Zagreb (1971), Rome (1975), Zaragoza (1979), Malta (1983), and Kevelaer (1987).[8] The bilateral discussions between the various confessional bodies have not given much attention to mariology, though there are valuable contributions in the Anglican-Roman Catholic International Commission (ARCIC),[9] in the Old Catholic-Orthodox Conversations,[10] and in the U.S. Lutheran-Roman Catholic joint studies.[11] Finally, a number of investigations by Anglican and Protestant scholars writing at both academic and more popular levels continue to appear.[12]

This impressive body of material and the continuing difficulties have been frequently evaluated.[13] It is clear that there have been unnecessary misunderstandings between Catholics and Protestants surrounding Mary. Some of these have been identified through patient dialogue. For example, it is now more generally recognised that the Catholic Church is firm in its affirmation of the one mediation of Christ. Thus the Reformed pastor, Henry Chevannes, showed that the doctrine of Mary's mediation can best be understood within a philosophy of participation,[14] a position also found in Vatican II.[15]

But such discoveries tend to be confined to mariological circles and do not come into the mainstream of ecumenical dialogue. Similarly, fresh presentations of the Marian dogmas[16] do not seem to find the critical attention they deserve from Protestant theologians. Dialogues and writings of mainline theologians who have not specialized in mariology seem continually dominated by a rather deadening application of the *sola scriptura* principle.

More positively it can be said that ecumenical studies on Mary are beginning to show a major convergence in agreement. The Marian and mariological congresses in particular have focussed on the Communion of Saints as a Christian dogma with rich possibilities for an innovative view of the position and role of Mary. Such a development calls out for further study.

II

Time and time again ecumenical discussion about Mary comes up against the two recent Marian dogmas of the Immaculate Conception (1854) and the Assumption (1950). Even the East, for all its deeply felt and exuberant mariology, is not at ease with these exercises of the papal magisterium.[17] There are two obvious Protestant and Anglican objections: the right of the Pope to define dogmas of faith is not accepted; and these dogmas are not seen as clearly taught in scripture. The 16th century confessional statements would seem to demand that doctrines be clearly taught in scripture or to be obviously deducable from the bible. Thus the *XXXIX Articles* read:

> Holy Scripture containeth all things necessary to salvation: so that whatsoever is not read therein, nor may be proved thereby, is not to be required of any man, that it should be believed as an article of the Faith, or be thought requisite or necessary to salvation.[18]

The *Westminster Confession* is similar:

> The whole counsel of God, concerning all things necessary for his own glory, man's salvation, faith and life, is either expressly set down in Scripture, or by good and necessary consequence may be deduced from Scripture ...'[19]

In practice ecumenical agreement on Mary tends to be confined to what can be established by historical critical scholarship. Other specifications, for example about the identity of the brothers of the Lord,'will in part depend on the authority which (scholars) allot to later church insights'.[20]

Another issue of enormous practical consequence is the way in which Mary is regarded by various churches. Here we should make a broad division between the Roman Catholic and Eastern Churches on the one hand, and the Churches of the Reformation on the other. In the former there is a rich body of doctrine and also a strong devotional life. The supreme lyrical expression of Eastern Marian piety, the *Akathistos* hymn, heaps up symbol upon symbol in a profuse outpouring of praise and intercession, and this is part of an enormous corpus of hymnody.[21] Again, the theology of icons emphasizes that the sacred painting is not a mere reminder of Christ or a saint, but a quasi-sacramental meeting place between the one who prays and the heavenly person whose image is represented. The centrality of icons of Mary on the iconastasis, along with the image of her Son, the Pantocrator, is a constant reminder to Eastern Christians of the person and role of Mary. Moreover she is usually depicted as the *Hodigitria* pointing to Jesus as the Way. The other main classical pose, the *Deisis*, shows Mary in intercession.

The Roman Catholic Church has its own treasure of art and poetry, as well as extensive liturgical celebration of the Virgin. There is also a rich devotional life, and in some countries widespread grass-roots religiosity focusing on Mary. Mary is seen as powerful, and quite different from us in her gifts and glory, yet at the same time close to human history as the Virgin patron of places, groups and events.[22]

In both the Roman Catholic Church and in the Churches of the East then, Mary is seen as a person deeply concerned with humanity. The human reaction to her is intercession and above all love. By contrast, Protestant Churches, rather than being concerned with the person of Mary, prefer to consider her rôle. At the lowest she becomes merely an instrument of the Incarnation, supplying a body for the Word whereby he was made flesh.

Is there a way out of the 'scripture alone' impasse, one that could provide a bridge between these different attitudes to the Virgin Mary? It would seem that the way forward will not solely be by exegesis, though this must continue. Nor will it be only through theological dialogue. A key might be found in spirituality.

III

Spirituality does not feature in a central way in any of the major ongoing conversations between the Churches. The recent U.S. Lutheran-Roman Catholic Dialogue, *The One Mediator, the Saints and Mary*, refers several times to piety and devotion, but these are not used as key heuristic or interpretative tools.

Spirituality is a term with many meanings. In general it refers to the personal appropriation of revelation and to the study of religious experience and of the means of Christian growth towards the perfection of charity.[23] Spirituality, then, involves a central emphasis on the human person. In recent years a deductive or an *a priori* approach has given way more and more to a study of Christian experience in the light of the gospel and the human sciences, particularly anthropology and psychology.

Spirituality begins when we move from the question, 'what does the doctrine mean?' (theology), to the question, 'what does it mean for me as a disciple of Christ?' The shift in the two questions is exemplified in the monastic tradition of the *lectio divina*, as one moves from *lectio* to *meditatio*. The *lectio* is concerned with the meaning of the text; the *meditatio* with the meaning for the one who is praying. In the highly developed tradition of the *lectio divina* we have a living encounter with the sacred text whose more specific meanings the Holy Spirit brings to light.[24]

The *lectio divina* is a means of escape from any wooden or exclusive concentration on historical-critical hermeneutics. An important statement of the recent response of the Vatican to the ARCIC documents was the observation: 'As is well known, the Catholic doctrine affirms that the historical-critical method is not sufficient for the interpretation of scripture. Such interpretation cannot be separated from the living tradition of the Church.'[25]

The *lectio divina* enables the believer to enter into the process which gives rise to doctrinal development: continual Spirit-guided reflection on the scripture, actualizing it for the present. It may be objected that it gives a subjective understanding of the scripture, one unsuitable as a basis for ecumenical dialogue. But the *lectio* is scripture read within a theological and liturgical tradition, and thus sharing in the objectivity of the faith community.

In Catholic circles some exegetes, for example Ignace de la Potterie and René Laurentin, have been voicing disquiet at the over narrow approach of contemporary exegesis.[26] The former looks to the patristic tradition of exegesis and the latter to hermeneutical tools additional to historical-critical ones. The classic study of Henri de Lubac opens out the whole sapiential approach to the sacred text.[27] One ancient author allows us to grasp the freedom and the depth of patristic exegesis:

> Lord who can grasp the wealth of just one of your words? What we understand is much less than what we leave behind, like thirsty people who drink from a fountain. For your word, Lord, has many shades of meaning just as those who study it have many different points of view. The Lord has coloured his words with many hues so that each person who studies it can see it in what he loves. He has hidden many treasures in his word so that each of us is enriched as we meditate on it.[28]

Now, though it is clear that no Church lives solely on the restricted results of historical-critical investigation, ecumenical dialogues tend to get locked into its limitations. Churches live through their liturgy, through the proclamation and preaching of the Word, and their preachers are not austere exegetes. The actualization of the Word takes place continually in ways considerably richer, because helped by the Spirit, than academic exegesis will allow. The recent Lutheran-Roman Catholic dialogue shows that the Lutheran party recognised the need for 'biblical extension', but did not use it extensively as an approach.[29] The Reformed-Roman Catholic Dialogue likewise acknowledged that 'all churches must perforce go beyond the immediate letter of scripture'.[30] The Old Catholic-Orthodox Conversations appeal to a deepening of comprehension of both Holy Scripture and Tradition.[31] We might speak also of a charismatic exegesis for the way in which the Word comes alive in the worship of the Churches and in the reflection of its members.[32]

Access to the question of Mary and the Churches by way of spirituality could be expected to shed some light on the crucial areas mentioned above. It is helpful to make a distinction between an objective Marian spirituality, viz. the path to God traced by the Virgin herself, and a subjective spirituality, in the rôle of the Virgin for the Churches today.[33] The sources for Marian spirituality are not limited to scripture, though this has of course the principal place. Dogmatic theology is also a source, as too is liturgy. But there are also other sources. If the ecumenical problem of Mary is not merely a theological one, but an affective one, then fields of experience that touch the area of feelings will have their own contribution. Thus the Arnold Bax setting 'Of a Rose I Sing' draws us through the complexity of its variations into a sense of the harmony and beauty of the Virgin. Again, a most important ecumenical book by Canon A. M. Allchin points another way forward as he studies poets and preachers in the Anglican tradition.[34] Further, whilst respecting the susceptibilities of Protestants with regard to religious images, great works of art contribute a sense of the aesthetic with regard to the Virgin Mary. Though we can with Pope John Paul II contemplate the place of Mary in the majestic sweep of Ephesians 1:3-10,[35] our sense of wonder and of awe can also be stimulated by literature and the arts. We can enter with joy into the divine plan for Mary and so avoid the danger highlighted by Max Thurian of considering Mary merely as an instrument allowing the appearance of God on the earth.[36]

IV

Just as we do not have in the gospels a resource for a psychology of Jesus, much less have we the potential for a detailed consideration of the interior life of Mary. But the scripture does give us a picture of Mary in broad outlines which nonetheless enables us to get to the heart of her spirituality and from there to a Christian spirituality with Marian dimensions.[37] But if we are to do so successfully we need to attend to the nature of the biblical witness in the case of each writer.

Luke tells the story of the infancy of Jesus from a paschal standpoint. With Raymond Brown, it is preferable to call the first chapters of Luke and Matthew infancy gospels, for they anticipate the main themes of the later life of Jesus.[38] In the light of Pentecost, Luke and Matthew had a deeper knowledge of the events of the infancy of Jesus than Mary or Joseph would have had as they were happening. A main theme of Luke-Acts is that of the Messiah committed to poverty and despoilment going to the cross, and thence to be glorified in order that the Spirit would come upon the Church. Mary can be seen as in some sense foreshadowing the paschal mystery of her Son. The famous question in Luke 1:34, 'How can this be since I do not know man?' is not a question arising from a vow or commitment to virginity, but a query about how she is to be inserted into God's plan; it means 'what am I to do?' The reply of the angel is to stress the omnipotence of God.[39]

Though the exact purport of the sword in Luke 2:35 is not clear, it indicates in some way that Mary is to share in the rejection of her Son and it implies suffering. If the sword is to be interpreted in the light also of Ezekiel 14:17, then Mary will be challenged to stand in faith under the discriminating judgement of God.[40] Her spiritual journey, described by the Second Vatican Council as 'a pilgrimage of faith',[41] is above all marked by *kenosis*: her life took on the mark of obedience to the divine plan (Lk 1:38); her Son distanced himself from family life with her and Joseph because of a higher obedience to the heavenly Father (Lk 2:49); she was to have no role in the ministry of her Son (cf. Lk 8:19-21 with Mk 3:31-34); she was to stand at the foot of the cross in a final surrender of her Son (Jn 19:25-27); finally in obedience to her Son (Lk 24:49; Acts 1:4) she was part of the nucleus of the early Church which received the Spirit at Pentecost (Acts 1:14; 2:4).

The key for the understanding of Mary's spirituality lies in the angel's greeting, *kecharitômenê* (Lk 1:28), which can be translated as 'favoured one' (*New Revised Standard Version*), 'you who enjoy God's favour' (*New Jerusalem Bible*), or 'most favoured one' (*Revised English Bible*). The Greek perfect passive participle implies that what was begun in the past is continuing in the present. As this greeting is found instead of her name, it clearly asserts a most important truth about Mary. Thus, as Luke first presents Mary, we have the clearest possible assertion of *gratia sola*: Mary has received God's favour and she continued to enjoy it.

She is told to rejoice, *kaire*, a word that has messianic overtones in some LXX texts (e.g. Zech 9:9; Zeph 3:14). Mary's response to the

Word of God is not a mere passive acceptance of the message: she declares herself to be a slave (*doulê*) of the Lord, and therefore she really wants (*genoito* – optative) what the angel has announced (Lk 1:38). This complete act of faith in God's saving word is the beginning of a life of faith. For Mary faith is darkness as well as light. The phrase, 'the angel departed from her' (Lk 1:38) is not just an *inclusio* with v. 26, but also the end of revelations for Mary. Henceforth her faith will, like ours, be mediated. She will learn God's will from others: Joseph (Mt 1:24), the shepherds (Lk 2:17), Simeon (Lk 2:28-35), Anna (2:38), her Son (Lk 2:49; 8:21), Peter (Acts 1:16-22). All these will reveal to her God's plan and the meaning of her Son's mission. She is presented as not understanding immediately (Lk 2:33.48-50); like the wise man (Sir 39:1-3) she ponders the events and words as they unfold (Lk 2:19.51). She is praised for her faith. Elizabeth moves from a praise of her motherhood to her greater blessing as one who believed (Lk 1:42.45), just as Jesus would later transfer praise of his mother to the more profound blessing of hearing the word of God and obeying it (Lk 11:27-28). In the *Magnificat* she is presented as one who has penetrated the deep secrets of God's way as he exalts the humble, the *anawîm*, and puts down the self-sufficient.[42] Along with the Annunciation account, the *Magnificat* is an assertion of unmerited grace, a point made strongly by Luther in his commentary.[43]

Though faith as the response to God's gracious initiative is the basis of the spiritual life, it is not sufficient in itself. As ARCIC II notes: 'Living faith is inseparable from love, issues in good works, and grows deeper in a life of holiness'.[44] It is customary to see in Mary's three month visit to her expectant cousin Elizabeth an exercise of charity (Lk 1:39-45.56). But her love turns firstly to her Son; Luke repeats that she wrapped him in bands of cloth (Lk 2:7.12), a traditional sign of caring for a child (cf. Ezek 16:4). Her dedication to her Son is not called discipleship in the New Testament; it is arguably greater as she is his Mother. Her attitude to Jesus is seen in her last recorded words at Cana, 'Do whatever he tells you' (Jn 2:5) an evocation of the Israelite covenant response (Exod 19:8). A key text is the difficult one of Jn 19:25-27. The significance of the passage is clear from v. 28a: 'After this (*meta touto*) Jesus knowing that all was now fulfilled (*tetelestai*) ...'. The preceding action has therefore a significance in the divine plan. Given the highly symbolic writing of John at this point, the meaning cannot be restricted to Jesus making filial provision for a home for his mother. An interpretation that gives major weight to the incident is confirmed by the word of Jesus, 'Woman', previously used in the Cana incident (Jn 2:4). It clearly parallels the Woman of Genesis 3:1-20. Though a developed New Eve theology belongs to the following century, there is some correlation between Mary and the first woman, just as there is an analogy between Adam from whose side Eve was formed and the blood and water from the side of Jesus as he slept on the cross (Gen 2:21-22; Jn 19:34). Nor must the significance of the Beloved Disciple be overlooked. Whether he was John, another disciple or an idealized figure, the Gospel presents him as the exemplary model of following. The true disciple is therefore one who takes Mary to himself, makes a home for her (*eis ta idia* – Jn 19:27).

V

Spirituality begins as soon as we begin to ask, what does the doctrine mean to me? What does it mean for my journey in the Spirit? Specifically with regard to Mary here, we ask what relevance does the outline picture of Mary's own journey have for the Christian community and its individual believer? An initial response can be made in terms of the text in John 19 we have just considered. The beloved disciple is one who makes room for Mary.

The *lectio divina* tradition invites us to a sapiential reading of the scripture. It is not enough to remain with the objective meaning of the text; it needs to be actualized and contextualized in believers and in their community. A first step is to empathize with Mary in the events of her life. Such reflection allows the person of Mary to emerge; it is the movement from knowing about Mary to knowing her. It is from within such a contemplation of her life, and seeking her mind, that the danger of substituting her for her Son will be avoided. Her obedient faith shines through her actions and words. She points from herself to her Lord – 'Do whatever he tells you' (Jn 2:5).

But her prophecy still remains: all will call her blessed (Lk 1:48). This is a challenge to the Churches to take seriously the Lucan picture of Mary and to join in her thanksgiving and praise for God's mighty deeds in her (Lk 1:47-50). Whilst many might argue that they do not feel the need to praise Mary, it must be stated that it is more in conformity with the scriptures to celebrate her praises. If the psalms sing of the beauty of creation and call on all creatures to honour God, then it is all the more fitting to celebrate God's blessings in Mary. Spirituality is concerned not with a minimum service that avoids moral failure, but with an entry into the fullness of God's ways. The example of Elizabeth is proposed by Luke to his readers: she saw God's plan fulfilled in Mary's motherhood and faith, and her response was praise (Lk 1:42-45). Moreover, the visit of Mary was a blessing for her and for her unborn son John (Lk 1:42-44; cf. 1:15).

The Catholic Church has always insisted that true devotion to Mary is concerned in imitation of her virtues.[45] If faith is the most basic response to God, the New Testament only gives us a few models for constant, unfailing, obedient faith: Mary, Joseph her husband, John the Baptist, Simeon and Anna, Nathaniel, Joseph of Arimthea, Stephen, Paul and the Beloved Disciple. The importance of Mary lies also in her being a feminine model for the Church's response to the divine initiative (doulê). This most basic note of devotion is itself of ecumenical importance, as it is an invitation to contemplate Mary in order to imitate her virtues. Such attention to Mary is another way in which she comes alive for the believer in her secondary but still significant role in salvation history.

A spirituality will consider not only Mary's earthly life but also her situation in the Communion of Saints. In ecumenical circles there is a new openness to seeing Mary as intercessor for the Church, even if many Anglicans and Protestants will not go as far as invoking that intercession. Those who are open to the idea that Mary intercedes for the Church might be further open to see the idea of praying to her as an expression of the wish to be included in her intercession. God respects our freedom. Invocation of Mary under Christ allows us to assert that we freely and gratefully accept her intercession in the family of God which is the Communion of Saints.

The doctrine of the Communion of Saints has not been so well developed in the Western Churches compared with the East. It calls out for contemplation of the relation of Mother and Son. Cardinal Léon-Joseph Suenens has frequently stated that Jesus in heaven does not have the attitude, 'you see that one over there, she used to be my mother'. Though human relations are transformed in glory (cf. Mt 22:30), the intuition of the Church in the East and in the Catholic Church in the West is that these are not abolished. There is now still greater love between Jesus and Mary than was possible on earth. Mary is still concerned with her Son's mission. Those who are united with God in glory will surely have a truly universal charity towards all God's children.

The liturgy has especial importance for an ecumenical growth in the understanding of Mary. The Presbyterian Donald Dawe remarks, 'a liturgy and a piety that give no function to Mary never raise the question of her meaning'.[46] The Catholic participants in the recent Lutheran-Roman Catholic Dialogue recognised the importance of liturgy: 'it is the golden norm of Christian piety, ... devotions should harmonize with its spirit, its themes, its seasons.'[47]

We have to be aware of a difference between the various Churches. In the East six of the major feasts of the Church year have a Marian character and there are hundreds of local Marian feasts. The liturgy of the Roman Church is not so developed from a Marian viewpoint, but it does have fifteen feasts in the universal calendar, as well as many local feasts. Recently the Vatican has published texts for forty-six more Masses in honour of Mary, each with its own preface and readings.[48] Some other Churches have feasts which have Mary as their object or have a strong Marian focus, such as the Presentation of the Lord (2 February) or the Annunciation (25 March). But other Churches have no such feasts, and if they lack a lectionary of regular scripture readings they may recall some biblical teaching about Mary only at Christmas. Liturgy is both worship and instruction. If feasts recalling Mary are not in evidence, and if the texts about her in the scripture are not used for worship, there is little chance that there will be an appropriate piety about the Virgin.

The 1987 Catholic new collection of Masses in honour of the Blessed Virgin Mary contains one based on a Carmelite liturgy,[49] 'Mary Mother and Spiritual Teacher' (*B.M.V. Mater et Magistra Spiritualis*). Its main prayer is that by her intercession we may reach Christ who is the Mountain. Other prayers, and the all-important Preface which always gives the character of each Eucharistic celebration in the Roman rite, stress Mary's example as well as her intercession. In the Preface she is presented as an image of evangelical life from whom we learn to love God above all, to contemplate the Word with her spirit and to love our brothers and sisters with her heart. The scripture readings for this celebration are either Proverbs 9:17-21.34-35 or Isaiah 56:1.6-7, and for the Gospel, Matthew 12:46-50 or John 19:35-27. The notion of mountain is taken up in Psalm 15.[50] Such a liturgy leads beyond the point of considering Mary as an example and invites one to enter into her mind and heart in order to discover deeper aspects of our discipleship and our search for holiness and union with God in love of him and of others. It combines the thought of Mary's own spirituality or spiritual journey, and our response in obedient faith to the example of God's grace triumphant in her.

VI

Ecumenical discussions are successful in removing the grosser misunderstandings between the Churches. Thus, those involved in ecumenical dialogue are generally prepared to recognise that Catholics do hold the sole mediation of Jesus, even though some may be worried about how this is compatible with some Roman religious practices. But here, as in other areas of ecumenism, there is the problem of the reception of dialogue documents by the wider Church. In many Protestant Churches there is much apathy about Mary; in the Roman Catholic Church there is need for greater sensitivity and openness to the ecumenical criterion for Marian devotion advocated by Pope Paul VI in his exhortation on Mary.[51]

The question of piety remains a neuralgic point for Protestants, and at times for reasons which are not strictly theological. Piety is a vast subject and in itself hardly suitable for initial ecumenical dialogue. Perhaps the time has come to focus on Mary's spirituality, the way in which she is exemplar for the Christian people. This will lead us to respond to what God has revealed to his people concerning her graced journey to him. Such dialogue will inevitably lead to a deepened consideration of the Communion of Saints, which is a theological truth with an ecumenical importance far beyond the issues of Mary and the saints.[52]

Much further work still remains to be done on the implications of the hierarchy of truths, especially if intercommunion is to be possible between the Roman Catholic Church and Churches which remain agnostic about the Immaculate Conception and Assumption, or otherwise do not accept the infallible statements of 1854 and 1950. But in the end the most challenging and perhaps the most fruitful road of advance will remain spirituality. Donal Flanagan observed some years ago: 'I do feel it (the question of sensibility) is the key to much of our differences in what concerns the blessed Virgin Mary'.[53] If he is right, and I feel that he is saying something very important, then the way ahead must be one in which scripture, theology, religious experience and feeling meet. This meeting point is spirituality, an area whose importance has not yet been sufficiently recognised in the whole area of ecumenical dialogue at every level.

Notes

1   *The One Mediator, the Saints and Mary.* 'Lutherans and Roman
     Catholics in Dialogue 8' (Minneapolis, 1992), passim.

2   *Church Dogmatics* (New York, 1956), 1/2, pp. 142-43; P.S. Fiddes,
     'Mary in the Theology of Karl Barth', *The Month* 22 (1989), pp. 300-9.
     For some modification in his mariological views see F. Courth,
     'Kontroverspunkte im ökumenischen Gespräch über die Mutter
     Jesu und Ansätze zu ihrer Überwindung' in H. Petri, (ed.),
     *Divergenzen in der Mariologie. Zur ökumenischen Diskussion um die
     Mutter Jesu.* 'Mariologische Studien 7' (Regensburg, 1989), pp. 14-7.

3   'Die marianische Prägung der Kirche' in (ed.), W. Beinert, *Maria
     heute ehren* (Freiburg-Basel-Vienna, 1979), pp. 263-279; C. Smith,
     'Mary in the Theology of Hans Urs von Balthasar' in A. Stacpoole,
     (ed.), *Mary and the Churches* 'Papers of the Chichester Congress,
     1986, of the Ecumenical Society of the Blessed Virgin Mary'
     (Dublin, 1987), pp. 142-8

4   Cf. H. Fries, 'Stein des Anstosses oder Chance für die Ökumene',
     Stimmen der Zeit 207 (1989), pp. 158-170

5   See collected essays: A. Stacpoole, (ed) *Mary's Place in Christian
     Dialogue* (Slough, 1982); id. *Mary and the Churches* (n.3); id. *Mary in
     Doctrine and Devotion* (Dublin, 1990); *The Way Supplement* 25
     (1975); 45 (1982); *One in Christ* 16 (1980).

6   E.g. *De mariologia et oecumenismo* (Rome, 1962); T.F. O'Meara,
     Mary in Protestant and Catholic Thought (New York, 1966); W.
     Tappolet, (ed.), *Das Marienlob der Reformatoren* (Tübingen, 1962);
     Bibliog. E.R. Carroll, *Understanding the Mother of Jesus*
     (Wilmington & Dublin, 1979), pp. 145-152; S.C. Napiórkowski,
     'Ecumenismo' in S. De Fiores and S. Meo, (eds) *Nuovo dizionario di
     mariologia* (Milan, 1985), pp. 518-27; M. O'Carroll, *Theotokos. A
     Theological Encyclopedia of the Blessed Virgin Mary* (Wilmington,
     2nd ed. 1983), pp.127-130. H. Petri, 'Reformatorische
     Frömmigkeit und Maria' in *Maria heute ehren* , pp. 64-81

7   *The One Mediator*, passim.

8   Texts: *Marianum, Ephemerides mariologicae* and combined in *Studi
     ecumenici* 5 (1987), pp. 529-52. See E.R. Carroll, 'Ecumenical
     Roundtables at International Mariological Congresses' in *Mater
     fidei et fidelium*. 'Marian Library Studies 17-23' (Dayton, 1991), pp.
     292-305

9   'Authority in the Church 11', *The Final Report* (London, 1982), pp.
     95-96. See E. Yarnold, 'Mary and the Work of ARCIC', *The Month*
     22 (1989), pp. 58-62

10   H. Meyer & L. Vischer, (eds.), *Growth in Agreement. Reports and
     Agreed Statements*. 'Faith and Order 108' (New York & Geneva,
     1984), pp. 399-401

11   *The One Mediator, the Saints, and Mary*. 'Lutherans and Catholics
     in Dialogue 8'; R.E. Brown et al. (eds.), *Mary in the New Testament. A
     Collaborative Assessment by Protestant and Roman Catholic Scholars*
     (Philadelphia & London, 1978).

12   E.g. 'Mary and the Churches', *Concilium* 168 (1983); J. de Satgé,
     Mary and the Christian Gospel (London, 1976); J. Macquarrie, *Mary
     for all Christians* (London, 1991); H.A. Oberman, 'The Virgin Mary
     in Evangelical Perspective', *Journal of Ecumenical Studies* 1 (1964),
     pp. 271-98; M. Thurian, *Mary. Mother of the Lord, Figure of the
     Church* (London, 1963).

13   E.g. annual surveys by E.R. Carroll in *Marian Studies*; W.J. Cole,
     'Mary in Ecumenical Dialogue', *Ephemerides mariologicae* 33
     (1983), pp. 447-54; S. De Fiores, *Maria nella teologiá contemporanea*
     (Rome, 2nd ed. 1987), pp. 230-55; J. García Pérez, 'La Virgen en
     el diálogo ecuménico actual', *Razón y fe* 219 (1989), pp. 547-52; R.
     Mackenzie, 'Mariology as an Ecumenical Problem', *Marian
     Studies* 26 (1975), pp. 204-20; B. de Margerie, 'Ecumenical
     Problems in Mariology', *Marian Studies* 26 (1975), pp. 180-203; H.

Petri, 'Maria und die Ökumene' in W. Beinert & H. Petri, *Handbuch der Marienkunde* (Regensburg, 1984), pp. 315-59. H. Petri, (ed.), *Divergenzen in der Mariologie*.

14   'The Mediation of Mary and the Doctrine of Participation', *Ephemerides mariologicae* 24 (1974), pp. 48-56 with responses 26 (1976), pp. 135-41

15   Constitution on the Church, *Lumen Gentium* 62; cf. C. O'Donnell, 'Mediatrix of Graces. Continuing Questions', *Milltown Studies* 22 (1988), pp. 95-110

16   E.g. W. Henn, 'Interpreting Marian Dogmas', *Gregorianum* 70 (1989), pp. 413-37; W. Kasper, *An Introduction to Christian Faith* (London & New York, 1980), p. 108

17   T. Ware, *The Orthodox Church* (Harmondsworth, 3rd ed. 1983) pp. 263-5

18   Art. 6 - J.H. Leith, (ed.), *Creeds of the Churches* (Atlanta, 2nd ed. 1973), p. 267

19   Art. 6 - ibid. p. 195

20   *Mary in the New Testament*, p. 72; cf. pp. 28-31

21   See J. Ledit, *Marie dans la liturgie de Byzance*. 'Théologie historique 39' (Paris, 1976).

22   *La religiosità popolare. Valore spirituale permanente* (Rome, 1978); G. Agostino, 'Pietà popolare', *Nuovo dizionario di mariologia*, pp. 1111-22

23   C.A. Bernard, *Teologia spirituale*. 'Testi di teologia 1' (Rome, 1983); A.M. Besnard, 'Tendencies of Contemporary Spirituality', *Concilium* 9/1 (Nov. 1965), pp. 14-24; B. Secondin & T. Goffi, (eds) *Corso di spiritualità* (Brescia, 1989), Introduzione generale, pp. 5-18

24   'Ecriture sainte et vie spirituelle', *Dictionnaire de spiritualité*, vol. 4, cols. 128-278; G. Giurisato, *Lectio divina oggi*. 'Scritti monastici 8' (Praglia, 1987); S.A. Panimolle, (ed.), *Ascolto della parola e preghiera. La 'Lectio divina'*. 'Teologia sapienziale 2' (Vatican, 1987) all with bibliography.

25   *Catholic International* 3/3 (1992) p. 129

26   I. de la Potterie, 'L'ascolto nello Spirito. Per una rinnovata comprehension "spirituale" della Scrittura' in *Ascolta! Quaderni di lettura biblica* (Rome, 1980), pp. 9-25; R. Laurentin, *Comment réconciler l'exégèse et la foi* (Paris, 1984).

27   *Exégèse médiévale*. 'Théologie 41/1-2, 42, 59.' 4 vols. (Paris, 1959-1962).

28   Ephraem, *Diatessaron* 1:18 - Tr. *Liturgy of the Hours* (London, 1974), vol. 1, p. 518

29   *The One Mediator, the Saints and Mary* , 'Lutheran Reflections' ad
      fin. and n. 102 on 'a deeper understanding of the scriptures'.
30   'The Presence of Christ in the World' (1977), n. 27 in *Growth in
      Agreement*, p. 440
31   'Ecclesiology' (1981) 2:2 in *Growth in Agreement* (n.10), pp. 412-13
32   M. Ouellet, 'Due modi di interpretare la scrittura' in AA.VV. *La
      missione ecclesiale di Adrienne von Speyr.'* Atti del 11 Colloquio
      internazionale del pensiero cristiano.' (Milan, 1986), pp. 158-61
33   J.A. de Aldama, 'Espiritualidad mariana', *Scripta de Maria* 3
      (1980), pp. 31-86
34   A.M. Allchin, *The Joy of All Creation. An Anglican Meditation on the
      Place of Mary* (London, 1984).
35   Encyclical *Redemptoris Mater* (1987) nn. 7-11
36   'Figura, dottrina e lode di Maria nel dialogo ecumenico', *Il
      regno/documenti* 28 (1983/7) p. 247
37   T. Goffi, 'Spiritualità' in *Nuovo dizionario di mariologia*, pp. 1362-
      78; S. De Fiores, 'Maria' in S. De Fiores & T. Goffi, *Nuovo dizionario
      di spiritualità* (Milan, 1985), pp. 878-902; S. De Fiores, 'Presenza di
      Maria nella spiritualità cristiana' in *Maria nella teologia contempo-
      ranea*, pp. 289-336
38   *The Birth of the Messiah* (Garden City, 1979).
39   T. Goffi, 'Spiritualità' in *Nuovo dizionario di mariologia*, pp. 1364-65
40   See R.J. Karris, 'Luke' in R.E. Brown et al. (eds.), *New Jerome Biblical
      Commentary* (Englewood Cliffs & London, 1989), p. 684
41   Constitution on the Church, *Lumen Gentium* 58
42   W.F. Maestri, *Mary: Model of Justice. Reflections on the Magnificat*
      (New York, 1987); S. Galilea, *Following Jesus* (Maryknoll, 1981),
      pp. 110-19
43   *Works* (St. Louis, 1956) vol. 21, pp. 295-353; see E.W. Gritsch,
      'Embodiment of Unmerited Grace. The Virgin Mary according to
      Martin Luther and Lutheranism' in Stacpoole, *Mary's Place in
      Christian Dialogue*, pp. 133-41
44   ARCIC ll, *Salvation and the Church* , (London, 1987), p. 14
45   Vatican ll, *Lumen Gentium* 64, 67. cf. Lutheran-Roman Catholic
      Dialogue , nn. 16, 27, 48, 103-14
46   'From Dysfunction to Disbelief. The Virgin Mary in Reformed
      Theology' in A. Stacpoole, (ed.), *Mary's Place in Christian Dialogue*,
      p. 147
47   *The One Mediator, the Saints and Mary*, Catholic reflections ad fin.

48   *Collectio missarum de Beata Maria Virgine.* 'Editio typica.' 2 vols.
      (Vatican, 1987).
49   C. O'Donnell, 'Mary as Prophet', *Studies in Spirituality* 1 (1991),
      pp. 181-98
50   *Collectio missarum*, vol. 1, pp. 126-8; vol. 2, pp. 126-9
51   *Marialis cultus* (1974) nn. 32-3
52   P.J. Cahill, 'Our Lady's Present Role in the Communion of Saints',
      Marian Studies 18 (1967), pp. 31-45; F.M. Jelly, *Madonna. Mary in
      the Catholic Tradition* (Huntington, 1986), pp. 148-167. Lutheran-
      Roman Catholic Dialogue passim; Marian-mariological
      Congresses passim.
53   'Mary: Some Problems in Ambivalence' in Stacpoole, *Mary and
      the Churches*, pp. 73-84 here p. 80

Religious Commitment
and Human Rights:
A Christian Perspective

José Míguez Bonino

Why should a Christian be concerned with human rights? What are the elements in Christianity which provide a basis for being concerned about human rights?[1] The first approach to these questions that comes to mind is the attempt to articulate a doctrinal platform, a Christian philosophy that would make the concern for human rights a 'logically necessary' corollary of the Christian faith. I will, nevertheless, avoid such an approach, because I think it would be historically inaccurate and, perhaps, not quite honest intellectually. What we today call 'human rights' – for instance as defined in the Charter of the United Nations – is the result of a long process, developed mainly in the West, in the course of which a number of forces have operated – economic, political, cultural, ideological – the Christian faith being one of them. We will not attempt to determine now what is the precise correlation of those forces or whether any one of them is ultimately determinative. But, whatever our view of the dynamics of history, I think we will have to admit that they have mutually stimulated, checked and shaped each other. We cannot, therefore, speak of a Christian understanding of human rights as something which had developed autonomously or in isolation.

It would be equally misleading to try to distinguish a Christian doctrine in itself from its historical embodiments. 'There is only the Christianity that is': so is said to have answered an American Indian when somebody tried to explain to him that 'that Christianity' under which they had suffered was not 'the true Christianity'. Religious doctrines, attitudes, norms of conduct, forms of worship, are born in response to historical circumstances – and, in turn, they influence that history. At each point in that history, a religion is a 'synthetic' historical phenomenon. Its permanent elements cannot, in any case, be found beyond or above that history but – if at all – in and through it.[2]

We must, therefore, choose a different path, an historical one. Our attempt will be to follow – no doubt only sketchily at this time – the historical process in which the Christian faith has attained a consciousness of itself in relation to the question of human rights. Only then will it be possible to try and abstract the 'motifs' which have become visible in that movement and which may point to the peculiar Christian understanding or the specific Christian roots of a conception of human rights. We will never find such a conception in a 'chemically pure' Christian form, but only in diverse historical formulations. For this purpose we must follow the movement of what has been called 'the history of freedom' in the Western world, in relation to which – at times supportively, at times in conflict – Christian theology and praxis have developed.[3]

I

The first form in which Christians faced the problem of human rights in a practical, existential way was in connection with religious freedom. The Roman Empire knew a type of religious tolerance as long as this did not conflict with the 'religion of the state'. When it became clear that Christians could not be subsumed – either religiously or ethnically – under the rights granted to the Jewish people, the problem of the 'legality' of the Christian faith could not be avoided. Two Christian claims made it particularly acute: the claim of universality – Christians would not accept ethnic, geographic or any other limitations to the extent of their mission; and the claim of exclusiveness – Christians would not accept any other 'supreme loyalty' alongside their obedience to the 'Lord'. The conflict was unavoidable, and the new 'ecclesia', made up mostly of the poor and marginal, held their ground.

In the process of defending its right, the early Christian Church resorted to two basic arguments. The first is the inherently free character of religious faith. 'It is a crime against religion', writes Tertullian, 'to deprive a man of his religious freedom, to forbid him to choose "a divinity"'.[4] 'Authentic worship cannot be given under external pressure,' adds Lactantius.[5] Although the argument is advanced in favour of the Christian religion, the principle has universal validity and left a permanent imprint on Christian doctrine. The other argument was but a consequence: if religious preference was exclusively a right of the human conscience, the state could have no competence on the matter. Peter and John's declaration according to Acts 4:19 is a first and terse affirmation of this principle: 'Whether it is right in the sight of God to listen to you rather than to God'. It was not a rebellion against civil authority as such: quite the contrary, even under very severe conditions, Christians were directed by their leaders to obey civil authority. But there was a clear limitation of the sphere of competence of political power: it had no right to interfere in the realm of conscience. The autonomy of the religious sphere was thus vigorously affirmed over against the predominant 'political theologies'.

The attitude of Christians concerning religious freedom was to change quite substantially in the course of time, when the Christian faith became itself the religion of the Empire. Religious compulsion was justified, the power of the state was enlisted in the service of Christianity, and a new type of 'Christian' political theology was articulated. The process is clearly reflected in the shifts that we can document between Augustine's early and late writings. Nevertheless, the earlier principle is attested by the very contradiction in which Christian thought becomes entangled. On the one hand, Christian theologians continue to assert 'the free character of the act of faith': faith cannot be imposed. A person confessing even the true faith against their conscience would be committing a sin. How could this be reconciled with the invitation to the civil power to forbid any religious practice other than the Christian? The only solution that medieval thought is able to find is the concept of tolerance as defined, for instance, by Thomas Aquinas. In spite of their contradictions and ambiguities, we must register these two basic contributions to the history of freedom: the freedom of the act of faith and the limitation of the competence of the state in religious matters.

Between the sixteenth and nineteenth centuries the initiative in the struggle for freedom changes hands. A great transformation in the social fabric of Europe found dramatic expression in France toward the end of the eighteenth century. People from the lower sector of the economy, largely emancipated from the cruder forms of feudalism, and growing in number in a sort of population explosion, had begun to press for better conditions. Meanwhile those in the new middle sectors – the bourgeoisie – aware of their increasing significance, took over leadership of 'the people', claiming for the 'third state' (*tiers état*) an amount of power equivalent to their importance in relation to the traditional power factors: the nobility and the Church. The result, as we know, was the French Revolution and, as the initial document, the 'Declaration of the Rights of Man (*Declaration des droits de l'homme et du citoyen*, 27 August, 1789). But thirteen years earlier, a new nation, the United States of America, led by the same social group – although within a different situation – had constituted itself around a very similar platform and issued the American Declaration of Independence.

Both statements were intended to embody what was believed to be an eternal and universal truth: States and political bodies do not create or grant such rights: they can only 'recognize' and 'proclaim' them. In fact, their very justification as States rests on this recognition, both in word and action. What is the source of these rights? In the American Declaration of Independence, the divine origin is explicit: all men are equal because they had been created with equal rights, 'endowed with them by the Creator'. The French Declaration substitutes nature for the Creator: all men are born with equal rights: these are of nature. But the religious background is here also unmistakeable: these rights are pronounced 'sacred'.

The *Déclaration des droits de l'homme* appeared originally in Paris in a pamphlet bearing above its title the picture of an eye within a triangle. The symbolism of the triune God is evident. At the bottom of the page, however, the symbol is explained otherwise: 'the supreme eye of reason that rises to dispel the clouds that darkened it'. When we put together the two kindred documents, one thing becomes clear: we have the mutual interpenetration, the fusion of two ideological interpretations, that had run at times a parallel, at times a common course, at least since the second century: an idealistic humanism of Greek origin and the Hebrew-Christian prophetic tradition. Creation and nature, human brotherhood with a common reason and a common father, the dignity of a rational self and of an object of God's love in creation and redemption – these two had together become the basis for a new self-understanding of man. The Christian motif had the upper hand in the US doctrine whereas the humanistic one was more prominent in the French; but both were children of this marriage.

Equality and universality are the distinctive concerns of these proclamations. A careful historical study would easily show that such basic notions were, in practice, understood under severe limitations. The French *Déclaration*, for instance, gives to 'property rights', which it proclaims 'sacred and inviolable' (Art. 17), a prominent place, and once it comes to determining who enjoys 'the rights of citizen', these constitute one of the decisive criteria. In fact, in a population of some 27 million, only 4,300,000 qualified. In the USA it was clear that the Indians, and later the blacks, were in practice not included among the 'men' (not to mention 'women') who had been 'created equal'. The proclamation of human rights was, towards the end of the eighteenth century, the embodiment of the concerns and aspirations of one social group, one sector of society – basically what we call today the bourgeoisie.

At this stage human rights are defined in terms of the individualism that characterizes Enlightenment thought, an individualism with a clear stress on economic factors. 'Every man is free to employ his arms, his industry and his capital as he deems fit and useful for himself; he can produce what pleases him as he likes' says the French *Déclaration*. But it is not limited to that area. The individual is also conceived as a 'citizen': a social order cannot be imposed from above or outside the will of the individuals: it must be 'contracted' or 'covenanted' by the free will of free individuals. As both expression of and foundation for these freedoms we find a philosophical conception which Hegel summarizes in this way:

> Against a faith in authority the subject's authority for himself was claimed, and the natural laws were the only thing that could bind the external and the internal ... Subsequently thought was also directed to the spiritual aspect: it was conceived that law and objective morality are based on man's will, while before these things existed only as commandments of God, imposed from outside ... The name 'reason' has been given to these universal determinations founded in the present consciousness ...[6]

I have said that Enlightenment freedoms emerged from a marriage between Christian faith and classical Greek humanism. But it was not easy for the Churches to recognize or acknowledge this fact. This is understandable in view of the anti-religious attitude that characterized the movement, in turn partly a reaction against the repressive character of an authoritarian structure of which the Church formed a part. Moreover, by locating religion also exclusively in the individual's free conscience and rejecting all revelation and authority, modernity seemed to do away entirely with dogma and Church authority. There was, nevertheless, a certain continuity between the early Christian claim for freedom in the act of faith and the Enlightenment claim for freedom of conscience. For reasons that are historically clear, this similarity was more easily visible for Protestantism. Hegel saw it in this way:

> This is the essential content of the Reformation: man remains self-determined for freedom ... It is of greatest importance that the Bible has now become the basis of the Christian Church: in the future, each individual, beginning with the Bible, should enlighten himself and should be able to determine his conscience according to the same source. This is the enormous modification that the principle has undergone ...[7]

This interpretation of Protestantism is certainly open to debate. But it can hardly be disputed that, objectively, the Reformation was part of the historical process that gave birth to modern society and its characteristic concept of freedom.

Again, for historical reasons which are not difficult to perceive, Roman Catholicism found it much more difficult to come to terms with Enlightenment freedoms. Its strenuous opposition to these throughout the nineteenth century is partly a legitimate rejection of a purely immanentistic form of humanist philosophy, partly a fear that, once deprived of the structures of authority that held Christendom together, men would drift away from religious truth and endanger both the peace of the earthly city and their eternal salvation. The new society, nevertheless, was here to stay. Slowly, the Catholic Church came to make its peace at the practical level, and then to appreciate the values of modernity. Vatican II marked the final seal on this rapprochement.[8]

On this basis, it becomes possible to explore the Christian contribution to the modern concept of freedom, although it is impossible to isolate it. One can also find a Christian basis for a commitment to human rights. It is not necessary to rehearse here the vast amount of theological work that has been done in this respect. It has rested basically on the doctrine of creation and/or the doctrine of redemption. The human being as God's creation and image, his or her dignity as God's steward and representative, the unity of the human race constitute a strong basis for asserting the rights of all. Equally, the Incarnation, the universal love of God attested by and operative in Christ's death and resurrection, the dignity of a humanity which in Christ has been exalted to the right hand of God, indicate an ultimate and unwavering commitment of God himself to the human, pointing to the value – the 'infinite value' as classical liberal theology used to say – of each human being.[9]

II

At the end of World War II, when the 'Universal Declaration of Human Rights' was proclaimed by the United Nations, a new concept appeared that was unkown in the classic formulations of human rights from the eighteenth century: 'social rights'. It was a timid and minimal recognition of a social and political reality which has been looming larger and larger in history throughout the previous century and a quarter: the growing masses excluded from the 'citizen's rights' defined by the bourgeois world; the industrial proletariat of the northern hemisphere and, later on, the hungering, exploited, culturally violated, deprived, repressed masses of the so-called 'Third World'.

The voice of those who, in the words of Gustavo Gutiérrez, had been 'absent from history' made itself heard in the struggles of workers for better labour conditions, a just salary, the right to work and the right to shape a society in which they would be actual subjects of their own history. For the peoples of the 'Third World', this does not mean merely a change in the internal conditions of their own societies but the 'rights' of the underdeveloped nations in international trade, the transformation of the conditions of the 'division of labour' among the nations of the world; in sum, nothing less than 'a new world economic order'. Thus, to the 'social, economic, political and cultural rights' (Art. 22) of the UN Charter, one would have to add 'the universal rights of peoples', which in the Algiers Conference of 1970 were defined as 'the right to freedom from all foreign intervention', the 'right to fight for their liberation' (if they are dominated by a foreign power), the right 'to own and use their own natural resources', and the right 'to determine the social and political system of their choice'. 'The respect for human rights implies the respect for the rights of peoples' reads the Preamble.

The relation of Christians and the Churches to this new phase of the human search for freedom is also varied and not without ambiguities. Given the fact that the claims for these rights are raised quite often over against the privileges and the domination of social classes and countries in which Christians have been conspicuously present, it is not surprising that there has been a resistance to the recognition of such rights in many Christian quarters. The struggle for the rights of the poor has been waged quite often under the impulse of ideologies that rejected and denounced religion as a means of social domination. On the other hand, many Christians in the oppressed sector of humankind – and with them not a few of their brothers and sisters in the affluent countries and classes – have discovered in their faith a basis and impulse for the struggle. Thus, the awareness of the question of 'the rights of the poor' has led to a rediscovery of the prophetic tradition of the Jewish-Christian faith.

A new fact begins to emerge. The Bible, it would seem, discovers and underlines another dimension of human rights. The books of the law, for instance, do not say anything in general about the rights of the human person. But they speak quite frequently of the judge who, at the gate, 'gives the poor man his right', of right done to the widow, the orphan and the alien (for example, Deuteronomy 10). The prophets are equally explicit. When Jeremiah wants to point out the good government – the god-like behaviour as king – of Josiah, he summarizes: 'He judged (that is, established the right of) the cause of the poor and the needy; then, it was well' (Jer 22:16). And the wisdom literature – a down-to-earth reflection on life as it is – does not hesitate in equating the 'rights of the poor' with 'the rights of God': 'He who oppresses a poor man insults his Maker' (Prov 14:31), 'Do not rob the poor because he is poor, or crush the afflicted at the gate (the place where justice ought to be rendered to the plaintiff); for the Lord will plead their cause and despoil of life those who despoil him' (Prov 22:22-3).[10]

The line of this reasoning is not difficult to follow. Everyone has somebody to protect and to uphold his or her right (interestingly, the Hebrew word that we translate 'redeemer' means also 'avenger'): the child has a father, the wife a husband, men have brothers, a tribe, a family. But the 'fatherless', the 'widow', the 'foreigner' have no avenger-redeemer when they are wronged. God, nevertheless, cares for them: he has protected their rights in law, he has pledged himself that no human life will be lost without vindication. A good government, therefore – a government according to God's own heart – becomes particularly responsible for the rights of those who have no protection, no power to vindicate their rights. The condition of the weakest in society indicates the quality of government. Respect for the rights of the poor is a sign of the nation's health. For this reason when God himself makes his 'good government' (his Kingdom) present among us in Jesus Christ, the 'rights of the poor' (women, children, the despised, the sick, above all 'the poor of the land') mark the thrust of his ministry. The jubilee, the great symbol of the restoration of all who had suffered dispossession, deprivation or oppression, becomes the paradigm of his mission (Luke 4). The universal scope and significance of the ministry, death and resurrection of Jesus, according to the Christian faith, is not restricted but rather defined and highlighted by the concrete priority of the poor that he taught and illustrated in his life. This is the heritage that the Church has received, and that it is beginning to rediscover and reclaim in this new phase of the historical search for freedom. Perhaps the Latin American Church – the largest sector of Christianity among the 'poor' – has been given the privilege of taking a lead in fostering this new awareness. In the very plain language of the Medellin Episcopal Conference, the Church is invited to take up the challenge of 'Defending, according to the commandment of the Gospel, the rights of the poor and oppressed'.[11]

III

The brief sketch that I have tried to draw of the history of the relation between the human quest for freedom and the Christian faith makes clear that we cannot speak of a ready-made 'Christian doctrine of human rights'. Rather, we see a development in which the historical experience of humanity stimulates Christians to explore the resources of their faith and this, in turn, inspires them to commit themselves more vigorously to the struggle for human rights. This process is not independent of the social conditions of Christians and Churches themselves. Consequently, it generates ambiguities, tensions and contradictions within the Christian communities as regards both doctrine and practice. On the other hand, it seems to me that we can discern, within this process, an ethical thrust, related to an understanding of God's relation to mankind and history. This ethical thrust moves towards a search for a 'more human life', the fulfilment, within the constraints of circumstances, of the best material and spiritual possibilities available for the human person and society. As we look at this, it seems that we can discern some insights which can be considered a permanent achievement.

'There is only one God and Father of all': this conviction is the basic ground on which the Christian faith rests. It is the basic confession of the Old Testament: 'Hear, O Israel, the Lord your God, the Lord is one' (Deut 6:4). Far from retreating from it, the New Testament makes it even more explicit in terms of its trinitarian faith: 'There is one Spirit … one Lord … one God and Father' (Eph 4:4-6). The consequence cannot be avoided: there is only one mankind. Within the New Testament this consequence is first drawn in relation to the new Christian community: all are one body, in which all members have equal dignity and value. Social, ethnic, cultural, even sexual distinctions – Jew and Greek, master or slave, man or woman – cannot justify any discrimination. But this universality overflows the limits of the community. Every human being bears the image of God; it is therefore absurd and sacrilegious 'to bless the Lord and Father … and to curse men, who are made in the likeness of God' (James 3:11). There is no doubt that it was the encounter with Platonic and Stoic philosophy which first gave to Christian theologians the possibility of articulating this conviction in theological terms (while also lending

to it something of the abstraction which was characteristic of
those philosophies). When Christians used this conceptual framework, however, they were not merely borrowing a Greek idea:
they were formulating something that was profoundly their own.
Centuries later Colonel Rainborough would give this conviction
a very concrete and explosive political formulation: 'Really I
think the poorest he that is in England hath a life to live as much as
the greatest he'.[12]

The North American theologian Paul Lehmann has coined a felic-
itous expression when he said that what God has been and is
presently doing in the world is 'what it takes to make and keep
human life human'.[13] It is a very modern formulation, but it expresses an insight which permeates the whole Biblical testimony.
Only a full biblical theology developed in the perspective of 'life'
as God's goal for his creation could do justice to this theme. But
perhaps it is not superfluous to mention briefly one of the very
early and pregnant expressions of such insight: the priestly
account of God's covenant with humankind in Noah, after the
story of the Flood (Gen 9:1-17). God voices and pledges his will
concerning 'fallen' humanity, humanity 'as it is' – vitiated by
wickedness, violence, sin. And he simply reiterates the promise
and commandment of creation: 'Be fruitful, and multiply, and fill
the earth'. Human life is still the key to creation. But three new
provisions are added: (1) Man has a right to put all existing life –
animal as well as vegetable – at the service of his life: 'every living
thing that moves shall be food for you ... I give you everything';
(2) Human life is sacred: God himself will avenge violence done
against man: 'of every man's brother I will require the life of man';
(3) Man himself is made responsible for respecting and enforcing
this provision: 'Whoever sheds the life of man, by man shall his
blood be shed; for God made man in his own image'. It is impossible to exaggerate the importance of this Biblical motif. God's
'covenant' with man has 'life', and particularly 'human life', as its
fundamental content. He is unconditionally and absolutely the
God of life. And consequently, he entrusts man with a mission:
the perpetuation, enriching and protection of life. This is God's
most precious treasure, so much so that not even his just and
necessary wrath against man's sin is cause enough to annul the
alliance. When the decisive time comes, the God-made-man will
protect the human race with his own life. He will take upon him-

self the just punishment and the senseless violence of the fallen world so that men may live. The new covenant 'in his blood' eternally seals and affirms the early covenant with mankind.

Once again, it took the Church a long time to explore the content of its affirmation of human life: the inviolability of the human conscience, the freedom to develop one's own intellectual and spiritual possibilities, the inalienable value of each human person, the unity of spiritual and physical life, the social character of human existence, emerge slowly in the encounter of the Christian faith with different historical circumstances and philosophical conceptions as the ever enlarging implications of this 'covenant'. But each new insight operates on the Christian conscience because Christians are faithful only when and to the extent that they – like their God – do in the world 'whatever it takes to make and keep human life human'.

IV

Universality and 'partiality' seem contradictory terms. But it is one of the deepest insights of the Biblical picture of God that his universality finds concrete expression in his 'partiality' in favour of the poor – the oppressed, the disadvantaged, the powerless, the marginal. In the strong words of one of the most important theologians of our century: 'God always takes his stand unconditionally and passionately on this side and on this side alone: against the lofty and on behalf of the lowly ...'.[14] At this point, the biblical concept of justice parts company with the classical tradition. It is not the blind rendering 'to each his own' – which presupposes a stable and basically unchangeable order – but the liberation of those who have been deprived of the conditions for an authentic human life. Such a vision does not mean a rejection of universality. What it does mean is that universality is never abstract. There are always historical tests for universality. In the Bible, this test is the condition of the poor. Here we have the basis for a deeper understanding of the struggle for human rights. When the Brazilian bishops, for instance, refer at length to the condition of the Indians, they are not arbitrarily selecting a special case: they are offering a witness which indicates the inhumanity of their whole society. 'The human rights of the Indian' are the test of the functioning of a society – just as those of the fatherless, the widow and the sojourner are for the biblical author.

This insistence on a particular focus for human rights, however much they remain universally defined, is crucial. For the vast majority of the population of the world today the basic 'human right' is 'the right to a human life'. The 'struggle for human rights' now means the struggle to vindicate the large masses claiming their right to the means of life. The defence of formal human rights is meaningful as a pointer to that deeper level. In that sense, the drive towards universality implicit in our Christian faith, which found partial expression in the American and French revolutions, and the aspirations expressed in the UN Declaration find their historical focus today for us in the struggle of the poor, the economically and socially oppressed, for their liberation. At this point the biblical teaching and the historical juncture coalesce to give the Christian Churches a mission. This is what it now means for Christians to be concerned with human rights.

Notes

1   The basis for this article was a presentation by the author at the 'Institute for Human Rights' of the Organization of American States (OEA) in April 1992 on behalf of the World Council of Churches.

2.   This article presupposes a concept of the development of Christian doctrine in which the historical circumstances and the encounter with trends of human thought play a significant role in 'activating' and helping to develop virtualities implicit in the Christian revelation.

3.   The 'history of freedom' has been a favourite subject of Hegel and the hegelian tradition. In recent theology J. B. Metz and J. Moltmann have developed this theme and assessed it from a theological point of view.

4.   *Apologeticum*, XXI, 30

5.   *Divinarum Institutionum* V, 21

6.   *Lecciones de filosofía de la Historia*

7.   Ibid.

8.   I have developed the interpretation of Vatican II in this sense in *Concilio abierto* (Buenos Aires, 1968), although rather uncritically in the evaluation of the values of the 'modern world'.

9. In the preceding section and parts of what follows I have quoted freely from my article 'Whose Human rights?', *International Review of Mission*, Vol. LXVI, No 263, (July 1977), pp. 220-24

10. Cf. the interesting study of this theme in wisdom literature by Hugo Etchegaray, S.J. `Direitos do pobre-direitos de Deus', *CEI*, Biblia Hoje-47; August 1978.

11. *La Iglesia en la actual transformación de América Latina a la luz de Concilio* (Buenos Aires, 1968), Doc. 'Paz', III/22

12. Quoted by A. S. P. Woodhouse (ed.), *Puritanism and Liberty*, (London) p. 53

13. *Ethics in a Christian Context*, (New York, 1963), p. 74

14. Karl Barth, *Church Dogmatics* (Edinburgh), Vol. II/1, p. 386

Justice, Ecology and the Quest for Christian Unity

Gabriel Daly

When Michael Hurley took *Floreat ut Pereat* as a motto for the Irish School of Ecumenics, he saw ecumenism as a task which is in principle achievable in finite historical terms. His vision for the School in a sense arose out of the dynamic and sanguine 1960s. He himself was an ecumenical pioneer who could see in the work of the Second Vatican Council a conciliar affirmation of values he already believed in and, within the confines of the age, practised. Roman Catholics had come to the ecumenical movement late and a trifle breathless. Indeed the 1960s in retrospect may strike one today as a period of ecclesial hyperventilation. Everything seemed possible, and breathlessness was a response only to be expected in those who were learning to use spiritual, theological, and ecclesial muscles which they never suspected they possessed, because they had previously had no opportunity to exercise them. Hope was in the air in those days, and it seemed to promise the hitherto unthinkable.

Floreat ut Pereat: may its very success bring about its own demise. It is an exceedingly idealistic motto, inviting, perhaps, some degree of ambivalence. To will one's corporate obsolescence is a difficult assignment for any institution. One can manage to do it largely because it seems so distant a prospect that its actual implementation can be safely left to a distant posterity. Ambivalence is therefore written into the whole enterprise. Augustine's prayer for continence comes to mind, with its all too human 'but not yet' codicil. It is not, of course, that we do not want unity. Rather it is that we can no more envisage what it might be like than we can envisage what heaven might be like; and so we pray 'Come Lord Jesus', but intend it to have the reassuring features of some realized eschatology: the Kingdom of God is here and now within and among you, if only you had the eyes to see it. You do not need to be anxious about the morrow.

Floreat ut Pereat. The motto may be taken both as a prayer and as an aspiration. The logo it underwrites portrays an ear of corn with all the evangelical resonances which that powerful symbol can evoke. There is the promise of a harvest awaiting the reapers who will bring it in with joy. So much for the 'floreat'. But what of the 'pereat'? Here the reaper is grim: the seed must fall into the ground and die. This is ecumenism as manifestation of the cross of Christ. It raises all sorts of questions about the nature of unity and its relationship with diversity; it is scarcely applicable to interfaith relations; and in respect of international peace, if it is eschatological, it also has a utopian ring to it. The experience of the Irish School of Ecumenics from its earliest days was that the quest for unity among Christians led ineluctably to a parallel interfaith dialogue and furthermore demanded a sociological component. This, of course, had been the experience of all genuine ecumenical ventures since the beginning of the century.

I

The World Council of Churches has been the body most affected by the inner logic and dynamic of ecumenical endeavour. As 'a fellowship of churches' it expressly wishes to avoid being regarded or treated as a superchurch. It is there to facilitate, support, express, foster and promote certain determinate aims and causes. The first of these is clearly articulated in its Constitution: 'to call the churches to the goal of visible unity in one faith and in one eucharistic fellowship expressed in worship and in common life in Christ, and to advance towards that unity in order that the world may believe'. However, the fourth clause in this list of aims illustrates the phenomenon of inner logic while at the same time demonstrating how that inner logic can set up an energetic field of tension and potential discord. The WCC has as its purpose 'to express the common concern of the churches in the service of human need, the breaking down of barriers between people, and the promotion of one human family in justice and peace'.[1]

Now, by any standards that is a very large aim indeed. Its nobility of purpose is matched only by its width of scope. It leaves no further frontier to be tackled (unless intelligent life is discovered elsewhere in the universe). The ecumenical impulse here achieves its fullest practicable span. It also raises the major questions which demand attention from ecumenical theologians. The first is what Willem Visser 't Hooft, the distinguished General Secretary of the WCC, has called 'christocentric universalism'.[2]

Konrad Raiser describes christocentric universalism as 'the paradigm for the ecumenical movement'.[3] It was formulated thus in a 1959 WCC study document: 'Christ's lordship over church and world provides the proper basis for a Christian social ethic … In every situation the Lord of the world is actively at work exercising his sovereignty over nations and peoples'.[4]

Raiser in his penetrating analysis of this 'paradigm', singles out its controlling elements as: christocentricity, concentration on the Church, universality of perspective, and history as the central category of thought. All of these elements were shortly to come under challenge and are now in fact challenged by Raiser himself.

It is worth recalling at this point that the WCC subscription to the salvation history paradigm was important for relations between itself and the Roman Catholic Church in the years immediately following the Second Vatican Council. In the 1960s many Catholic theologians were emerging from a non-historical scholasticism, and were delighting in their discovery of salvation history as a master category in their new theological hermeneutic. For many this represented a major shift in perspective from a pervasive and unchecked essentialism to the existential and relativising influence of historical consciousness. It greatly facilitated dialogue with theologians of other Churches and it provided an interpretative grid for the incorporation of biblical studies into Roman Catholic systematic theology.

In this, as in other matters, Catholics were soon to find that much of what they were embracing with enthusiasm in the immediate aftermath of Vatican II was already itself coming under critical fire from within. Development of thought in the WCC provides an apposite illustration of this. In March 1960 sixty-seven black South Africans were killed by the police at Sharpville. The WCC subsequently organized a consultation at which an ecumenical delegation met a group of black and white Church leaders. The consultation affirmed that no Christian could be excluded from any Church on grounds of race or colour; it also denounced the injustices of apartheid. The South African prime minister rejected the consultation statement, and three South African Dutch Reformed Churches withdrew from the WCC. It had become plain that institutional ecumenism could not avoid a political agenda if it wished to retain the credibility of its Christian witness. This thrust to ever wider universalism, however, poses real problems for those of its members who see the Church, in theological terms, as an inner-related sanctum of salvation, or, in sociological terms, as a culture with structures which mirror those of the secular world. The remainder of the decade was to underline the tension between Faith and Order on the one hand and active socio-political engagement on the other.

II

When the Assembly met at Uppsala in 1968, socio-political matters were high on its agenda. In the following year the WCC set up the Programme to Combat Racism. The Programme committed the Council to give financial support to groups actively involved in opposition to white racist regimes. This raised the question of whether these monies were being used to buy arms.[5] Debate on the matter within the WCC was lively. Baldwin Sjollema has observed that 'The WCC would never be the same again: it had taken sides with the racially oppressed. Charity was being replaced by solidarity. The WCC became more relevant to the majority of Christians and even to people of other faiths. Concrete action against racism had severely tested the ecumenical fellowship, but it was not broken'.[6]

The same debate was also taking place in the Roman Catholic Church with the birth of Liberation theology in Latin America. The Pastoral Constitution, *Gaudium et Spes*, of the Second Vatican Council, on the Church in the Modern World, exhorted local Churches and their pastors to contextualize their faith by relating it to the concrete cultural situation in which they lived. In Latin America that situation was preponderantly one of endemic poverty, tyranny, and injustice. In 1968 the Second General Conference of Latin American Bishops met at Medellín in

Colombia and issued a statement which committed the Church to large-scale action on behalf of the poor and oppressed. Within a remarkably short time Liberation theology became a powerful influence on the Catholic theological scene, and it set up tensions similar to those being faced by the WCC. In many respects Liberation theology qualifies for inclusion under Visser 't Hooft's characterization of the ecumenical movement as 'christocentric universalism'. The Church is there not for itself but for the world. The category of liberation must of its very nature be universal.

According to Konrad Raiser, 'The decisive symbolic break with the universalist paradigm came with the initiation in 1969 of the Programme to Combat Racism'.[7] When the world mission in Bangkok in 1972 'interpreted the universal "Salvation Today" in terms of the liberation struggles, open conflict broke out in the ecumenical movement, for this in fact represented a basic challenge to the universalist paradigm'.[8] Significantly this was the decade when the word 'sustainability' entered ecumenical parlance. It pointed to a further widening of the borders of the *oikoumene:* There are future generations to be thought about. We can no longer continue to think of development in terms of the extension of Northern capitalism, operating through transnational corporations, to the undeveloped world. What is the wider world? Who wants to develop it? And for what reasons? Raiser answers forthrightly.

For the first time it is now possible to speak of a closed world system, which follows its own rationality and logic, independently of human needs, and either rejects the goals of justice, participation and sustainability as illusory and irrational, or else recognizes them only to the extent that they do not disturb the balance which the system demands.[9]

This agenda is plainly irreconcilable with the ideals of the ecumenical movement, and a WCC study published in 1983 said so in unvarnished language.[10]

Raiser advances and strongly argues the thesis that the WCC's active solidarity with the racially oppressed marks a break with the paradigm of universalism. It is the transnational corporations which have created, in Míguez Bonino's expressive phrase, an *'oikoumene* of domination', which stands and operates over against the 'oikoumene of solidarity'.[11] Raiser does not shrink from asking whether the *'oikoumene* of solidarity' 'is at best utopian, or at worst nothing more than an illusion'.[12] He is able to accept the despair implicit in his question because he proposes to use it as a springboard for leaping out of what is for him the obsolete and constraining paradigm of universality which has hitherto provided the ecumenical movement with its controlling model for understanding and implementing its task.

We have here a radical proposal and one offering no small matter for controversy. Visser 't Hooft's vision had been christocentric universalism. What, however, happens to the christocentricity if the universalism is rejected? Raiser tackles this question by first addressing the question of salvation history. He makes two points which call for closer examination. (1) History as a whole cannot be seen as the work of God. (2) Historicization of nature constitutes a serious assault on the future both of humankind and of the planet.

That universal history cannot be simply regarded as the work of God is clear to anyone who contemplates the evil and suffering which have been so obvious a feature in it. J. B. Metz's concepts of theology after Auschwitz and a theology of victims has placed, for many Catholic theologians, a firm question mark over both transcendental theology and the theology of salvation history understood as continuous and coterminous with universal history. There is too much suffering in both the history of enslavement and in liberation movements. Metz, however, refuses to treat universal history and salvation history in a dualistic fashion. The history of salvation is universal history 'shot through with a constantly threatened and disputed but unshakably promised hope: the hope of God's justice, which also includes the dead and their past sufferings, and forces the living to be interested in justice for all'.[13]

Raiser is particularly concerned to reject the notion of history as development. God's presence in history is manifested not in development but in creative breakthroughs to something new. It is eschatological rather than 'natural'. History possesses unity only in the light of its end.[14] Liberation theology, with its analytical separation of history into that of the colonial victors and that of the indigenous victims, provides a further argument against in-

voking a univocal notion of history to serve as vehicle of salvation. He thus serves an eviction notice on the theological construct of salvation history, which has had such a prominent role
to play in WCC self-understanding and in Roman Catholic theology after Vatican II.

Raiser's second objection to the theology of history paradigm is
related to the ecological crisis which is so clearly upon us today.
This crisis bears not merely upon the world of capitalist eco-
nomics, but also, and more painfully, upon the quest for justice
and peace in the developing world. This is a very large question
indeed, and I shall restrict my attention here to its ecumenical implications, and especially to Raiser's thesis that 'the reduction of
history to human interaction ... proves to be a dangerous – and
indeed potentially lethal – abstraction'.[15]

III

The ecological crisis faces all humankind, believers and non-be-
lievers alike. If we continue to poison our soil, water, and air; if
we continue to emit gases which trap heat in the earth's atmo-
sphere and thus intensify global warming, and gases which produce acid rain that kills off forests; if we look on while huge areas
of rain forest are cut down with consequent loss of irreplaceable
flora and fauna and with serious effect upon the stability of
climate and soil; if, in short, we refuse to take this crisis with the
seriousness it demands, we shall quite simply bring about the de-
struction of our planet as a habitation for living creatures of all
species, including our own.

The onset of this crisis – or rather of the perception that it is a crisis – confronts all humankind, but especially governments, industry, commerce, and the media. The theological community
has now begun to intensify its interest in how religious attitudes
may have contributed to the global situation which faces us
today and also its interest in how a sound theology and spirituality of creation could contribute to setting things right again.
Three areas of central importance to Christian theology need to
be reconsidered in view of the ecological crisis.

(1) Christianity, Protestant and Catholic, has frequently empha-

sized God's transcendence at the expense of God's immanence. There have been many reasons for this, not least of which was its Jewish monotheistic inheritance together with an intense suspicion of animism: God must not be identified in any way with nature. Early Christian theology, influenced by Platonist metaphysics, emphasized the difference between matter and spirit and promoted the desire to escape from the physical world to the unchanging eternal realm of God. The birth of modern science as an autonomous discipline unbeholden to religious dogma, coupled with the rise of deism as a reaction against what it saw as Christian sectarian bigotry, conspired to place nature at a distance from God. For a variety of reasons Christian theology appeared content to hand nature over to the scientists while itself concentrating on the realm of grace.

(2) Closely related to the exaggerated concern with divine transcendence has been the preoccupation with redemption as the interpretative key to all Christian theology and spirituality. Readers of Matthew Fox's influential *Original Blessing* will have noted the wide gulf he engineers between creation spirituality on the one hand and fall/redemption spirituality on the other.[16] The book is an exuberant essay in compensatory discrimination, but it also sets up a new and needless exclusivism: it forces a choice between, 'Augustinian pessimism' and creation-centred optimism, on the assumption that they are mutually exclusive. The case to be answered, however, cannot be rightly treated on the basis of this assumption. What needs to be recognized and redressed is the dialectical balance between the respective theologies of creation and redemption. Action taken on behalf of an ecologically stricken world is redemptive, at least in principle, and can give the word 'atonement' a new meaning and reference.

In respect of all this the Orthodox bring a case against Western theology. Thus Paul Evdokimov claims that the West has been preoccupied with grace and freedom, original sin and predestination. It has taken its anthropology from Augustine, its soteriology from Anselm, and its philosophy of knowledge from Aquinas. Scholasticism, in short, has resorted to rational analysis. On the other hand, '*l'Orient préfère la connaissance sapientielle, où convergent le dogme, la contemplation mystique, la théologie et la philosophie*'.[17] Vladimir Soloviev had already in the 19th century seen 'the two opposing tendencies in Western life, one seeking to glorify man at the expense of God, the other seeking to glorify God by denigrating the human – the conflict between Renaissance optimism and Augustinian pessimism'.[18] Paul Gregorios convicts Augustine of making the human mind the constitutive foundation of reality and pits him against Gregory of Nyssa. Per Lønning comments:

> Western alienation from creation is here seen in dual perspective: on the one hand, there is the epistemological estrangement, which sees the realm of objects as submitted to the human mind; on the other, there is the hamartiological estrangement, which makes nature in itself evil. The latter of these two errors, then, tends to provoke its own opposite: the admiration of the goodness of nature that seems to make a saving divine presence unnecessary.[19]

The WCC Conference on Faith, Science and the Future , meeting in 1979 in the Massachusetts Institute of Technology, made these Eastern Orthodox accusations its own. Modern Western Christian theology has strengthened the opposition between nature and humanity, even introducing the opposition into its interpretation of the Bible: creation and salvation have been separated to the detriment of creation.

The slight whiff of triumphalism here should not be allowed to prejudice Western Christians against giving very careful consideration to the points being made by Orthodox theologians. It has to be conceded that Augustine did deal a serious blow to creation-centred theology, but we may be expecting rather too much of Gregory of Nyssa if we think that he will speak convincingly to our post-Enlightenment world without serious hermeneutical adjustment. The best we can do with Gregory and other patristic writers who put forward a theology favourable to creation is to recognize how this strand of thought was more or less obliterated in Western theology and is ripe for recovery and further development today. It will, of course, have to stand in what David Tracy calls 'mutually critical correlation' with contemporary culture. There is no question of its simply standing in judgement over that culture. There has to be a hermeneutic of suspicion as well as of retrieval: patristic fundamentalism is as unacceptable as biblical fundamentalism.

(3) The charge of anthropocentrism, commonly brought not merely against Augustinian pessimism but also against post-Enlightenment theologies of experience, has to be faced with openness of mind and readiness for conversion. Anthropocentrism is an inevitable consequence of allowing soteriology to overshadow the theology of creation, unless one has a developed theory of cosmic redemption. Creation has been traditionally made to serve as the backdrop to salvation and has been unwittingly devalued in the process. Animate and inanimate nature have been seen as being there for the sake of the human species. Certain biblical texts appear to lend themselves to the sort of interpretation which sees human beings as dominators and exploiters of their world. The Priestly account of creation in Genesis, while bringing Eve into a closer and less inferior relationship to Adam than she has in the Jahwist account, nevertheless gives both Adam and Eve supremacy over the rest of creation more or less on the lines of Psalm 8: 'Thou hast given him dominion over the works of thy hands; thou hast put all things under his feet, all sheep and oxen, and also the beasts of the field, the birds of the air, and the fish of the sea, whatever passes along the paths of the sea.' (vv.5-8) These and other biblical texts easily scandalize our contemporary and ecologically sensitive ears. The point is really not so much what the authors of these and similar texts intended to say but what later generations have made of them.

The biblical writers cannot be justly accused of contributing to our late 20th century anxieties about the future of our planet or of offending against our ideas of 'political correctness'. It is hermeneutically naïve to expect to find that the biblical writers shared our anxiety and guilt about the way in which we have treated our world. We can, and must, however, learn to read the Scriptures with an eye which is ready to notice how the anthropocentric texts have gone unredressed in our imaginations by other texts such as Psalm 104, the covenant with Noah, and the great fanfare of divine celebration of nature in the book of Job.

Bishop John Austin Baker, in a preparatory study for the WCC Assembly at Canberra, gives a valuable warning against taking these and similar texts as evidence for biblical insouciance about human responsibility towards nature.

> The Hebrew Scriptures ... do nothing to justify the charge

that they bless an exploitative, humanly self-centred attitude to nature. They recognize man's preying on nature as a fact, but characterize that fact as a mark of man's decline from the first perfect intentions of God for him or as a defect to be eradicated in God's perfect future'.[20]

Bishop Baker makes the interesting point that we need the Hebrew Scriptures as a corrective to the salvation-centred thrust of the New Testament. He notes that whereas the Hebrew Scriptures are largely rural in culture, the New Testament is predominantly urban. Christians simply have to recognize that there is little in their foundational documents about 'corporate or global issues'.[21] It is this that makes Raiser's call to abandon the paradigm of christocentric universalism at the same time both radical and seemingly imperative.

We have already noted how the WCC found it impossible to restrict its attention and concern to purely internal church relations but was drawn into the struggle against racism and into other causes of a socio-political character. This process of ever-widening concern and engagement is one of the most heartening signs of our times. Perhaps more than any other ecclesial body, the WCC Assemblies and sub-groups have identified the logical and ethical connection between social, political and, now, ecological issues.

IV

At Nairobi in 1975 the fifth Assembly of the WCC produced a theme which has been unfolding ever since, namely, the search for a just, participatory, and sustainable society. The theme of justice had been long established. Participation was rapidly emerging as a necessary feature of the movement for justice. People need to participate in the movements which seek to free them. They must be subjects and not merely objects of the development process. 'Sustainability', however, marks a new and vitally important concern which has been coming inexorably to the fore since the early 1970s. This is the stark recognition that there are limits to growth. The planet cannot meet the demands which are being made on it by an open-ended and unrestricted drive to further development. Sustainable development was later to be defined by the Brundtland Report, *Our Common Future*, (1987), as the kind of development that allows us to meet our current needs without trespassing on the rights of future generations to enjoy the same access to the world's natural wealth as we do today. Jonathan Porritt, in his fine book, *Save the Earth*, credits the Brundtland Report with being the first to bring to the world's attention the fundamental concept of sustainable development.[22] Well, not perhaps the very first. Ecumenists have reason to take pride in noting that the WCC had been doing so for more than a decade before Brundtland.

The internal logic and coherence of the justice, participation and sustainability theme received an important development at the Sixth Assembly in Vancouver (1983). The theme now became *Justice, Peace and the Integrity of Creation* (JPIC). This not merely incorporated the ecological concerns of today into a process already concerned with justice for the poor and oppressed of the world and with peace in a world threatened by constant possibility of nuclear war; it combined the three in a unified programme in search of a difficult theological coherence. The WCC thereafter set in motion a series of important studies which emphasized this unity.[23]

Justice and peace are properly analysed and discussed in terms of human history with its record of both, but also of war and exploitation of the weak by the strong. The integrity of creation calls for different, or at least modified, categories. As Konrad Raiser sees it, 'The reduction of history to human interaction ... proves to be a dangerous – and indeed potentially lethal – abstraction'.[24] The reason is that history as a category of thought is almost inevitably anthropocentric unless great care is taken to relate it to nature, animate and inanimate. Yet history-as-event takes place within a world of natural cycles, while history-as-record frequently adverts to the influence of nature and its cycles on human affairs.

There is a built-in tension between justice and peace, on the one hand, and the integrity of creation, on the other. As we know, tensions can be healthy and productive as long as they are recognized for what they are and are allowed for. Ecological concern is easily seen, especially by committed workers for justice, as an aesthetic indulgence on the part of the affluent. Even where the developed world has advanced far beyond purely aesthetic considerations and has truly grasped the frightening implications of the ecological crisis, one may wonder with Raiser whether there is within the evironmental movements of the industrialized nations 'a latent evasion of the demands for social and economic justice throughout the world'.[25] It is easy for the developed world to call for the saving of the great life-teeming forests of the tropics; are we prepared, however, to reimburse poor nations which cooperate in the preservation of these forests and in other ecologically responsible projects? The question has implications for us voters as well as for the governments we elect.

This tension between the demands of justice, on the one hand, and the condition of the natural environment, on the other, has been realistically faced during several meetings of the WCC. Perhaps the provision of fora for discussion and debate upon these contentious matters is precisely what a body like the WCC does well enough to serve as a model for others engaged in similar debates. It has long experience of handling the tensions which arise between people who are committed to noble but sometimes conflicting causes.[26]

At Vancouver in 1983 the Assembly decided not merely to consider the issues of justice, peace and the integrity of creation, but to do something far more active, namely, 'to engage member churches in a conciliar process of mutual commitment (covenant)'. This was a daring course of action, since the WCC is traditionally anxious not to be thought of as a superchurch. What form would this 'conciliar process' take? And how would the mutual comitment be expressed? These questions are still with us. Their ecclesiological implications make some Churches suspicious. This may well be seen as a disturbingly clear illustration of the sin precisely of ecclesial disunity. Why do Churches (some more than others) put matters of authority so high on their agenda that the great central truths of Christianity and the crises which face the world today are forced into subordinate positions?

Per Lønning puts his finger on the major challenge to the ecumenical movement today when he refers to 'the obvious discrepancy between the ecumenical understanding produced through official studies and dialogues and the lack of practical consequences drawn in and by the churches'.[27] Interestingly, Lønning refers to this communicative failure in terms of 'reception'. Such an excellent document as the Lima Text of 1982, *Baptism, Eucharist, and Ministry*, is a particularly frustrating example. It is widely praised as a fine exemplar of ecumenical dialogue; yet nothing practical seems to happen in response to it.

The trouble about reception is that it is expected to take place away from the process that generated the document. In ecumenical encounter, as in most other forms of healthy communication, the process of dialogue is more important than the document that results from it. The document is the fruit of a successful dialogical process, usually undertaken by a small number of very committed people. Separating the text from the process which generated it is as devitalizing as it is inevitable. What is needed is a further process designed to re-kindle the dynamism of the original one. That original process, when successful, may have demanded of its participants an intellectual, spiritual, and moral conversion for which there is simply no substitute. The absence of this conversion renders clinical evaluation of its text not only useless but harmful because of the discouragement it fosters.

V

Ecumenical conversion normally results from sharing the experience of striving to overcome inherited divisions and suspicions by trying to get behind the formulas which harbour the divisions. (The Aristotelian term 'transubstantiation' would be an instance in eucharistic theology.) To have to 'freeze' this experience in words suitable for documentary expression is hard enough; but to hand the document over to be scrutinized cold by those who have not been through the conversion encounter must be one of the most frustrating experiences possible. Ecumenists have to be a tough breed. More than twenty years ago Michael Hurley wrote:

> A pessimistic attitude to ecumenism is so widespread among Christians that it might well be considered the greatest obstacle to the cause of reconciling the Churches and the clearest sign of the evil and sinfulness of our disunity. In various ways this pessimism provides an excuse for the indifferent, a difficulty for the interested and a

temptation for the committed.[28]

If these words were apposite in the ebullient sixties, they are doubly so now in what has become for Roman Catholics the retrograde nineties, when so many of the hopes kindled by Vatican II are being slowly but steadily extinguished. Nor can Roman Catholic ecumenists console themselves with the thought that elsewhere in the ecumenical movement things are very different. Reporting to the Assembly of the WCC at Canberra in 1991, Emilio Castro noted a lack of ardour and impatience. 'It is taken for granted that we cannot get beyond our confessional divisions'.[29]

Per Lønning believes that 'the present age of ecumenical rapprochement is nearing its end and that new patterns of progress will have to be sought'.[30] He suggests that widening the ecumenical agenda could help to revitalize the ecumenical movement, and that the theology of creation might well serve the purpose admirably. His book, *Creation – An Ecumenical Challenge?*, records and reflects on several WCC initiatives which were taken in response to the Vancouver Assembly programme. This is an area where interfaith dialogue could feed back into interchurch dialogue. The methodological principle is a simple one: dialogue with other faiths can alert us to elements in our own faith which we have neglected. Nature-orientated cultures and religions have much to say to Christians about the first article of the Christian creed on God as creator. Lønning's point is that this lesson given to us by other faiths and cultures could send us back together to the study of a seriously neglected area of our common Christian faith.

He is of course aware of the dangers. There are those who would exhort us to let sleeping dogs lie. If we have neglected creation theology, at least we have not quarreled about it. This timorous and minimalist exhortation to avoid the risk of opening up fresh divisions overlooks the fact that Orthodox theologians are already critical of Western Christianity's traditional dichotomy between creation and redemption. Dialogue between West and East within Christianity on the topic of creation could serve to alert the West to its neglect of such Eastern *theologoumena* as *theosis*, just as it might alert the East to the (at least ecumenical) necessity of confronting the challenge offered to Christianity, Eastern as well as Western, by modernity.

One way or the other, I believe that a serious and open discussion on the relationship between creation and redemption could give a fresh perspective to some of our inherited ecumenical problems. It could help us to look anew at such classical problems as divine transcendence and immanence, nature and grace, nature and history (noting here the inescapable ambiguity of the term 'nature'), Christ and culture, sacramental symbolism, justification by faith, primordial and new creation, protology and eschatology, providence and evil, creation and chance, alienation and reconciliation, world and Church ... The list could be extended. What I hope I have suggested is that there is in this matter of creation a fertile source of further dialogue between divided Christians. It could take us back beyond inherited denominational divisions. We could find ourselves looking at pluralities and ambiguities (to use David Tracy's terms) which would allow us to transcend earlier disputes. Roman Catholics might find themselves resonating with Luther's *simul justus et peccator*. Lutherans might find themselves envisaging a world which could be changed by Christian action which did not offend against the *sola fide* principle. There is no end to the possibilities, not merely in interchurch but also in interfaith dialogue.

Perhaps the WCC Assembly at Vancouver was pointing to a badly needed and potentially very fruitful initiative when it called for a conciliar process aimed at facing up to, and doing something about, questions of justice, peace and the integrity of creation. There is nothing to be lost by all Christian Churches sponsoring such a programme as soon as possible. At least it would demonstrate that we are capable of concerning ourselves with something more important than ecclesiastical pretensions, obsession with authority and hierarchical structures, and the sacralization of power. It might even suggest to the secular world that Christians were taking the ecological crisis of today with the seriousness it deserves.

Notes

1 M. Kinnamon (ed.), *Signs of the Spirit: Official Report Seventh Assembly* (Geneva, 1991), p.358

2 W. A. Visser 't Hooft, *No Other Name: The Choice between Syncretism and Christian Universalism* (London, 1963), p.103

3 K. Raiser, *Ecumenism in Transition: A Paradigm Shift in the Ecumenical Movement?* (Geneva, 1991), p.41

4 Cited in Raiser, *Ecumenism in Transition*, p.41

5 M. Van Elderen, *Introducing the World Council of Churches* (Geneva, 1990), pp.60-2

6 B. Sjollema, 'Programme to Combat Racism', in N. Lossky et al. (eds.), *Dictionary of the Ecumenical Movement* (Geneva, 1991), p.827

7 Raiser, *Ecumenism in Transition* , p.60

8 ibid. p.61

9 ibid. p.63

10 *Churches and the Transnational Corporations: An Ecumenical Programme* (Geneva, 1983), p.14; cf. Raiser, p.63

11 T. Wieser (ed.), *Whither Ecumenism? A Dialogue in the Transit Lounge of the Ecumenical Movement* (Geneva, 1986), pp.29-30

12 Raiser, pp.64-5

13 J. B. Metz, 'Theology in the Struggle for History and Society', in M. H. Ellis and O. Maduro (eds.), *The Future of Liberation Theology: Essays in Honour of Gustavo Gutierrez* (New York, 1989), pp.168-9

14 This could be interestingly correlated with W. Pannenberg's second thesis on revelation: 'Revelation is not comprehended completely in the beginning, but at the end of the revealing history'. W. Pannenberg, (ed.), *Revelation as History* (London, 1969), p.131

15 Raiser, p.68

16 M. Fox, *Original Blessing: A Primer in Creation Spirituality Presented in Four Paths, Twenty-Six Themes, and Two Questions* (Santa Fe, 1983).

17   P. Evdokimov, *L'Orthodoxie* (Paris, 1980), p.17

18   P. Gregorios, *The Human Presence: An Orthodox View of Nature* (Geneva, 1978), p.79

19   P. Lønning, *Creation – An Ecumenical Challenge: Reflections Issuing from a Study by the Institute for Ecumenical Research, Strasbourg, France* (Macon, 1989), p.9

20   J. A. Baker, 'Biblical Views of Nature', in Birch et al, (eds.) *Liberating Life: Contemporary Approaches to Ecological Theology* (New York, 1990), p.16

21   ibid., p.21

22   J. Porritt (ed.), *Save the Earth* (London, 1991), p.37.

23   Geraldine Smyth, O.P., a former student at the Irish School of Ecumenics, is at present engaged in doctoral research into the JPIC process. Her main concern is to examine its overall theological coherence.

24   Raiser, *Ecumenism in Transition* , p.68

25   ibid.

26   The stresses and strains were particularly evident at Canberra in 1991. On this see several references in *Minutes of the Meeting of the Faith and Order Standing Commission, Rome, Italy 1991* (Faith and Order Paper No. 157 (Geneva, 1992).

27   P. Lønning, *Creation – An Ecumenical Challenge?* p.27

28   M. Hurley, *Theology of Ecumenism* (Cork, 1969), p.86

29   M. Kinnamon (ed.), *Signs of the Spirit* , p.166

30   Lønning, *Creation* , p.26

The Missionary Challenge
to the Church
at the End of the 20th Century

Emilio Castro

We approach our topic with the understanding that the mission- ary dimension is a non-negotiable component of our Christian faith. To be Christian is to be engaged, to be a participant in God's own mission. The invitation to conversion is an invitation to ac- cept the responsibility to participate. God is a missionary God. From the first page of the Bible, when God creates and establishes relationship with the creation, to the central event, the incarna- tion in Jesus Christ, and to the final apocalyptic visions in the book of Revelation, God is calling, rebuking, judging, absolving, always loving. There is no way in which we can eliminate the missionary dimension from the Christian message and it still re- main the Christian message.

I would like to define the missionary perspective of the Christian faith as an attitude of sharing in God's invasion of love through- out human history. Every Christian, every human is called to participate in a global human venture. Our personal salvation is not personal in the sense of selfishly related only to my personal destiny, but I am a human being in community, belonging to the family of God, and in this way my personal calling is an invita- tion to integrate myself in the body of Christ, in the Church, in the community of the missionary people of God. Our Christian iden- tity, that means our missionary identity, sends us into the world to live in love, to be salt, leaven, light. We are invited to be in our worshipping communities an anticipation of the Kingdom to come. I begin by recalling this basic assumption of our Christian conviction because it is necessary to protect ourselves from two errors commonly found among Christians today:

1) First, that Christian mission can be reduced to, or can give special priority to, the numerical and geographical expansion of the Church; that the reality of our missionary engagement is

130

measured by the numbers of missionaries whom we send abroad or by the numbers of new converts who are added at home. Important as this dimension is, it is not in itself the full manifestation of our missionary being and could become and has become very often an alibi for not confronting the total demands of the Gospel of the Kingdom, the total demands of God's love for a particular situation.

2) But we also need to protect ourselves from the other error, namely, that the age of world mission is over and what really matters today is not so much the number of people who come to church but the expression of justice in solidarity with others. Due to or perhaps in reaction to the initial understanding of mission which I described before, this new vision tends to substitute development, dialogue, solidarity, justice and liberation, etc. for the notion of mission. Once again, while all these components are normal and integral parts of the dynamics of the Kingdom of God, they do not in themselves amount to the whole of Christian life.

All those elements belong as fundamental entry points to the eschatological dynamics of the Kingdom of God. Depending on the place, the moment, the circumstances, the personal vocation, we are called to assume our entry point, whether it is actual direct proclamation of the Gospel, or participation in solidarity with the suffering people nearby or far away. The important thing is the perception that this is done in response to the invitation of God in Jesus Christ, and that this is our way to enter into, to add to the total liberating purpose of God manifested in Jesus Christ. The people who respond to God's invitation are always sent, travelling, entering into new territories. The perspective of the Kingdom is wide – always detecting places and moments where a Christian presence is necessary.

In this essay I should like to concentrate on the missionary challenges at the end of the 20th century and discuss those points of entry which seem to be of essential priority for today. My list, of course, will not be exhaustive, but I hope perhaps to discern something of the cutting edges of the encounter between this people sent by God into God's own world, and the dynamics which are operational in that world.

I

Let me begin by indicating what to me is the most important challenge with which we are already confronted now, and which will be with us in the years to come. This is well summarized by one of our old Sunday school hymns, 'Tell me the old, old story, tell me of Jesus and his love'. I do not see any greater urgency today than to develop the capacity of transmitting the story of Jesus Christ within and outside the Christian community. While we are all aware of the secularization prevailing in Western Europe, we are also aware of the fact that the majority of the population still likes to be called Christian. In some countries of continental Europe this can be measured even by the payment of Church taxes. Those taxes are there, providing for many services which the Churches are able to offer, but the bodies, the minds, the hearts of the people are not there. Make an inquiry about the meaning of some of the official holidays celebrated in some of our countries, like Pentecost or Ascension Day or even Christmas and you will get the most extraordinary responses from the people.

But we are talking only of the region called previously Western Europe. We need to look also to the regions belonging to Central and Eastern Europe. We are obviously excited by the new perspectives which have opened up for the Churches there as a result of the overthrow of the party monopoly, within the ideological system. However, we should not be blind to the fact that during the past 45 or even 75 years the population has been deprived of a living relationship with the Churches. In a city like Erevan in the Armenian S.S.R. there were five churches in 1917 for a population of 30,000 people. In 1990 there were five churches for a population of 1,100,000 people. It is impossible to know how many churches have been closed, but it is estimated that under Khruschev alone some 2,000 churches were taken away from the Russian Orthodox Church. Religious instruction was prohibited; and the mass media were forbidden to report on any action taken by a Church. Today we are witnesses of a religious revival; we have a tremendous unity of ethnic groupings and religion. We can watch great feelings, great emotion and the attempt to recover the tradition, but without the actual content, without the actual knowledge. There is curiosity, there is even partisan passion, but there is no knowledge. It is very significant that the Churches in those countries are concentrating their efforts on getting hold of vast quantities of Bibles and religious books – an absolutely necessary resource for conveying the substance of the Christian message.

I have dictated this paper in Nanjing, China, during a visit there to the Amity Printing Press, a joint effort of the China Christian Council and the United Bible Society. Here millions of Bibles are being printed for the benefit of the Chinese people. The National Council of Churches of (South) Korea is coordinating a big campaign among Churches of that country to raise together the means to provide one million Bibles for the Churches in the former Soviet Union.

We could add here the need of the rapidly developing Pentecostal and African Instituted Churches for substantial basic knowledge of the Christian tradition. I do not need to elaborate on rapid growth in world population which represents enormous challenges for the formation of Christian communities and the evangelistic task of the Church. Training, Christian education, the spreading of the Bible – all this is today a fundamental challenge in our missionary outreach. We know there are many dimensions of the mission of the Church which have greater glamour, but the sterling work of the Bible distributor and the Sunday school teacher is fundamental if we want to go into the new millenium as Christians. The capacity to point to Jesus Christ, 'Lo, the Lamb of God who takes away the sins of the world' is fundamental, and a central component in this particular period of history.

II

Notwithstanding the progress of humankind and the radical changes taking place in some parts of the world, enormous sectors of the population in numerous countries live under inhuman conditions of poverty. The slogan of the 70s and 80s about the priority of the poor is not only still with us but it points to an ever more dramatic reality. The population growth in Africa, and the growth in slums in Asia and Latin America, indicate the tragedy of an economic system which is unable to cope with the needs of the masses. The economy of a country may appear to be good, yet substantial sectors of the population may be very poor. As Christians who know the gospel of Jesus Christ, who himself was born among the poor and died among the outcast and despised of society, we cannot be merely accomplices of this. A concern to relieve poverty should become one of the most important components of our missionary vocation. The only way to proclaim the gospel is to be in solidarity. The poor of the earth, the majority of humanity, are also those deprived of the knowledge of Jesus Christ.

The Christian missionary response to the growing poverty in the world implies a prophetic denunciation of the structure of division and power which have resulted in the continuing deterioration of the situation of the poor at the same time that there is an improvement of living conditions for the privileged ones in the world. It is startling to see how plans to build the Europe of the future are basically concerned with its protection. The wall which was destroyed in one part of the continent will be built elsewhere through law, regulations and police actions as protection even from the physical presence of the poor of the earth. The current discussions of GATT (the General Agreement on Tariffs and Trades) on liberating the international trade of agricultural products, indicate the lack of international solidarity and the prevailing selfishness of our own societies, which remain indifferent to the consequences of their actions for the masses of the world.

Something similar could happen in the fight against drug traffic. Countries are being encouraged to use the military and the police to attack plantations, but there is no willingness to encourage the substitution of other agricultural products which would provide other sources of income for the poor of the earth.

But our prophetic solidarity will not be credible unless it is accompanied by practical solidarity. Relief operations like the one which the Churches and the international community are organizing in relation to Ethiopia and the Sudan on a recurring basis are expressions of our Christian concern on a personal and community basis. While ideally the prophetic task should be to change the rules of the game in such a way that this kind of charitable action should not be necessary, we need to be aware of the fact that today it is essential. Even in a better tomorrow we know that no system will be perfect and it will always be necessary to respond in a personal way to personal needs. We need to be alongside the poor of the earth to help them in their own survival, their own organization, so that they can develop their own capacity in the struggle to overcome the situations of need in which they find themselves.

Our imagination will need to be stretched to discover ways and means to act out our solidarity. Our life-style should certainly be challenged. It is impossible to dream that all people of the earth can reach the level of consumerism of the North Atlantic society. The energy capacity of the world as we know it today makes that simply impossible. One of the most important findings of the conciliar process on Justice, Peace and the Integrity of Creation is that those three components belong together and are the expression of our communion, our conciliarity. It is impossible to speak about justice unless we assume our ecological responsibility, unless we reduce our energy consumption in such a way that we contribute to the overall health of the planet and to the overall solidarity of humankind. It is impossible to speak of peace unrelated to justice and ecological responsibility. Perhaps this is one of the bitter but necessary lessons which the Gulf conflict will teach all of us.

Advocates of the poor, solidarity with the poor, learning from the poor – such criteria test our missionary faithfulness. They are very high on the agenda of our missionary reality today and will be essential for the missionary challenge of the coming millenium.

III

While the encounter with other religions is not new in the life of the Church or in the theological reflection on the mission of the Church, it is currently taking specific dimensions which call to our attention one of the main challenges to be faced today and in the years to come. It is interesting to read the materials of the Jerusalem missionary conference of 1928, where it was taken for granted that the religions of the world would not be able to cope with the progress of western science and that only Christianity, being precisely the cradle of that science, would be in a position to resist. Today we see that almost the contrary has happened. Christianity is having great difficulties in fighting a secularity strongly permeated by philosophical pre-suppositions deriving from modern science, while the other religions seem either to accommodate quite well or else simply bypass that world by ignoring it and providing a mystical or disciplinary outlet to people who continue their own scientific research untouched in their religious pre-suppositions. The fact is that the main religions of the world are here to stay. They cannot be thought of merely as hunting grounds or as potentially Christian. Even the phrase coined by German theologians about the 'anonymous Christians' – which describes those who follow their conscience within other religions – is conceived today from the perspective of those religions as pejorative and as an indication of our pride and our spirit of superiority. Of course, as I have already indicated at the beginning of this paper, the missionary dimension is essential to the Christian faith and there is no way to accommodate a relationship with other religions at the price of our withholding the Gospel of Jesus Christ from other people. I do not have any right to decide for myself who is being called into the Church to fulfil the mission which belongs to the Church in the whole economy of God.

At the same time I cannot risk confrontation with people of other religious convictions because there are fundamental Christian values at stake as regards the peace which is possible and necessary in the world. We have first of all to think in terms of survival. There exist already situations where Christianity and Islam, or Christianity and the main oriental religions, are at the point of confrontation. Equally sad is the reality of the situation in the world where Christians of different confessions, sometimes representing different ethnic groups and social situations, see each other as enemies. But of course the conflict is not limited to the internal life of the Christian community nor to the relation of the Christian community with other religions; it has also to do with the conflicts within those religions. Our first duty is to create conditions for collective survival. It will be absolutely necessary for all to work together in the creation of a climate of reciprocal trust and to establish the rules which will ensure the stability of this trust.

It is also necessary to see the potential for mutuality available in the encounter with different religions. When the Programme on Dialogue with People of Living Faiths of the WCC invites religious leaders to attend its main meetings, it is trying to create a climate of trust and confidence, showing that the internal discussion of the Christian Church has nothing to hide from the other religious communities. Also, when His Holiness the Pope or the Community of San Egidio in Rome, or more especially the World Conference on Religion and Peace call together religious leaders to pray or to prepare conditions for peace, they are helping to create a network of friendship and trust which will harness the potentials of those different religious movements in order to foster a common peace and a common future for humankind. It is here, perhaps, where world opinion is eager to receive from people with religious convictions some indication of their real contribution to the future of humankind. This is not easy because our histories divide us and because the caricatures which we have of one another can easily lead to mutual distrust destroying the possibilities of working together.

We Christians would like to render testimony to Jesus Christ according to the will of God. But the only way to give testimony to Christ is to allow the Spirit of Christ to guide our own attitudes in relation to our neighbour: he who did not impose himself on anybody; he who accepted that others can do good and do not need to be controlled; he who was eager to encounter the Samaritan woman or appreciated the faith of the Roman centurion.

Obviously the theological task must be continued, namely that of identifying the tension between the testimony to Jesus Christ and the recognition of the value of other organized religions in the light of the Kingdom of God. Personally I am helped by a reflection on the position of the Apostle Paul in relation to Israel in Romans 9:9-11. I believe that there we have a clue to keep the tension constructive between the passion to communicate the Gospel, and the acceptance that, in the mystery of God, other religions also have a role to play. All this will be fully revealed only in the eschatological manifestation of God's mercy.

IV

Finally, our being the Church of Jesus Christ, our theological reflection, our proclamation and our daily lives should all bear witness to the spiritual quality of life. We have seen the collapse of the socialist systems in Eastern and Central Europe and are now heading for a real discussion on the kind of society which is worth building and which preserves fundamental human values. Summarizing the debate, one could say that a radical reduction of what human beings are to the notion of *homo faber*, to the notion of a proletarian, a producer, has been discarded, but that today we risk replacing it by a similar reduction of the human being to a pure consumer, and by regarding each other merely as potential market targets. This can happen in politics, in marketing and even in evangelization.

It is absolutely necessary to find alternative models which will preserve values of different systems from past experiments and which will indicate potential for the future. But those models should be shaped by convictions, philosophical affirmations,and alternative orientations which come from our understanding of what human beings are. The World Council of Churches called all its member Churches to come to Canberra in Australia for the Seventh Assembly under the prayer, 'Come, Holy Spirit – Renew the Whole Creation'. We were led to the selection of this theme by several concerns; one of those concerns was for freedom as a fundamental category of our being. How can we speak of freedom in a situation where the progress of modern science implies that there is no limit to the capacity of the researchers or the practitioners to influence the type of persons that our children will be? The whole field of genetic investigation and research is full of promises but also of threats to our present and our future. Essential convictions regarding the dignity of the human person, the notion of freedom, the awareness of a spiritual dimension that cannot be reduced to measurement – all these belong to our Christian convictions, but now they are coming back to us as intellectual and practical challenges to be translated into life-choices for the future of mankind.

We have been led to the theme of the Spirit because we realise how, in the social contemporary fabric, forces are at work which tend to condition our reactions. Public opinion polls not only help to assess the cultural climate within a population but also give guidance to people who would like to influence that climate and change our thinking habits and prevailing values. We cannot simply go back to an authoritarian society imposing perceptions and values that must be freely accepted by all. We have grown into maturity in the recognition of our freedom and in allowing society to risk itself by confronting conflicting points of view. But the question remains: How do we strengthen the dimension of spiritual life, the reflective dimension, so that in the use of our freedom we shall not be victims of clever manipulations which lead us in the direction of slavery once again?

Our Assembly theme was a prayer, because prayer symbolizes the dimensions of mystery, of dialogue, of meaning, of which our world is in desperate need. When ideologies to shape, change and transform the historical development of humankind fail, and hidden ideologies which sacralise 'market' or 'consumerism' are admitted as occupying the empty territories, we need to ask ourselves if our Churches' liturgical and spiritual traditions, and our basic convictions of the Spirit's activity can help contribute to an important and vital dimension of the human.

The charismatic movements in our Churches and the popular religiosity prevailing all over the world are pointers towards the need for a dimension of sacredness and mystery which does not find satisfaction in the supermarkets of today. It is up to the theologians of the Church, to the pastors of the Church, to the life of our congregations, to highlight this spiritual dimension. In the end, this will be our fundamental contribution towards the present and future of humankind.

I have limited myself to these four dimensions which I consider central to the present and future of the mission of the Church: the communication of the name of Jesus Christ; the close relation with the poor, the downtrodden, the poor of the earth in which Jesus Christ himself wants to encounter us; an awareness of the presence of other religions and the need to cope with their permanent existence constructively; and finally, the need for a testimony to the spiritual dimension of life. 'Come, Holy Spirit – Renew the Whole Creation'; maybe in the answer to this prayer we will have the beginning of a missionary charter for the end of this century.

This paper was first delivered as a public lecture at The Queen's University of Belfast on 18th October 1990.

PART II

Reconciling Faiths

On Salvation through a Desire of Belonging to the Church

Francis Sullivan

Since the time of Robert Bellarmine, a standard solution to the problem of reconciling the possibility of salvation for non-Catholics with the necessity of belonging to the Catholic Church, has been to explain that those who do not actually (*in re*) belong to the Catholic Church can be saved through their desire (*voto*) of belonging to it. With the Encyclical *Mystici Corporis* of Pius XII, and the 1949 letter of the Holy Office to Archbishop Cushing, this became the official solution of the Catholic Church to the problem. However, while this solution was proposed in earlier drafts of *Lumen gentium* at Vatican II, it is not found in the final text, nor does it appear in any other document of the Council. This raises the following questions, which have obvious implications for a Catholic theology of ecumenism.

1. How was the *re-voto* solution used prior to *Mystici Corporis*?

2. Why was objection taken to the way it was used by Pius XII in 1943 and by the Holy Office in 1949?

3. What is the significance of the fact that this solution was dropped from the text of *Lumen Gentium*, and does not appear anywhere in the documents of Vatican II?

4. Does the idea of a salvific *votum ecclesiae* still have a place in post-Vatican II Catholic theology?

I

Against the reformers who held that the true Church consists only of the elect, or of the predestined, or of those justified by faith, St Robert Bellarmine argued that such a Church would be invisible, since God alone would know who belonged to it. Bellarmine insisted that there is only one Church; that it is visible; and that everyone can know who belongs to it. This led him to the conclusion that all the conditions required for membership in the Church must also be visible. For this reason he described the true

Church as the community of people joined together by the visible bonds of the profession of the same faith, the reception of the same sacraments, and communion with the lawful pastors under the Roman Pontiff. Preoccupied as he was with maintaining the visibility of the Church, he proposed a 'definition' of the Church which named only the external elements by which one can know who belongs to the Church and who does not.[1]

It is a common mistake to take Bellarmine's definition to mean that he thought that the Church consisted exclusively of visible elements. The truth of the matter is that he saw the visible elements as constituting the 'body' of the Church, but he also insisted that the Church has a 'soul,' which he identified with the inner gifts of the Holy Spirit, such as faith, hope, and charity. Obviously, Bellarmine recognized that the soul is the higher and more noble part of the Church; and yet he insisted that membership in the Church depended uniquely on participation in the visible elements which constitute its 'body'. As he saw it, to require any interior qualifications for membership in the Church would conflict with its visibility.

On the other hand, he recognized the possibility that a person might partake of the 'soul' of the Church, by having faith and charity, without being actually a member of the Church. He mentioned two examples: that of a catechumen who has made a perfect act of charity, and that of a person under sentence of excommunication who has regained the state of grace through perfect contrition.

Bellarmine held that neither of these persons could be described as actually belonging to the Church as one of its members, since the catechumen lacked the sacrament of baptism, and the excommunicated person lacked communion with the pastors until he or she was officially reconciled. On the other hand, he recognized that such persons could have the faith and charity by which they would be on the way to salvation. In his terms, they could partake of the 'soul' of the Church without actually being part of its 'body'. This led him to propose and reply to an objection based on the axiom: 'No salvation outside the Church'.

With regard to catechumens, he replied: 'The saying "Outside the Church no one is saved," should be understood of those who belong to the Church neither in reality nor in desire, just as theologians commonly speak about baptism. Because catechumens, even though not in the Church *re* (in reality), are in the Church *voto* (by desire), and in that way they can be saved'.[2] Then, with regard to the excommunicated person who has regained the state of grace before being officially reconciled with the Church, he replied: 'Such a one is in the church *animo sive desiderio* (with his mind or by desire), which is sufficient for his salvation; however, he is not in the church bodily, that is, by external communion, and it is the latter which makes one in the strict sense a member of the church on earth'.[3]

In these passages of Bellarmine's treatise *On the Church Militant*, we have, for the first time, an interpretation of the axiom: 'No salvation outside the Church', which explicitly recognizes that a person who is not actually a member of the Church can be saved by the desire of belonging to it. As Bellarmine himself points out, this is really a further application of the doctrine which had been common among Catholic theologians, to the effect that the lack of actual baptism might be supplied by the desire of receiving it. St Ambrose and other Fathers had justified their optimism about the salvation of catechumens who died suddenly without having actually been baptized by explaining that God would accept their desire of baptism in lieu of its actual reception.[4] St Thomas Aquinas spoke of the possibility that even an implicit desire for baptism might suffice for justification.[5] The Council of Trent confirmed the common doctrine of theologians by saying that after the promulgation of the Gospel no one could be justified without the sacrament of baptism or the desire of it.[6]

Since it is by receiving the sacrament of baptism that a person enters the Church, there is an obvious connection between the necessity of baptism and that of belonging to the Church. However, it would seem that Robert Bellarmine was the first theologian to apply the *re-voto* solution to the problem of reconciling the possibility of salvation for people who are not actually members of the Catholic Church, with the axiom *Extra ecclesiam nulla salus*. With regard to the doctrine of Bellarmine, it is important to note that in his view, it was not enough that a person partake of the 'soul' of the Church (i.e. faith and charity) in order to be saved; lacking actual membership in the 'body' of the Church, the person would have to belong to that body at least 'by desire.'

Francisco Suárez followed Bellarmine on this point, but went beyond him, arguing that as a person could be justified by having an implicit desire for baptism (as St Thomas had taught), so also a person could be saved by having an implicit desire of belonging to the Church. Such an implicit desire would be contained in a person's dispositions of faith and charity.[7]

At this point the question could well be raised: if the dispositions of faith and charity are really the essential conditions for justification, why do these theologians insist that such dispositions must also involve a desire for baptism and membership in the Church on the part of those who are not actually baptized? The answer is that, at least from the time of St Ambrose, it had been understood that baptism was so necessary for salvation that if it could not be had in actual fact, it must be had at least in desire. This implies that baptism is necessary not merely because it was commanded by the Lord, but because it is a means of salvation, which must enter into the obtaining of its effect, at least through the person's desire of receiving it. This is undoubtedly the notion behind the Decree of Trent to the effect that justification cannot be obtained except through baptism or the desire for it.[8] If baptism were necessary merely by virtue of a divine precept, there would be no need of the desire of the sacrament on the part of those who were invincibly ignorant of that law. Bellarmine and Suárez applied the same reasoning to the necessity of membership in the Church; this also is necessary as a means of salvation, but like baptism, its lack can be supplied by the desire of it.

It is well known that the principal collaborator with Pope Pius XII in the preparation of the encyclical *Mystici Corporis* was Fr Sebastian Tromp of the Gregorian University. Given Fr Tromp's great esteem for the theology of St Robert Bellarmine, it is not surprising that Bellarmine's solution re-appears in the encyclical. But before looking at this point, we should recall that a fundamental thesis of *Mystici Corporis* was that the Roman Catholic Church, and it alone, is the Mystical Body of Christ, and since only Roman Catholics are really members of the Church, only they are really members of the Mystical Body. However, a later passage of the encyclical shows that Pius XII recognized the possibility of salvation for those inculpably outside the Catholic Church.

In section 100 of the encyclical, Pius XII urged Catholics to pray for 'those who are not yet members of the Church'. He made it clear that he meant both Christians and non-Christians by mentioning two groups: those who have not yet been enlightened by the gospel, and those separated from the Catholic Church by a breach of faith and unity.[9] In section 101 he went on to say that he desired nothing more ardently than that those who do not belong to the visible structure of the Catholic Church should 'have life and have it more abundantly'. For this reason, he said:

> We urge each and every one of them to be prompt to follow the interior movements of grace, and to seek earnestly to rescue themselves from a state in which they cannot be sure of their own salvation. For even though, by a certain unconscious desire and wish, they may be related to the Mystical Body of the Redeemer, they remain deprived of so many and so powerful gifts and helps from Heaven, which can be enjoyed only within the Catholic Church.[10]

While Pius XII does not say in so many words that non-Catholics can be saved, neither does he say that they cannot; rather, they are in a state in which 'they cannot be sure of their own salvation', and in which they are deprived of many helps to salvation. In other words, salvation is possible, even though more problematic, for non-Catholics.

Secondly, the Pope explains how the salvation of non-Catholics can be reconciled with the principle that there is no salvation outside the Catholic Church. While such people are not really (*reapse*) members of the Catholic Church, and therefore not really members of the Mystical Body, they can be related (*ordinantur*) to the Mystical Body 'by a certain unconscious desire and wish' (*inscio quodam voto ac desiderio*). In this phrase, papal authority has been given to the solution which Bellarmine proposed back in the sixteenth century: those who are not actually members of the Church can be saved by the desire of belonging to it. Furthermore, the Pope has confirmed the teaching of Suárez that even an implicit desire can suffice.

The language used by the Pope was carefully chosen. Given the strict identification between the Catholic Church and the Mystical Body which was the theme of the encyclical, he did not say that non-Catholics could be saved by being members of the Mystical Body; rather, they could be related to it, by wish and desire. He admitted that such a desire could be 'unconscious' (*inscio*); thus he excluded an interpretation which would have limited the possibility of a saving relationship to the Mystical Body 'by desire' to those who explicitly intended to join the Catholic Church. Presumably he recognized the fact that most non-Catholics would not have an explicit wish to be Catholics, and yet he did not exclude the possibility of their salvation.

Some critics questioned the notion of an 'unconscious wish,' asking how it was possible to have a wish of which one was not conscious, and how one could attribute a desire to join the Catholic Church to people who insisted they had no such desire. The answer which the Pope did not give, but which he no doubt expected Catholic theologians to supply, was that such a desire was implicit in the person's dispositions. Those who sincerely wished to do the will of God implicitly desired what God required of them, even if they did not know what that was. Speaking more accurately, it was not the desire as such, but a specific object of desire of which they were not conscious.

The most common criticism of this part of the encyclical was that it made no distinction between Christians and non-Christians when it said that those outside the Church could be related to the Mystical Body of Christ by an unconscious desire. It was objected that this ignored the fact that, by virtue of their baptism, Christians are sacramentally incorporated into Christ, and must belong to his Mystical Body in a way that the unbaptized do not. As one might expect, this criticism was most often voiced by those committed to the ecumenical movement.[11]

However, criticism of this passage of the encyclical came also from some Catholics who would have preferred it if Pius XII had simply re-affirmed the ancient doctrine that there was no salvation outside the Catholic Church, and left it at that. The most vociferous of these were Fr Leonard Feeney and his followers at St Benedict Centre in Cambridge, Massachusetts. They were convinced that membership in the Roman Catholic Church was so necessary for salvation, that if non-Catholics truly corresponded with divine grace, they would be led to an explicit desire to enter this Church, and would normally become Catholics before they died. They rejected as absurd the idea that Protestants, Jews and other non-Christians had an 'unconscious desire' to be Roman Catholics, and that they could be saved by such a desire.

After Fr Feeney had publicly accused the Archbishop of Boston of heresy for allowing that non-Catholics could be saved, an appeal was made to Rome for an authoritative interpretation of the axiom *Extra ecclesiam nulla salus*. The response came in the form of a letter of the Holy Office, addressed to Archbishop Cushing.[12] The key section of the letter reads as follows:

> The Saviour did not make it merely a necessity of precept for all nations to enter the Church. He also established the Church as a means of salvation without which no one can enter the kingdom of heavenly glory.
>
> As regards the helps to salvation which are ordered to the last end only by divine decree, not by intrinsic necessity, God, in His infinite mercy, willed that their effects which are necessary to salvation can, in certain circumstances, be obtained when the helps are used only in desire or longing. We see this clearly stated in the Council of Trent about the sacrament of regeneration and about the sacrament of penance.[13] The same, in due proportion, should be said of the Church in so far as it is a general help to salvation. To gain eternal salvation it is not always required that a person be incorporated in reality (*reapse*) as a member of the Church, but it is required that he belong to it at least in desire and longing (*voto et desiderio*). It is not always necessary that this desire be explicit, as it is with catechumens. When a man is invincibly ignorant, God also accepts an implicit desire, so called because it is contained in the good dispositions of soul by which a man wants his will to be conformed to God's will.
>
> It must not be imagined that any desire whatsoever of entering the Church is sufficient for a man to be saved. It is necessary that the desire by which a man is related to the Church be informed by perfect charity. And an implicit desire cannot have its effect unless a man has supernatural faith.

As is so often the case, the controversy had the beneficial effect of bringing forth an official and more detailed explanation of the *re-voto* solution than had been given before. However, it failed to satisfy Fr Feeney and his followers, who remained adamant in their literal interpretation of 'No salvation outside the Catholic Church'. On one important point the letter of the Holy Office failed to satisfy ecumenically-minded Catholics as well: for, as was the case in *Mystici Corporis*, the letter made no distinction between non-Catholic Christians and non-Christians as far as their relation to the Mystical Body is concerned. In either case, their salvation depended on their being related to it by desire. No reference is made to the fact that by their baptism, Christians have been sacramentally incorporated into Christ, and thus are related to his Mystical Body in a way which non-Christians do not share. We must now see how the Second Vatican Council handled this question.

III

After Pope John XXIII had announced the convocation of the Second Vatican Council, a preparatory theological commission was formed in 1960, with Cardinal Ottaviani, Prefect of the Holy Office as its head, and Fr Sebastian Tromp, chief collaborator with Pius XII in the writing of *Mystici Corporis*, as its secretary. It is no surprise that on the question of salvation for those outside the Catholic Church, this schema echoed the teaching of Pius XII, and the 1949 letter of the Holy Office to Archbishop Cushing.

In its first chapter, 'On the Nature of the Church Militant', it repeated the fundamental theme of *Mystici Corporis*, that only the Roman Catholic Church is the Mystical Body of Christ.[14] The question of the necessity of belonging to the Catholic Church for salvation was taken up in chapter 2, whose first section reads as follows:

> The holy council teaches, as the holy church of God has always taught, that the church is necessary for salvation, and that no one can be saved who, knowing that the Catholic Church was established by God through Jesus Christ, would refuse to enter or remain in it. Moreover, just as no one can be saved except by receiving the sacrament of baptism, by which one who puts no obstacle in the way of in-

corporation becomes a member of the church, so also no one can obtain salvation unless he is a member of the church, or is related to it by desire. However, in order that a person reach salvation, it is not enough to be a member of the church or to be related to it by desire; it is further re-
. quired that a person die in the state of grace, united with God by faith, hope and charity.[15]

The following section further explains who can be related to the Church by desire:

It is not only catechumens who, moved by the Holy Spirit, aspire to enter the church with a conscious and explicit intention, who are related to the church by desire; but others also who do not know that the Catholic Church is the only true Church of Christ, can, through the grace of God, obtain a similar effect through an implicit and unconscious desire. This is the case whether they sincerely wish what Christ himself wishes, or, not knowing Christ, they sincerely desire to fulfill the will of God their Creator. For the gifts of heavenly grace are by no means lacking to those who, with a sincere heart, wish and seek to be renewed by divine light.[16]

This preparatory draft of the constitution on the Church was discussed for one week (December 1-7, 1962), during which it received such strong criticism from the bishops that at the end of the first period of the council, it was withdrawn without having been put to a vote. During the spring and summer of 1963 a new draft was prepared, which incorporated a good deal of material from the preparatory one, but differed substantially from it in tone and general approach. This new draft was presented to the council at the beginning of October, 1963, and was discussed for the whole of that month. It followed the previous text in asserting that the one and only Church of Christ is the Roman Catholic Church, but it added the significant admission that 'many elements of sanctification can be found outside its total structure', and that these are 'things properly belonging to the church of Christ'.[17]

The necessity of belonging to the Catholic Church for salvation was treated in the new draft in the following terms.

> The holy council teaches, with Holy Scripture and Tradition, that the church is an institution necessary for salvation, and that therefore those cannot be saved who, knowing that the Catholic Church has been established by God through Jesus Christ as necessary, refuse to enter it or to remain in it. For what revelation affirms about the necessity of baptism (cf. Mk 16:16; Jn 3:5), undoubtedly applies also to the church, which one enters through baptism as by a door.[18]

The new draft also follows the previous one in insisting that only Roman Catholics are really (*reapse*) members of the Church. It then explains that those who are not really members can be related to the Church by desire.

> Catechumens who, moved by the Holy Spirit, knowingly and explicitly seek to be incorporated in the church, are joined to her by desire [*voto*], and Mother Church already embraces them as her own with her love and care. In its own way the same is true of those who, not knowing that the Catholic Church is the one true church of Christ, sincerely, with the help of grace, seek with interior faith, hope and charity to do the will of Christ, or, if they lack distinct knowledge of Christ, to do the will of God the Creator, who wishes all to be saved.[19]

The phrase: 'In its own way the same is true' clearly means that those who are ignorant of their obligation to join the Catholic Church can have a saving relationship with it by desire (*voto*). This will be 'in its own way' however; they will not have an explicit desire as catechumens do, but one that is implicit in their sincere intention to do the will of Christ, if they are Christians, or of God the Creator, if they are not. The new draft, therefore, continues to apply the *re-voto* solution to the question of the salvation of those outside the Catholic Church, following *Mystici Corporis* and the 1949 letter of the Holy Office in applying this solution to other Christians as well as to non-Christians. However, at this point the revised schema introduced a paragraph which supplied something that was lacking in the previous texts, namely the recognition of the many ways in which the Catholic Church is joined with other Christians in the common sharing of the goods of salvation. Among such goods it mentioned faith in Christ, baptism and other sacraments, belief in regard to the Eucharist, sharing in prayer and other spiritual benefits, and a certain communion in the Holy Spirit, who works with his sanctifying power not only within the Catholic Church but also among other Christians.[20]

The following section of this draft has the title: 'Concerning non-Christians as people to be drawn to the Church'. The main theme of this section, as the title indicates, is the missionary task of the Church to evangelize the non-Christian world. However, it includes a positive statement about the values to be found in other religions, which are described as a 'preparation for the Gospel and light given by God'. After this we find the following statement about the possibility of salvation for non-Christians.

> Those who, without blame, do not know Christ or his church, but with a sincere heart seek God and his will, as it is known to them through the dictates of their conscience, and who, with the help of grace, try to fulfill God's will in their actions, can hope for eternal salvation...[21]

We can presume that the dispositions which are mentioned here as justifying the non-Christian's hope for salvation, are those in which the same draft would recognize the presence of an implicit desire of belonging to the Catholic Church.

This 1963 draft of the conciliar text on the Church met with general approval, but received a very great number of proposals for emendation. During the interval before the next period of the council, a considerable revision was made in the light of those proposals. When the bishops gathered in the autumn of 1964 they were working with a large volume entitled *Schema Constitutionis de Ecclesia*, which contained the 1963 draft and the revised text, along with the reports of the Theological Commission, explaining the reasons for each change that had been made in the text. One such change was that in the new text, the only persons who are said to belong to the Church by desire (*voto*), are catechumens. The idea that non-Catholics are saved by virtue of an implicit desire to belong to the Catholic Church disappeared from the revised schema, which on this point remained unchanged as the final text of *Lumen Gentium*. As we have seen above, this idea had been present in the sentence of the previous draft that began with the words: 'In its own way the same is true'. The explanation given by the Theological Commission for dropping this sentence reads as follows:

> The words of the previous text: "In its own way the same is true..." are not retained by the Commission. The idea is now better expressed below, in no. 15. In any case, non-Catholic Christians do not have a desire of baptism, but baptism itself. Hence they are not to be put in the same category with the non-baptized. Many of the Council Fathers spoke to this point.[22]

This explanation of the change that had been made undoubtedly reflects the dissatisfaction of many bishops with the fact that previously no distinction had been made between non-Catholic Christians and non-Christians as far as their relationship to the Church was concerned; of both it was said that they could be related to it by desire. Now official recognition is given to the fact that other Christians are related to the Church by the sacrament of baptism, which obviously distinguishes them from those who are not baptized.

In section 15 of *Lumen gentium*, to which the Theological Commission refers here, another emendation was made, which has an important bearing on the question of the salvation of other Christians. This is the section which described the many ways in which the Catholic Church is joined with other Christians. Among such links, the previous text had mentioned the fact that those Christians also receive baptism and other sacraments. The final text makes an extremely significant addition, with the phrase 'in their own churches and ecclesiastical communities'. Here we have a concrete application of the Council's decision no longer to identify the Church exclusively with the Roman Catholic Church. If other Christian bodies are rightly called 'churches and ecclesiastical communities', they must also participate, in varying degrees, in the reality of Christ's Church. Furthermore, they participate in the saving function of Christ's Church, inasmuch as it is in these Churches and communities that people are brought to Christian faith and receive the sacraments of salvation. Christians are not saved in spite of, or independently of, the Churches to which they belong, but rather through the ministry of word and sacrament which their own Churches provide for them.

The Decree on Ecumenism spells out the saving function of these Churches and communities even more explicitly in the following passage of its chapter entitled: 'Catholic Principles of Ecumenism'.

> The brethren divided from us carry out many of the sacred actions of the Christian religion. Undoubtedly, in ways that vary according to the condition of each church or community, these actions can truly engender a life of grace, and can be rightly described as capable of providing access to the community of salvation.
>
> It follows that these separated churches and communities, though we believe they suffer from defects already mentioned, have by no means been deprived of significance and importance in the mystery of salvation. For the Spirit of Christ has not refrained from using them as means of salvation which derive their efficacy from the very fullness of grace and truth entrusted to the Catholic Church. (*Decree on Ecumenism* 3)

It is the doctrine of Vatican II that it is only in the Catholic Church that the fullness of the means of salvation is to be found. Whatever 'elements of sanctification and of truth' are present and operative in other Christian Churches, are derived historically from the one Church of Christ which 'subsists in' the Catholic Church. In some way, which the council does not further specify, their efficacy as means of salvation is also derived from that fullness which is found in the Catholic Church. But this does not conflict with the basic assertion of the text: that the Catholic Church now recognizes that other Christian churches and communities are used by God as instruments of salvation for those who belong to them in good faith. The necessary role of the Church in their salvation is explained by the role which their own Churches play in their salvation. In those Churches, the one Church of Christ is effectively present and salvifically operative, even if it does not 'subsist' there with the same unity and the same fullness of the means of grace with which it subsists in the Catholic Church. The conclusion which I draw from this teaching of Vatican II is that 'No salvation outside the Church' is no longer a problem for Catholic theology as far as the salvation of other Christians is concerned. Their own Churches are the ecclesial means by which they reach salvation.

But another, and even larger question remains: what about the salvation of non-Christians, who are two-thirds of the world's population? Must they have a saving relationship to the Church, and if so, can this still be understood as an implicit *votum ecclesiae*?

IV

Apart from the reference to catechumens, there is no mention in *Lumen Gentium*, or for that matter, anywhere else in the documents of Vatican II, of the necessity of a *votum ecclesiae* on the part of those who are not Catholics. Does this mean that Vatican II intended to reject the *re-voto* solution to the problem of the salvation of those 'outside the Church'? As far as non-Catholic Christians are concerned, I believe the answer is yes. But there is reason to doubt whether this was the council's intention with regard to non-Christians. Given the doctrine of Trent, that at least the desire to be baptized is required for justification, and the fact that it is by baptism that one enters the Church, it seems logical to say that if non-Christians need to have an implicit desire of baptism, they must also need to be related to the Church by implicit desire. While Vatican II did not retain this traditional formula, it is fully consonant with the way it explained the necessity of the Church, in the following passage of *Lumen Gentium*:

> Basing itself upon sacred Scripture and tradition, [this sacred Synod] teaches that the Church, now sojourning on earth as an exile, is necessary for salvation. For Christ, made present to us in His Body, which is the Church, is the one Mediator and the unique Way of salvation. In explicit terms, He Himself affirmed the necessity of faith and baptism, and thereby affirmed also the necessity of the Church, for through baptism as through a door men enter the Church. Whosoever, therefore, knowing that the Catholic Church was made necessary by God through Jesus Christ, would refuse to enter her or to remain in her, could not be saved. (*LG* 14)

At the First Vatican Council, the draft of the constitution on the Church contained a paragraph on the necessity of the Church, which specified that this was a necessity not only of precept but of means.[23] At Vatican II, several of the bishops requested that the text of *LG* 14 be emended to include explicit reference to the idea that the Church is necessary with necessity of means. The Theological Commission replied that such necessity was sufficiently indicated by the analogy with the necessity of Christ as mediator, and the necessity of baptism.[24]

The necessity of Christian faith and baptism explains why the Church is a necessary means of salvation for non-Christians, who would otherwise lack such means. Non-Catholic Christians find these necessary means of salvation in their own Churches. But, as we have seen above, it is because baptism and the Church are necessary for salvation with necessity of means, that when they are not had in actual fact, they must be had at least in implicit desire. From this we conclude that it is consonant with the teaching of Vatican II, to maintain that the dispositions which non-Christians need in order to be saved, must involve an implicit desire of belonging to the Church. It is true that Vatican II does not use this language. But it can hardly have intended to repudiate the doctrine of Trent about the need of a *votum baptismi* on the part of the unbaptized. How then can we explain the fact that the idea of a saving *votum ecclesiae* on the part of non-Christians is found nowhere in the documents of Vatican II?

The explanation provided by the Theological Commission shows that when they emended the text so as to eliminate the *votum ecclesiae* on the part of others than catechumens, their attention was focused on the application of this idea to non-Catholic Christians. A number of bishops had insisted that consideration be given to the fact that by virtue of their baptism, non-Catholic Christians have a real relationship to the Church of Christ that is much more than the 'desire' by which non-Christians can be related to it. It was to satisfy this request that the sentence beginning: 'In its own way the same is true...' was eliminated from the text.

If I am not mistaken, the fact that this emendation also eliminated the *re-voto* solution to the problem of reconciling the salvation of non-Christians with the necessity of the Church was overlooked and unintended. I see no good reason for thinking that this solution no longer has a place in Catholic ecclesiology. It is a corollary of the teaching which the Theological Commission said was intended, even though not spelled out, in *Lumen Gentium* 14: namely, that the necessity of belonging to the Church for salvation is a necessity not merely of precept but of means.

In making the point that the traditional *re-voto* solution to the problem of the salvation of non-Christians is consistent with the doctrine of Vatican II, it is of course not my intention to imply that this remains the last word of the council on the question. In my book, *The Church We Believe In*, I have a chapter on Vatican II's notion of the Church as 'universal sacrament of salvation', which I consider its most important contribution to Catholic thought on the role of the Church in the economy of salvation.[25] Likewise important is the council's assertion that everyone in the world either belongs to the Church or is related to it (*LG* 13), and its description of the ways in which various categories of non-Christians are related to the Church (*LG* 16). In my opinion, the thrust of the conciliar teaching favours the view that there is no salvation without the Church being in some way involved in the process, and without some relationship to the Church on the part of those being saved. It has been alleged that to hold this would involve one in unacceptable 'ecclesiocentrism'. I think, rather, with Karl Rahner, that since all grace is the grace of Christ, it must also be grace of the Church, since this is the historical presence of Christ's grace in the world.

Notes

1   *De Controversiis*, vol. 2, lib. 3, *De Ecclesia Militante*, cap. 2
2   *De Ecclesia Militante*, cap. 3
3   *De Ecclesia Militante*, cap. 6
4   *De obitu Valentiniani consolatio* 51, J. P. Minge, *Patrologia Latina*, (Paris, 1844-64), (hereafter *PL*) Vol. 16:1435
5   *Summa Theologicae*, III, q. 69, a.4, ad 2
6   H. Joseph D. Denzinger, *Enchiridion Symbolorum*, (hereafter *DS*) 1524
7   *De fide theologica*, disp. 12, cap. 4, n. 22
8   *DS* 1524
9   *Acta Apostolicae Sedis*, (hereafter *AAS*) 35 (Rome, 1943) 242. The section numbers are those provided by Sebastian Tromp in his edition of the encyclical (Rome, 1958).
10   *AAS* 35 (1943) 243

11   This view was expressed, with varying nuances, by J. Gribomont, 'Du sacrement de l'Eglise et de ses réalisations im parfaits. Essai de théologie du schisme,' *Irénikon*, 22 (1949), pp. 345-67; by L. Richard, 'Une thèse fondamentale de l'oe-cuménisme. Le baptême, incorporation visible à l'Eglise,' *Nouvelle Revue Theologique*, 74 (1952), pp. 485-92; and by Thomas Sartory, *The Oecumenical Movement and the Unity of the Church*, (Oxford, 1963), pp. 141-53

12   The letter is referred to by the opening words: *Suprema haec sacra*. The full Latin text, with an English translation, was first published in *American Ecclesiastical Review*, 127 (1952), pp. 308-15. The Latin text is also given in *DS* 3866-72

13   *DS* 1524, 1543

14   Ch. 1, no. 7; *Acta Synodalia Sacrosancti Concilii Oecumenici Vaticani II*, IV Vols., (Vatican City, 1970-80), (hereafter *AS*) I/4, p. 15

15   Ch. 2, no. 8; *AS* I/4, p. 18

16   Ch. 2, no. 9, *AS* I/4, p. 18

17   Ch. 1, no. 7, *AS* II/1, p. 220

18   Ch. 1, no. 8; *AS* II/1, p. 220

19   Ch. 1, no. 8, *AS* II/1, p. 220-1

20   Ch. 1, no. 9; *AS* II/1, p. 221

21   Ch. 1, no. 10; *AS* I/1, p. 221

22   *AS* III/1, p. 203

23   J. D. Mansi, *Sacrorum Conciliorum nova et amplissima collectio*, (1759-1927) Vol. 51:541

24   *AS* III/1, p. 202

25   (Mahwah and Dublin, 1988).

Is Interfaith Dialogue undermining Interchurch Dialogue?
Ecumenics as the Framework for an Integral Ecumenism

John D'Arcy May

From an early stage, Michael Hurley conceived his ecumenical project in the framework of what he called – following continental rather than English-speaking usage – 'ecumenics'. As it became clear to him that not only social ethics but interfaith dialogue, too, is an integral part of Christian ecumenical endeavour, this framework allowed him to accommodate them both in his thinking.[1] For him 'Ecumenics as the scientific study of ecumenism is necessarily multidisciplinary and interdisciplinary' and is 'a whole of which ecumenical theology is … only a part'.[2] In the same way, what I was proposing to call 'fundamental ecumenics' was defined by my colleague Heinz-Gunther Stobbe as 'multi- and interdisciplinary problem-oriented research'.[3] In his preface to the collected papers of a consultation on human rights, organised by the Irish School of Ecumenics in 1978, Michael Hurley referred to ecumenics as 'an interdisciplinary science, including in its scope not only topics of Interchurch and Interfaith Dialogue, but also Religion and Society topics such as Human Rights', describing the 'ecumenical ideal' as 'a unity of believing communities in the service of the world'.[4] Ecumenics is thus not restricted to the tractates of traditional theology or to the classical doctrines still in dispute among Christians. 'The unity it seeks to promote is not just a unity of beliefs, but a unity of believing peoples in all their diversity'.[5]

Leonard Swidler, another veteran of all three areas of ecumenism, is fond of saying that ecumenists have to engage on two fronts at once: their dialogue *ad extra* with those beyond the confines of their particular denomination or religion has to be protected by conciliating *ad intra* those of their own faith who feel betrayed by such openness.[6] After over two decades of interfaith dialogue under the auspices of the Vatican's Pontifical Council for Interreligious Dialogue (the new name for the Secretariat for Non-Christians established in 1964) and the World Council of Churches' Office on Inter-Religious Relations (the reorganised form of the Sub-Unit on Dialogue with People of Living Faiths set up in 1971), it has become abundantly clear that one of the most divisive issues among Christians worldwide is the marked divergence of their attitudes to dialogue with other faith communities and religious traditions.

At the risk of undue generalisation it is probably fair to say that the line of demarcation runs roughly as follows: the Vatican is cautiously open to interfaith relations as symbolised by Pope John Paul II's day of prayer for peace with other spiritual leaders in Assisi (27th Oct. 1986) and endorsed in his recent encyclical *Redemptoris missio*,[7] though it has problems with what it takes to be the political naïveté of the WCC in allowing its agenda to be set by social activists not representative of its member Churches, whose positions have only the most tenuous theological basis. The WCC on the other hand sees the Vatican's reaction to Catholic liberation theologians as unduly restrictive, but because of its large evangelical constituency and the concerted opposition of the Orthodox it has the greatest difficulty in facing up to the theological implications of interfaith dialogue.[8] Summing up the discussions of an ecumenical consultation on interfaith dialogue at Baar, Switzerland, in January 1990, Paul Knitter pinpointed a 'Christological reservation' made by participants from all the major Christian traditions:

> It animated the Orthodox concern that in extolling the mediating role of institutions or religions we might forget that the saving grace of Christ works primarily in the hearts of individuals. It was pointed out that similar fears of diminishing the central role of Jesus were, most likely, the reason why Vatican II, despite all the positive things it said about other religions, could not bring itself to state explicitly that these religions serve as 'ways of salvation'. For the WCC, too, the fear of many member churches that all these new calls for dialogue with other religions would lead to a decentering of Christ in God's plan has been one of the main reasons why in its official statements the WCC has so far not been able to give systematic theological substance to its ethical appeals for interreligious dialogue.[9]

The place of interfaith dialogue in the Christian ecumenical movement, then, is a long way from being secure, and in the other world faith communities it is even less so. My purpose in this essay is to show that this is at least partly because the meta-discipline of ecumenics is so little developed that theologians – and their equivalents in other traditions – are unable to make a convincing case for dialogue to their respective communities. I propose to look first at Christianity's as yet untapped potential for diversity-within-unity, showing that its future in an increasingly pluralistic world depends on its realising to the full its inherent catholicity or universality. I will then make a special case for the globalisation of ethics in the new multi-cultural and future-orientated environment, going on to show that interfaith dialogue will need a fully developed theory of interreligious communication if it is to be equal to these demands. In conclusion, I will ask whether the resulting vision of an integral ecumenism is indeed, as many suspect, the antithesis of traditional ecumenism, or rather its fulfilment.

I

To raise the question of catholicity, in the words of Hans Küng, is 'to see that the question of unity arises again here, in markedly more acute form'.[10] This is because catholicity is not a matter of size, geographical extent or cultural composition, but touches, like unity, the ultimate question of the Church's identity. Is it the same Church, founded on the one gospel, that we find embodied in the languid Catholicism of southern Italy, the wary tradition-alism of Catholic Ireland, or the strident nationalism of the Polish Church? Do the 'State' Churches of England, Sweden and Germany owe the same debt to the Reformation? Is Orthodoxy in Ethopia, India, Russia and Romania equally commensurable with the tradition of the Greek Fathers? Do the aggressive evang-elistic sects emanating from the United States have anything in common with the spirituality of the Wesleys from which many of them sprang? Are present-day peace-loving Mennonites recog-nisable as the offspring of the Anabaptists, the radical wing of the Reformation? Are any two of these 'Christian' in the same sense, and are the new religious movements emerging in their thous-ands from Asia and Africa Christian at all in any acceptable meaning of the term?[11] One could make similarly bewildering surveys of the various inculturations of Buddhism, whose origins are in India, in Thailand, Sri Lanka, Tibet, Japan and now the West, or of the forms taken by Islam in Indonesia, Pakistan, Iran and its Arabian heartland.

The prospect of interfaith dialogue raises the question of catholicity itself 'in a markedly more acute form'. The fundamental objection to such dialogue is that it presupposes relativism and encourages syncretism.[12] The acknowledgement that each religious tradition is true in its own way and the claim that elements of each of them may therefore be incorporated into any other touch the all-important question of identity. Is there a transcendental unity underlying all religious experiences, doctrines and practices, and if so is it then a matter of indifference which ones we adopt? All such 'inculturations' of Christianity already involve 'dialogue' with the cultures, religious or otherwise, in the midst of which Christians find themselves. The question at issue, however, is the extent to which other people's 'ways' are actually ways of salvation or, if they are not, what is their relationship to the Christian way? This question tends to be more clear-cut when Christians are confronted by the so-called 'world religions', especially where the Christians form tiny minorities and the other faiths are socially predominant, as in much of Asia. In principle, however, the question arises wherever Christians are challenged to enter into the meanings that other people's myths and rituals, truths and certainties have for those who live by them.

Serious consideration of the salvific significance of other religious traditions invariably activates what one writer has called 'theological inhibitions' specific to the various confessional strands of Christianity.[13] These have now fallen into the fairly well-defined pattern of 'exclusivism', 'inclusivism' and 'pluralism'. Exclusivists insist on a complete discontinuity between God's saving work in Christ and the efforts of human beings to discover the truth and attain salvation. Inclusivists acknowledge that followers of other ways are included in God's plan of salvation, but what salvation is can only be determined by reference to Christ. Pluralists, dismissing the devices of inclusivists – such as Karl Rahner's 'anonymous Christians' – as 'Ptolemaic epicycles' (John Hick), have moved from a Christocentric to a theocentric and on to a soteriocentric theology of what Hick calls the transition from 'self-centredness to reality-centredness', but at the price of rejecting as 'mythical' any identifiably Christian symbols. None of these solutions is entirely satisfactory. The search for a framework that would accommodate all their worthwhile insights continues.

One thing, however, is clear: increasingly, the traditions are encountering one another from 'centre to centre' as the importance of their various scriptures, institutions, rituals and doctrines is relativised by familiarity and comparison. The relationship between the 'autonomous centre' of each identifiable tradition, be it the experience of a founder or the time-beyond-time enshrined in myth, and the 'social media' in which this becomes historically accessible, is roughly equivalent to that between the autonomous 'I' and the socially constructed 'me' in the genesis of the individual self.[14] Communication worthy of the name must engage the centre of the personality as of the tradition. Adepts of dialogue are thus not merely engaging in polite conversation but are 'passing over' (John S. Dunne) empathetically into the very heart of other traditions, experiencing from within what it is like to believe what their adherents believe.

Inter-religious dialogue is also seen to presuppose 'intra-religious dialogue' (Raymond Panikkar), in which believers and their communities come to terms with the implications of other people's convictions for their own faith, e.g. when Christians assimilate the significance of ethnicity and the land for Jews or encounter the splendour of Muslim monotheism, or when Buddhists and Hindus are brought up against the urgency of Christian concern for active love and social justice. Already, we must reckon with the 'other ecumenisms' of communities like world Buddhism or Islam and the growing solidarity among indigenous peoples worldwide, which will take their place alongside Christian ecumenism, challenging and complementing it in ways as yet undefined.

For Christians, the process of 'inculturation' and the emergence of indigenous 'contextual' theologies remains the laboratory of interfaith dialogue, though the connection is not always made. The reconceptualising and reinstitutionalising of faith in the

wake of successful evangelisation is the classical origin of properly 'ecumenical' problems, for the resulting re-embodiments of
Christianity must remain communicable to the wider *oikoumene*.
A synthesis must be achieved between cultural autonomy and
Christian authenticity. This will take widely differing forms according as the Christian faith, with its peculiar combination of
the incarnational and the transcendent, encounters traditions
which are 'biocosmic', arising out of an organic unity with the
cycles of nature and structured by kinship and ritual, or 'metacosmic', characterised by efforts to find salvation entirely beyond
the transitory framework of this world.[15] Any adequate theology
of interfaith dialogue must be able to come to terms with all conceivable varieties of both.

This contemporary restatement of the problem of catholicity as
the intensification of the traditional problem of unity already
tries to envisage the equivalent problems faced by other traditions as they deal with the plurality of faiths and ideologies, each
of which is becoming aware of the claims, values and dangers of
all the others. In such a situation it is simply not enough to continue advocating dialogue whilst presupposing a scheme of
things in which one's own faith is at the centre of successive con-
centric circles representing the other traditions of humankind
according to one's own evaluation of them. The meta-discipline
we have been calling 'ecumenics', if it is to justify itself as an ecumenical method, must offer the prospect of taking us beyond
this perspective whilst retaining the uniqueness of each tradition. The globalisation of ethics presents us with an appropriate
way of exploring the possibilities of ecumenics.

II

Common causes are not enough; we need common grounds for
pursuing them. The inadequacy of that slogan from the early
days of the ecumenical movement, 'doctrine divides, service
unites', demonstrated the social activists' dependence on assured and agreed convictions. Today the attempt is often made
by those who are committed to abolishing apartheid, protecting
the environment or promoting liberation to shield their cooperation from the intrusion of religious differences. But it is also be-

coming apparent that, in order to be really sure of our common commitment, we need to be able to understand and share in some way the spiritual sources from which it springs.[16]

There is no lack of incentive for interfaith dialogue on the great issues of our time such as peace and development, human rights and economic justice, but the dialogue about ethics prompts us to raise the question of the ethics of dialogue itself. What generally remains implicit in the many-layered interreligious communication that characterises so much social intercourse in our multicultural environment quickly becomes explicit in the 'centre-to-centre' dialogue or serious interreligious conversation. Hidden layers of interest must be laid bare if communication is not to be distorted. Prejudice, dogmatism and ideological attachment of any kind are exposed as unethical because detrimental to the common pursuit of the faith that does justice, the truth that sets free. Only when subjected to this scrutiny in the course of pursuing it does interfaith dialogue reveal itself to be an intrinsically rational process with implicitly universal scope.[17]

Such reflection is made all the more difficult, however, by the stubborn fact that, on the face of it, the central doctrinal assertions of the various religious traditions are logically contradictory. One cannot assent to both the doctrine of rebirth and the unrepeatability of each human existence; either one accepts the existence of a transcendent God or one does not; Jews believe the Messiah has not yet come, Christians that Jesus was he, Muslims that Jesus was but a great prophet.[18] To give but one example of how this applies to the problem of formulating a common ethic, both Muslims and Africans have felt constrained to draw up alternative charters of human rights to compensate for what they perceive as the Western Christian bias of the UN's 'Universal' Declaration.[19]

The communities defined by religion are communicating with one another within the only community to which their discussions of ethics and values ultimately refer, that of all humankind. The unity of humankind, understood as the basis of equality, is a moral postulate rather than an empirical fact, but it marks out the horizon within which consensus must be achieved, and its empirical realisation remains the goal of all practical ethical endeavour. However, practical recognition of human unity in the form of ethical conduct provides more than just a pragmatic justification for interfaith dialogue. Indeed, the dialogue could be said to consist in the recovery of humanness through the medium of religion as it 'constructs meaning' for alienation, suffering and death, including and especially that of history's victims, those without name and number who are unjustly deprived of their human dignity and of life itself.[20]

As a working hypothesis I would like to propose that the seedbed of interreligious understanding is the deeply buried but intensely felt 'consensus of the suffering' which, if brought to explicit awareness in the course of dialogue, could correlate our apparently irreconcilable attempts to make sense of the inescapable unsatisfactoriness of life, the *dukkha* or 'unease' discerned by the Buddha and the *mataiotes* or 'futility' to which, for St Paul, all creatures are subjected (Rom 8:20).[21] It is on the basis of this hidden consensus that spiritual, as opposed to intellectual, dialogue takes place. It marks out the parameters within which the specifically religious 'meaning' implicit in efforts to bring about both personal and social liberation may be symbolised.

This shared awareness of the inescapability of suffering constitutes the properly religious dimension of that 'consensus of the committed' which, on the same hypothesis, sustains those bent on practical action in pursuit of justice and represents the most accessible level of mutual understanding between them. In the struggle between classes, races and sexes, however, differences are likely to arise about the legitimacy of actions, and in such cases appeal may be made to the more fundamental consensus about the ultimate meaning embodied in actions. Such meaning-consensus is absolutely basic to all social activity, giving immediate and unquestioned assurance about what counts as 'reality', how one is to act and why 'our' norms and customs are in harmony with the cosmos (hence such norm-laden symbols of ultimate order as *dharma, Tao, Torah, shari'a*).[22] Ethical injunctions may not logically be derived from religious assertions, as Hume demonstrated and Kant confirmed, but their practical import as norms for action in communities only becomes operative in the communicative milieux created by shared convictions which are 'religious' in the sense indicated above.

If common causes are really to find common grounds, however, the consensus envisaged by interfaith dialogue must include, at least in principle, a 'consensus of the reasonable' which makes explicit the claim implied by participation in such dialogue that the religious convictions under discussion are 'true'. This is not, however, a good point at which to begin dialogue, for then people tend to get bogged down in the semantics of doctrines or simply pit one self-contained view of the world against another, omitting to clarify their own relationships and the interests that motivate them. The question of truth arises naturally once the meanings that underpin socially sanctioned actions become problematic, either by a developing opposition of viewpoints held by those within the community or by the shock of confrontation with a totally different worldview coming from outside. Only then does the need arise to translate one system of beliefs into the symbolism and terminology of the other, and this demands recourse to a meta-language, analogous to the grammar of 'deep structure' in linguistics. The construction of this meta-language can only be undertaken in the course of dialogue itself. Interfaith dialogue thus makes considerable and simultaneous demands at spiritual, practical and intellectual levels.

Reason in interfaith dialogue is always practical reason, though those religions that have developed philosophical traditions have always found limitless scope for theorising about views of the world, what the Buddha called *ditthi* and steadfastly refused to discuss. Truth, like the language in which it must be expressed, has its roots in action and in the meanings that make action purposive. A theory of truth would thus include criteria for the internal coherence of discourse (analogous to syntactics in the constitution of language), for corresponding between discourse and its intended referents (semantics), and for consensus as the practical basis for asserting truth in real life situations (pragmatics).[23]

Is it feasible to enshrine religious truth in a category of its own, beyond the reach of rational criticism because it is concerned only with personal experiences or metaphysical beliefs inaccessible to 'conventional' reason? Religious discourse is primarily directed to explicating and sanctioning courses of action as 'liberative' or 'salvific', but ways must be devised in the course of dialogue itself and with the linguistic means elaborated therein of raising and if possible deciding questions of truth. It is perhaps misleading to conceive of this as a contest of rival 'truth-claims'. The truth of each 'way' as embodied in proposals for action and backed up by proposals for belief will be vouched for precisely in practice, and may well turn out to be complementary to the truth of other 'ways'. Above all, if interfaith dialogue is to come to grips with the problems of practical life and politics in a world dominated by a-religious scientific and technological thinking, the question of truth cannon be shirked.

At the same time, it is not enough to 'apply' criteria of rationality elaborated in the allegedly 'neutral' sphere of philosophy or science to the exigencies of interreligious conversation. Though the biocosmic traditions of tribal societies have generally not been constrained to develop such criteria, the metacosmic traditions of the world religions generally have, and they are always implicit in any socially viable view of the world. For interreligious dialogue, we need criteria of rationality according to which we can raise and decide questions of religious truth. A lot of work still needs to be done on the 'comparative hermeneutics' of religious traditions and the meta-dialogue of religious philosophies.

Interfaith dialogue, then, from the point of view of its ethical objectives, aims at nothing less than what I have called a 'panhuman consensus' in the three dimensions of action, meaning and truth.[24] But what could this mean in terms of the properly religious preoccupations of its participants? Ecumenists of all traditions who are capable of adopting such a perspective will not be satisfied until this question is answered.

III

Perhaps the most precious potential of religious traditions is their ability to symbolise the goal of truly universal human community as a real possibility, whether in the form of the Kingdom of God as the universal rule of love in Christianity, the expectation of the Messianic age in Judaism, or the outpouring of *metta* (loving kindness towards all beings) in Buddhism. But religious communities, like languages, are ineluctably and irreducibly particular. Their symbols and rituals, however universal in intent, function primarily to maintain their own social identity and coherence. That is why they fiercely resist compromising their integrity by trading off their symbols and rituals against those of others for the sake of a supposed doctrinal consensus.

The ethical norms the religions inculcate into their adherents are regarded by them as universal, but in fact they are the internalised norms of the particular community and are therefore easily regarded as incompatible with those of others. How is it conceivable that a world community could be built with such unpromising material? Now that the universalist international structures, such as the EC in a reuniting Europe and the UN as an agency of world development and security, are beginning to be put in place and become effective, we observe recrudescences of regionalism, nationalism and ethnocentrism, often fuelled by religious fanaticism. In the same way, the erection of ecumenical structures such as the WCC and the network of bilateral dialogues seem to provoke sectarianism and fundamentalism in those who cannot acquiesce in them. The deplorable role of religion in the ethnic strife in Sri Lanka and the former Yugoslavia, or in the communalism of India and the internecine violence of the Middle East and Northern Ireland, may well have a similar explanation.

Interreligious communication thus has an intrinsically social dimension. The norms, whether of truth or action, appealed to by individuals engaged in face-to-face dialogue are non-negotiable for them precisely because they are the internalised norms of their respective communities (though these may be communicating and interacting at a variety of levels, mostly beneath the surface of explicit awareness). Each such community, through its individual representatives, brings to the dialogue a long-established, socially validated and firmly institutionalised consensus about the way to ultimate salvation. For the group, this functions as social meaning and underlies the 'utterance meaning' of all statements made, whether verbally or in ritual enactment.[25] It is into this basic consensus of the other's faith community that the serious participant in interfaith dialogue must enter, intentionally and intuitively adopting the other's viewpoint, expressed in symbols which may be painfully alien, on the most fundamental questions, practice and experiences of the religious and spiritual life.

At this point we are carried well beyond the mere pragmatic justification of interfaith dialogue as a sort of pooling of non-renew-

able spiritual resources, the better to tackle the problems pressing upon all of us. Dialogue has its own intrinsic value and is thus
an end in itself, as is the universal human community which it envisages. The fundamental problem posed by dialogue is how to
transcend the normative beliefs of each religious tradition
without breaking the link of faith with what each takes to be the
transcendentally Real and True. For Christian ecumenists, this
problem has reduced itself to the choice between a generalised 'religious' and a particularised 'Christological' approach to dialogue.[26] Whereas 'generalists' like John Hick and Wilfred
Cantwell Smith strike out boldly towards a complete restatement
of faith detached from any anchoring in traditional symbols,
drawing Christian ecumenists like Paul F. Knitter and Leonard
Swidler in their wake, 'particularists' like John B. Cobb and Hans
Küng attempt to universalise the Christocentrism of the Pauline
vision of the cosmos. The uniquely personal synthesis achieved
by Raimundo Panikkar, who has been called the 'mutational
man' for his ability to enter simultaneously into Christian, Hindu
and Buddhist spiritual experience, is in a class of its own. The
generalists owe much to the tolerant inclusivism of Indian spiritual philosophy, whereas the particularists hold out the possibility
of remaining in touch with the rootedness of religion in ethnicity,
territoriality and historical awareness.

At such a juncture there is little point in talking about a 'theology
of' interfaith dialogue, as if it could be drawn ready-made from
the treasure house of tradition and 'applied' to the new situation.
Rather, we must reconcile ourselves to an era in which all theology will be intrinsically dialogical, placing the meaning of our
most central and sacred symbols continually at issue.[27] Our aim
will not be to create a new religion, as Mircea Eliade was sometimes accused of doing and as one has the impression Hick is prematurely attempting,[28] but to salvage these symbols from ideological misuse and irrationalist debasement, allowing syntheses
to develop wherever genuine complementarity emerges from dialogue and preserving and developing their meanings for the
spiritual benefit of all. One can scarcely sing and celebrate a generalised religion; one cannot rightly exclude others from participating in a particularised one: that is our present dilemma, and it
is ecumenical in the most basic meaning of the word.

IV

I see the way ahead for interfaith dialogue as lying in a threefold transformation of Christianity: a transformation of Christian spirituality by entering the light-filled darkness of the Spirit in the hope of thereby eliciting the long-awaited contribution of the Orthodox and of facilitating collaboration with the spiritual traditions of Asia; a transformation of Christian theological reasoning in the encounter with the teaching of absolute nothingness in the various schools of Buddhism; and a transformation of Christian praxis by learning from those cultures, once dismissed as 'primitive' and now acknowledged as 'primal', how to embed a nurturing relationship with nature in the life of communities. The transformation will be mutual; Christianity too will continue to have its unique impact, though it will no longer be one-sidedly missionary.

Interfaith dialogue could thus become the instrument of what I like to call a 'realised universality', expanding the concept of catholicity to embrace the truth of every tradition in all its integrity, yet allowing each its proper autonomy until the process of dialogue shall have shown us the way towards a synthesis beyond syncretism. Far from 'betraying' evangelism and 'undermining' ecumenism, interfaith dialogue will then be seen to fulfil their promise in as yet unimagined ways, including within its scope the human and ecological problems that beset us at present. But in order to conceive of such an 'integral' ecumenism and ensure that it remains truly evangelical, it will be necessary to develop much further that intellectual framework which Michael Hurley envisaged more than twenty years ago, and far-sightedly called 'ecumenics'.

Notes

1   It was on the occasion of publishing an article in the *Journal of Ecumenical Studies* 14 (1977), pp. 304-12, entitled 'From Ecumenical Theology to Fundamental Ecumenics: A Proposal for the Future of Ecumenical Theory from the Catholic Ecumenical Institute, University of Münster, West Germany', that I first became aware of the existence of a School of Ecumenics in Ireland. On sending a copy of the article to Milltown Park, I received in return Michael Hurley's article, 'Ecumenism, Ecumenical Theology and Ecumenics', *Irish Theological Quarterly* 45 (1978), pp. 133-39, which accorded pretty well exactly with the ideas my colleagues, Peter Lengsfeld and Heinz-Gunther Stobbe, and I were developing in Münster. Unlike this earlier paper, 'Ecumenics: What and Why?', *The Furrow* 21 (1970), pp. 416-27, which was in effect the founding charter of the Irish School of Ecumenics, the 1978 article contained an explicit reference, prompted by the thinking of Jesuits in Asia, to the new situation: '... all over the world, although only in a small way and very tentatively, interfaith dialogue is now considered to be a necessary part of ecumenism' (p. 134).

2   Hurley, 'Ecumenism', p. 138

3   cf. May, 'Fundamental Ecumenics', p. 308

4   cf. Alan D. Falconer, (ed.), *Understanding Human Rights: An Interdisciplinary and Interfaith Study*, (Dublin, 1980), p. ix.

5   Hurley, art. cit., p. 138

6   cf. Leonard Swidler, 'The Dialogue Decalogue: Ground Rules for Interreligious, Interideological Dialogue', *Journal of Ecumenical Studies* 20 (1983) pp. 1-4 (rev. 1984), 'Second Commandment', p.2

7   cf. *Origins* 20 (1991), p. 557. The pope goes out of his way to stress that 'the church sees no conflict between proclaiming Christ and engaging in interreligious dialogue', though 'without detracting in any way from the fact that salvation comes from Christ and that dialogue does not dispense from evangelization', par. 55. This approach is further developed in a paper jointly issued by the Congregation for the Evangelisation of Peoples and the Pontifical Council for Interreligious Dialogue on 20 June 1991 and entitled *Dialogue and Proclamation*, cf. *Origins* 21 (1991), pp. 121-35

8   The WCC's VIIth Assembly in Canberra (February 1991) was only able to declare: 'We witness to the truth that salvation is in Christ and we also remain open to other people's witness to the

truth as they have experienced it'Michael Kinnamon, (ed) *Signs of the Spirit: Official Report, Seventh Assembly*, (Geneva and Grand Rapids, 1991), p. 104, cf. p.59. cf. John D'Arcy May, 'The Dance of the Spirit: A Theological Reflection of the VIIth Assembly of the WCC,' *Doctrine and Life* 41 (1991) pp. 309-310

9   Paul F. Knitter, 'A New Pentecost? A Pneumatological Theology of Religions', *Current Dialogue* 19 (Jan. 1991), p. 34

10   Hans Küng, *The Church*, (New York, revised edition, 1976), p. 383

11   A 'phenomenological' examination of Christianity as a religion has been made by Ninian Smart, *The Phenomenon of Christianity*, (London, 1979), with the stated object of demonstrating the difficulty of claiming that such diverse manifestations point to a readily discernible underlying indentity.

12   I question the usefulness of syncretism as a theological category, cf. John D'Arcy May, 'Syncretism or Synthesis? An Anticipatory Sketch of Religious Change in the Pacific', *South Pacific Journal of Mission Studies* 1 (1991), pp. 18-21. Whereas official bodies such as the Vatican and the WCC warn about the limits of diversity, I should like to explore the Church's capacity for diversity, its potential to realise its universality in an increasing variety of situations.

13   cf. Arnulf Camps, *Partners in Dialogue: Christianity and Other World Religions*, (Maryknoll, 1983), pp. 22-7

14   cf. John D'Arcy May, 'Essence - Identity - Liberation: Three ways of Looking at Christianity', *Religious Traditions* 6 (1984), pp. 30-41; *Meaning, Consensus and Dialogue in Buddhist-Christian Communication: A Study in the Construction of Meaning*, (Berne, 1984), ch 7; 'Integral Ecumenism', *Journal of Ecumenical Studies* 25 (1988) pp. 579-80, 585-6

15   cf. John D'Arcy May, *Christus Initiator. Theologie im Pazifik*, (Dusseldorf, 1990), ch. 7

16   Hans Küng, *Global Responsibility: In Search of a New World Ethic*, (London, 1990), has outlined an ambitious research programme aimed at establishing a common ethos to which the different ethics of the great religions could contribute.

17   Jürgen Habermas has developed a theory of 'communicative reason' as the intellectual framework of 'discourse' – dialogical communication reflecting on the historical and rational conditions of its possibility – in which the attainment of consensus is an integral part of the pursuit of truth, for every speech act implicitly

envisages the ideal communicative situation free of domination
by 'interests', cf, Jurgen Habermas, *Nachmetaphysisches Denken.
Philosophische Aufsätze*, (Frankfurt, 1988); *Habermas und die
Theologie. Beitrage zur theologischen Rezeption, Diskussion und Kritik
der Theorie komunikativen Handelns*, (ed.), Edmund Arens,
(Dusseldorf, 1989).

18   The problems involved have been definitively formulated and
      analysed by William A. Christian, *Oppositions of Religious
      Doctrines: A Study in the Logic of Dialogue among Religions*,
      (London, 1972).

19   cf. Martin Forstner, "Inhalt und Begründung der allgemeinen
      islamischen menschenrechtserklarüng', *Bregründung von
      Menschenrechten aus der Sicht unterschiedlicher Kulturen*, (ed.),
      Johannes Hoffmann, (Frankfurt, 1991), pp. 249-73; text of 'The
      Banjul Charter: The African Charter of Human and Peoples'
      Rights', *Catholic International* 2 (1991) pp. 631-2.

20   This insight, which was the insistent theme of Walter Benjamin in
      the formative years of the Frankfurt School of social philosophy
      from which Jürgen Habermas comes, is the centrepiece of the
      masterly reappropriation of the human sciences for theology by
      Helmut Peukert, *Wissenschaftstheorie - Handlungstheorie - Funda-
      mentale Theologie. Analysen zu Ansatz und Status theologischer
      Theoriebildung*, (Dusseldorf, 1976 & Frankfurt, 1978), ET *Science,
      Action and Fundamental Theology*, (Cambridge Mass.,1984).

21   On the central role of a 'consensus of the suffering' in interfaith
      dialogue see May, *Meaning, Consensus and Dialogue*, pp. 224-34.

22   For a further explication of this account of social meaning-con-
      sensus, cf. Heinz-Gunther Stobbe and John May,
      'Übereinstimmung und Handlungsfähigkeit. Zur Grundlage
      ökumenischer Konsensbildung und Wahrheitfindung',
      Okumenische Theologie. Ein Arbeitsbuch, (ed.), Peter Lengsfeld,
      (Stuttgart, 1980), pp. 304-6.

23   cf. May, 'Integral Ecumenism', pp. 584-85, n. 31. In an otherwise
      appreciative review of my *Meaning, Consensus and Dialogue* in *The
      Journal of Religion* 67 (1987) pp. 426-7, Paul J. Griffiths is unable
      to accept the logical priority of 'consensus as to how it is reason-
      able to behave' over 'agreement about the way the world is', i.e.
      'Buddhist (or Christian) ethical and soteriological practices make
      sense only if their respective metaphysical positions, their truth
      claims, hold water'. My point, however, is not an either-or priority

of action over truth or vice-versa, but complementarity; the structure of my argument is spiral: action-consensus, while revealing
the need for meaning-consensus, is simultaneously modified by
the truth-consensus to which meaning consensus gives rise, as I
tried to explain as carefully as I could in my book, pp. 213-5.
Griffiths 'classical' position on the logical priority of an already
constituted truth cannot accommodate the insights into the primacy
of praxis coming from liberation theology and critical theory.

24   cf. May, art. cit., p. 586.

25   For this terminology, see John D'Arcy May, *Meaning, Consensus
      and Dialogue*, p. 204.

26   The terms of the debate are well represented in *Toward a Universal
      Theology of Religion*, (ed.), Leonard Swidler, (Maryknoll, 1987),
      and the issue of the *Journal of Ecumenical Studies* 26 (1989), on the
      theme 'Universality and Uniqueness in the Context of Religious
      Pluralism'. Some of the contributors to *The Myth of Christian
      Uniqueness*, (ed) John Hick and Paul F. Knitter. (Maryknoll, 1987),
      push pluralism beyond the limits of compatibility with traditional
      theology, as is pointed out by Robin Boyd,
      'A Barthian Theology of Interfaith Dialogue?', *Pacifica* 3 (1990),
      pp. 288-303 in support of David Lochhead, *The Dialogical Imper-
      ative: A Christian Reflection on Interfaith Encounter*, (London, 1988).

27   A brilliant, if somewhat idiosyncratic essay in what he calls
      'inter-theology' has been offered by Kenneth Cragg, *The Christ
      and the Faiths: Theology in Cross-Reference*, (London, 1986), and a
      foretaste of what may be in store can be found in John P. Keenan,
      The Meaning of Christ: A Mahayana Theology, (Maryknoll, 1989).

28   It had already occurred to me to ask whether Hick is not stretch-
      ing the Christian story, and the language in which alone it can be
      told, to breaking point when I chanced upon the same expression
      in a sympathetic and careful review of his *An Interpretation of
      Religion* by C. Robert Mesle, *Journal of the American Academy of
      Religion* 58 (1990) pp. 710-14: '... he stretches too far, putting new
      wine in old skins ... Hick now rejects the literal truth of any lang-
      uage, including his own theodicy, which 'speaks about the Real,
      as a personal being carrying out intentions through time ... '
      (359), p. 713. In an M. Phil. thesis completed at the Irish School
      of Ecumenics in 1991, John O'Grady has brilliantly exposed the
      mistakenness of Hick's supposed dependence on Baillie's
      Christology.

The Meeting House:
The End of Interfaith Dialogue

Robin Boyd

I grew up in the North of Ireland, among Presbyterians who, at least in the country, often spoke of their church as the 'meeting-house'. Going to church was 'goin' to meetin''. This clearly distinguished the Presbyterian place of worship from the Anglican 'church', and from the Roman Catholic 'chapel'.

'Meetinghouse' is a good word, with its echoes of the synagogue (*sunagoge*) of the Jewish Diaspora, as of the earlier 'tent of meeting' in the wilderness. One of the Scottish Paraphrases (1781) which we frequently sang, especially on nostalgic occasions like anniversaries and farewells, was 'O God of Bethel! by whose hand Thy people still are fed' – a very much expanded translation of Genesis 28: 20-22, where Jacob, after his dream of the ladder, promises that if God brings him again to his father's house, 'then the Lord shall be my God'. The fourth verse of the paraphrase (always sung to the tune 'Salzburg') is

> O spread thy covering wings around,
> Till all our wanderings cease,
> And at our Father's loved abode
> Our souls arrive in peace.

When and how will all the wanderers come home? And what will that home be like when they get there? That was the concern of the man whose name was also Israel.

It is the concern of Israel still. And it has become the concern of Christians also, not only for themselves, but for people of other faiths, with whom they are now in dialogue. What is the end of interfaith dialogue? Could it be a meeting in our Father's home? And what will that home be like?

In the early days of the Irish School of Ecumenics, Michael Hurley introduced interfaith dialogue to the curriculum: if dialogue between Christians and Muslims was possible, then why not between Roman Catholics and Presbyterians, even in Ireland? It was an important decision. As one who was privileged to be his first successor at the school, I believe it appropriate to risk considering what might be the end point not only of the Christian ecumenical movement, but also – even more dangerously! – of interfaith dialogue. In what follows I attempt an answer to that question.

I

Ecumenists do not hesitate to draw up blueprints for eschatology in matters of faith and order. 'Convergence' is the model in many multilateral and bilateral interchurch dialogues.[1] The World Council of Churches' agenda on justice, peace and the integrity of creation (JPIC) envisages convergence in these areas, as does the concept of 'the unity of the Church and the renewal of human community', crystallised in the 1990 report Church and World.[2]

For various reasons, however, theologians seem reluctant to apply eschatological criteria to interfaith dialogue. It was not always so, and a hundred years ago the talk in Protestant missionary circles was of 'the evangelisation of the world in this generation'.[3] The eschatology of interfaith dialogue was a vision of a world won for Christ. By the 1920s, however, things were changing: in the area of interfaith dialogue, 'the eschatological office closed'[4] though it opened for faith and order, social ethics, and eventually ecology.

While conservative evangelicals have continued to hold an exclusivist view of the ultimate victory of the Cross, ecumenical Christians have preferred to concentrate on interfaith dialogue. Proper sensitivity has made it impolite to look towards the end-time.

The thesis of this essay is that the time has come when, in company with our friends from other faith-communities, we should look towards the end-time – the *telos* when God's goal will be reached – and ask what, at that point, the relation of the great world faiths to each other will be. When there is no more war, when women and children are no longer exploited, when the lion lies down with the lamb, when the whales are safe, when all

Christians are in communion with each other, – what will be the state of interfaith relations? We need to think eschatologically; for 'if we turn off the lighthouse of eschatology we can only grope around in the darkness of despair'.[5]

The options for eschatological models are limited. They are (i) The victory of one of the present world faiths, in substantially its present form; (ii) The emergence and victory of a new world faith, possibly formed from a fusion of the present ones; (iii) The joint survival of the present world faiths in a pluralism which has either a nondescript 'God' or 'the Real', or 'faith' in a series of optional traditions at its centre;[6] (iv) The 'homecoming' of all peoples into communion with one God whose very being is communion[7] – a homecoming in which people of all the traditions will know that this is the place for which they have long been homesick, the place where they belong.

People of the different world faiths long for the time – or the 'moment out of time'[8] – when they will enter God's immediate presence, or share in God's life, or experience release (*moksa*) through the soul's unity with the supreme soul.[9] This micro-eschatology of the individual is usually associated with a macro-eschatology of the whole of creation, when 'a new heaven and a new earth' (Rev.21:1) will be established.

In the Jewish tradition, for example, Zechariah gives a vision of humanity converging on Jerusalem, with people of other cultures clutching, as it were, at the sleeve of a Jew, saying 'Let us go with you, for we have heard that God is with you'.[10]

Similar images of a society transformed by a relationship with God are found in the New Testament[11] and in other faith-communities.[12] It is a recurring image of unity through communion with God, realizable momentarily and imperfectly in this life, more fully after death, and above all at the *eschaton*, when it will apply not only to individuals but to the human race.

We have been using the term eschatology; but as G.B. Caird points out,[13] the neuter word *eschaton*, so beloved of theologians, does not occur in the New Testament. The personal *eschatos* does, however, and is applied to Christ, and to God, as the first and last, the Alpha and Omega. 'The end is not an event but a person',[14] Caird writes. It is probably more helpful, then, to speak of the *telos*, the goal of history, rather than of the *eschaton*. What we are looking at here is 'not the victory of one religion, but God's immanent reign'.[15] In the end, all humanity will find itself somehow caught up into the life of God, its source and its final home.

II

At the beginning of the 19th century the influence of a unitarianism of the first Person of the Trinity was strong, and found an interfaith response, for example in Hinduism, in the work of the great Bengali social reformer Ram Mohan Roy.[16] The exclusivist missionary theology of the 19th and 20th centuries tended to concentrate on the second Person of the Trinity, as has the inclusivist approach of the 'hidden Christ' type.[17] Today there is a tendency to stress the universal activity – in creation, nature and people of other faiths – of the Holy Spirit.[18] But the classical Christian faith in its fullness is Trinitarian, not unitarian, and any reduction in this fullness is fatal for honest interfaith dialogue.

When Christians confess their faith in the triune God, they are reaffirming the early Fathers' scriptural insight that God's unity is not the unity of a monad:

> We should not be afraid to face seriously the differences between trinitarian and other forms of monotheism. The Trinity teaches us that unity should be conceived personally and relationally, not logically and mathematically (and therefore impersonally).[19]

John Zizioulas points out that in the work of the Cappadocian Fathers, God's being is ultimately identified with a person (the Father) rather than with an impersonal substrate like *ousia*. Their position, he writes, is that 'the final assertion of ontology in God has to be attached not to the unique *ousia* of God but to the Father, that is to a hypostasis, a person'.[20] He continues:

> The only way for a true person to exist is for being and communion to coincide. The triune God offers in himself the only possibility for such an identification of being with communion; He is the revelation of true personhood.[21]

We are saying, then, that at the *telos*, when all humankind arrives home, we shall find ourselves involved not in annihilation, nor in identity with an impersonal absolute, but in communion with a personal God who already has an inner life of communion in the threeness of Father, Son and Spirit. 'The goal of salvation,' says Zizioulas, 'is that the personal life which is realized in God should also be realized on the level of human existence'.[22] At the human level, our fullest and most satisfying life is life lived in relationship, in communion. The witness of the Christian scriptures points to communion at the heart of Godhead: and, astonishingly, we are called, in Christ, to share in that life. At the *telos*, we hope to share in it completely and for ever, both personally and cosmically. Yet even now we can have a foretaste of it in worship; as we share in the life of the 'God whose being consists in communion'.[23] 'We are most truly human – most truly personal – when at the eucharist we participate, through the Spirit, in the communion that is Christ's relation to the Father'.[24]

Here, in Christian terms, is the *telos* – our homecoming. We shall see in the sequel how this affirmation is one in which followers of other faiths might ultimately, if not immediately, join us.

It is because of Jesus of Nazareth that we know and share in the tri-unity of God. In Jesus, God is for ever involved with humankind, in all its earthiness, its suffering – and its joy. And it is 'in Christ' that we human beings are caught up into the life of the Trinity – the only place where we find the ultimate meaning, the *telos* of our existence.

If we are to enter – now or eschatologically – into the *koinonia* of the Godhead, then he is the way. 'God (the Father) remains the goal and end. Jesus Christ is at the centre of the mystery as obligatory Mediator ... as the way leading to God'.[25]

It has always been tempting for Christians to speak of the *logos* rather than of Jesus. The Fourth Gospel's insight into the identity of the second person of the Trinity with the *logos* points the way to comparable identifications in other cultures. But 'the Word became flesh and pitched his tent in our camping-ground'. (Jn 1:14). He is the point at which God touches us in our ordinariness, and we respond. And it is in his loving, healing, forgiving, suffering, dying life that we know what the triune God is like 'on the inside'.[26]

Zizioulas describes the temptation of the *logos* - Christology for the early Church: could it be an effective instrument for allowing the Greeks to feel that the Gospel was indeed for them, that they could be 'at home' in it? St Athanasius' answer was 'Yes' – 'but subject to one essential condition: the doctrine of the *logos* can be maintained only if the *logos* becomes identical with the Son as part of the Trinity'.[27]

When Christians talk about God, then, there is no way in which they can remain silent about Jesus of Nazareth, the Christ. It is because of him that they were first called 'Christians' in Antioch. We are not mere theists, much less deists: we are Christians, and are faithful to our tradition only if we tell the story – the good news (*euangelion*) – of Jesus of Nazareth. The only worthwhile gift we have to offer the world, the only thing that makes us interesting or unusual, is our witness to Christ - his life, suffering, death and resurrection. Everything else we have to offer can be bettered by somebody somewhere. There is no point in Christians taking part in interfaith dialogue unless they affirm an unreduced Christology.[28]

III

In considering the 'scandal' of the Trinity in relation to other faiths, we shall limit ourselves to Hinduism and Judaism – Hinduism because it is the alternative world-faith with which I am best acquainted, and Judaism because it was within Judaism that this dialogue originally began.

The writings of Swami Abhishiktananda (Henri Le Saux, 1910-73) and Fr Bede Griffiths have made us familiar with the term *Saccidananda* (from *sat* = being, *cit* = intelligence, *ananda* = bliss) used in advaita (non-dualist) Hinduism to describe the absolute Brahman.[29] The Christian exegesis of this term goes back to the great Bengali Christian theologian, Brahmabandhab Upadhyaya (1861-1907) and before him to another Bengali who never became a Christian, Keshub Chunder Sen (1838 - 1884). Using a phrase from the Upanishads, Abhishiktananda speaks of a Hindu-Christian meeting point 'in the cave of the heart'.[30] He is speaking primarily of the experiential spirituality of dialogue, but the phrase could be applied also to the cordial eschatological meeting of Hindu and Christian, as they share with one another their experience of the 'pluriform fullness of the One-without-a-second'.[31]

Keshub Chunder Sen expounded the correspondence – pointing towards an eschatological identity? – between *sat, cit, ananda* and the Christian belief in God as Being, I AM; the *logos* as Word/intelligence; and the joy of the Spirit. The temptation with regard to the second element here is to stop short with the *logos*, and avoid the scandal of the incarnation of the *logos*. Brahmabandhab Upadhyaya, however, resisted that temptation in a wonderful Sanskrit hymn on the incarnation, which complements and 'fleshes out' – in the deepest sense of the term – his equally profound hymn on the Trinity as *Saccidananda*.[32]

What is happening here is that Brahmabandhab – followed by Abhishiktananda and others – has outlined a fully Indian, even Hindu,[33] doctrine of the Trinity. This has proved helpful, if not to all, yet certainly to some Indian Christians. They and their Hindu friends have felt that 'in the cave of the heart' they were really sharing together, at this point, in the inner colloquy of the one, absolute God. At present only a limited number of people have had that experience, and use that particular language of dialogue. But might it not be that in 'our Father's loved abode' many Christians and Hindus might find that together they share this experience, this language? Might they not realize that in the bliss of experiencing Being as that communion they are acting faithfully towards their own heritage, and the way by which they have come?

Development of doctrine is needed here, for advaitin Hindus think of the final liberation (*moska*) as ontological unity with the impersonal Brahman, rather than as communion. In fact they would see the idea of communion as belonging to a lower level of religious experience than their own, to the level of *bhakti*, devotion to God in personal form. Yet the separation between these two different strands of Indian thought – personal and impersonal[34] – is by no means rigid, and several thinkers have effectively 'developed doctrine' across it. Brahmabandhab, for example, showed how the doctrine of the Trinity lifted the Christian faith out of the individual piety which many people thought was its only level to the highest possible level, that of the absolute

Brahman: yet he affirmed that even at that height it made sense
only because of the inner relations of Saccidananda, exegeted as
Father, Son and Spirit. Mahatma Gandhi is another example.
Neither a Brahmin, nor an advaitin, nor a Christian, he was devoted both to *satya* (truth, or the self-consistency of a thing with
its *sat*, being), and *ahimsa*, that non-violence which for him was
active love akin to the Christian agape.[35] By this twin devotion he
demonstrated that the realisation of our unity with supreme
being (*sat*) is not to be found in silent contemplation, but in active,
self-sacrificing love. When our deeds are characterised by love,
we cross over from low-level existence to the supreme level,
where life is not so much a matter of being as of doing, a life of
love in action – being as communion.[36]

What is of special significance here is that in each of these cases of
development in Hindu doctrine the person of Jesus of Nazareth
has been an active agent. It was Brahmabandhab's evangelical
conversion through the Church Missionary Society which inaugurated his pilgrimage to Saccidananda. It was very considerably Gandhi's involvement with Christian friends (mainly
Quakers) in England, and his study of the New Testament as well
as of writers like Ruskin, Thoreau and Tolstoy, which led him to
preach and practise the ideal of non-violent, self-sacrificing service and partnership with the poor in a way that few have
achieved. The road to 'being as communion' keeps crossing the
Emmaus road.

The two friends joined by a stranger on that Emmaus Road were
Jewish, as was the stranger. None of the three had any intention
of setting up a new religion separate from Judaism: the task before them was rather the forging of a reformed Judaism which
would be a light to the gentiles for the glory of Israel and Israel's
God. (Lk 2:32) Yet things worked out differently: and by the time
the followers of Jesus' reformed Judaism – reinforced by recruits
from the gentile world – had developed their belief in one God
into a Trinitarian formula, the division between Christian and
Jew had hardened into a reality.

Yet Christians must accept that eschatologically – as originally –
we and the Jewish people are one. Christians are not independent: Judaism is the tree, the trunk, of which we are an engrafted
branch (Rom 11:17ff). And Christians realise that most of the

blame for the separation, the devastating misunderstanding, rests with them. As in the Crusades against the Muslims, so in the Holocaust and Christian involvement in it we have sinned against our own people, and there is no possible self-justification.

Is there, then, any hope of a paradigm shift in Jewish-Christian relations, any way in which Christians could find forgiveness, and Jews and Christians as one people find a welcome in our Father's loved abode? Could the catalyst be Jesus Son of Mary, Jesus the Jew whom Christians, from the days when they were still simply a particular Jewish group, have acknowledged as the Messiah, the Christ? Christians by their anti-semitism have made it very difficult for Jews to encounter Jesus the Jew. Now at last, perhaps, through dialogue and the effort at mutual understanding, the door is opening again for the first time since the New Testament era. Might it not be, as T.F. Torrance has suggested, that the Jewish people might find in Jesus one who in solidarity has shared their suffering, and enabled them, in that suffering, to share his love-relationship with the God of Abraham, Isaac and Jacob?

Torrance writes:

> The Christian Church can never be the same after the Holocaust, for all its understanding of divine revelation and salvation, mediated through Israel, must be, and cannot but be, affected by the Eli, Eli lama sabachthani? in which Israel and Jesus Christ are for ever forged together in a new and quite irreversible way. The Christian Church and the Jewish Church are now harnessed together ... for witness, service and mission ... toward the end-time, when Christ will come to take up his reign and make all things new.[37]

That suggestion points towards the possibility of Jews and Christians discovering a development of doctrine which could bring them together in an eschatological sharing within the communion of God's inner life. God's Spirit is active throughout the Hebrew scriptures. And God's special emissary Jesus, on whom the Spirit rests, offers today the possibility of divine reconciliation with a world which, in the 20th as in the first century, has wanted only to reject, torture and destroy him and his people.

IV

Ecumenical Christianity since about 1960 has been afflicted by an unresolved dichotomy. On the one hand there has been a lively appreciation and practice of Trinitarian worship, and a corresponding liveliness in theological debate on matters of faith and order, especially baptism, eucharist and ministry. On the other hand there has been an equally lively concern with issues of justice, peace and the integrity of creation (JPIC), accompanied by some pressure on the Churches to refrain from Christocentric witness. God as creator and God as Spirit are, on the whole, non-offensive categories. Jesus Son of God and Messiah is a *skandalon;* so the pressure has been to reduce the scandal by reducing the Christological content of discourse.

The paradigm shift within Judaism created by Jesus and his first followers was the result of the proclamation – in word and deed – of the good news (*euangelion*) of the new life-style (the Kingdom) which he brought. The good news we have to offer is the good news of the coming of Christ, his life and his life-style, his death and resurrection, his ongoing presence with his people in the power of the Spirit. As Christians we have nothing so important as this to share with the world – the good news that through Jesus and his Spirit we are called to invite the cosmos to share in the inner communion of the triune God, in that bliss (*ananda*) of which Indian spirituality so rightly speaks. We have no right to keep this to ourselves: the whole world has a right to hear us. In the fine words of *Mission and Evangelism - an ecumenical Affirmation*, WCC 1982, 'Christians owe the message of God's salvation in Jesus Christ to every person and to every people'.[38]

In the past the Church's evangelism has sometimes been associated with civil or military power, or with financial, commercial or cultural imperialism. As a result, Christianity has been seen as a foreign system, hostile to the local cultural tradition. By their mode of telling the story of Christ, Christians have made the story unacceptable, and so the road towards an acceptable eschatology of interfaith relations has been blocked. It is here that the contribution of liberation theology is so important, and should not be discredited despite the collapse of Marxism, whose method of social analysis it often draws on. Liberation theology in its origins brought freedom, new life and hope to oppressed and marginalised people. It affirmed their communion with and their following of the human, suffering, justice-affirming Jesus of Nazareth. Here was no imperialism, but the gospel working 'from below'.

Today the only acceptable method of evangelism is what Leslie Newbigin calls 'mission in Christ's way'.[39] That means the way of humility, of sharing, of friendship, of suffering. Newbigin sees the classic definition of mission in 2 Cor 4: 7-12, where Paul describes the Christian agents of mission as 'always carrying in our body the death of Jesus, so that the life of Jesus may also be manifested in our bodies'. In a world of violence and self-centred power-seeking this implies 'a totally uncompromising yet totally vulnerable challenge to the powers of evil in the name and in the power of the Kingship of God present in the crucified and risen Jesus'.[40] Jesus sent out his disciples to bring peace – *shalom* – to the world (Jn 20: 19-23). And as he did so he 'showed them the scars of that atoning passion by which alone peace is made between sinful men and women and their holy Creator'. Their mission had to be 'always in conformity with the way by which peace was made, the way of the cross'.[41] Where mission in Christ's way is happening, the Church is 'recognizable as his body because it bears the scars of his passion'.[42]

In *Truth to Tell* Newbigin speaks of 'world mission not as proselytism but as exegesis'.[43] We sit down beside secularised people in industry, politics and the arts – and other faiths, we might add! – and together we explore and expound the Gospel, learning from each other as we learn from the good news which is also public truth.[44] In this way evangelism becomes a dialogical process in which both partners share in the exegesis and exploration of the good news.[45]

The great achievement of Christian mission in the 19th century was the planting of the Church in virtually every nation and cultural environment. In a significant sense, 'the evangelisation of the world in this generation' was in fact carried out by the generation which witnessed Edinburgh 1910. It has taken many decades, however, for the western churches to accept the fact that the agent of mission is no longer the cross-cultural missionary or missionary society, but the local eucharistic community. Meanwhile, the mainline western Churches have seemed to lose their missionary nerve, except in its social justice component, and at the same time their own surrounding society at home has become progressively secularised. It is time for an awakening to the essential role in mission of the local eucharistic community both in the former sending and in the former receiving countries.

This means that the local church, in every situation where it is not positively prevented by persecution – and such situations are markedly fewer in 1993 than they were some years ago – must engage in sharing with others the *euangelion*, both in deed and word. Raymond Fung, urging Christians to combine in an 'Isaiah agenda' for social justice with other people of good will,[46] has pointed out that evangelism – in the widest sense of witness in deed as well as word – must start from the worship of the local church, a worship which must be open and welcoming to those who share the social justice agenda.

In worship the story of Jesus of Nazareth is repeatedly told, both in the ministry of the Word, and in the symbolic action of the eucharist. It is in worship that the triune God is approached, that the power of the Spirit is experienced, that God is glorified in doxology. In worship the people of God share, for a significant moment, in the inner life of the Trinity and so are empowered for their mission to the world around them. In Zizioulas' words:

> If the Church wishes to be the place of freedom, she must continually place all the 'objects' she possesses within the communion event … Christians must learn to live in an epicletic way, i.e. leaning on the communion-event in which the structure of the Church involves them. Truth liberates by placing beings in communion.[47]

The true missionaries today are lay people, based in the eucharistic community, who tell the story to their neighbours, live out the Isaiah agenda in partnership with them, and, when the Spirit prepares the way, invite them first to worship, and ultimately to discipleship. The local church, using the local language and the local cultural milieu, is, under the Spirit, the effective agent of mission in Christ's way and the demonstration of real life as communion with God. It is the key to that 'epicletic' living which is a foretaste of the *telos*, when the whole cosmos will share in the inner life of the triune God. In Newbigin's words, the local eucharistic community is 'the primal engine of change in society'.[48] The local church, as a community which is a sign of the inner community of the Trinity, is also a sign of a humanity transformed by its participation in the life of the triune God.

V

In the past, as today, Christians have been divided between those with a burning concern to preach the Gospel and win converts, and those with a conviction that a major – perhaps the major – component of mission is the pursuit of justice and peace. It is an unfortunate dichotomy, and in the early days of the Protestant missionary movement – for example in people like William Carey or William Wilberforce – it was simply not present. In recent decades it has found institutional expression in the Lausanne Committee for World Evangelism on the one hand, and the World Council of Churches on the other.[49]

In the context of the eschatology of interfaith dialogue, the question at issue here is this:

(a) Are we hoping for, and working towards, a time within human history when followers of the great world faiths will find themselves converging into a single faith-community worshipping the triune God, and caught up into the inner communion of the Godhead? This outcome would also be associated with the emergence of a human society from which violence, injustice and exploitation of people and the environment had been banished. Or (b) Are we looking to an event beyond history, beyond the parousia, when God will intervene in the life of the earth, and all saved humanity will become one in a Kingdom beyond the limits of time and space? In this scenario the duty of Christians is to ensure that by their conversion before the end, as many human beings as possible will participate in that salvation.

I believe that this is a false antithesis. Certainly the time is coming when, through a 'big bang' or cooling off, or in some other way, the history of this planet will come to an end, and all our known creation will find its *telos* in the mercy of the triune God. Yet the mission of Jesus himself makes it clear that God's will is that even on this earth we should reflect God's love in a society where the hungry are fed, the sick are healed, women and children are respected, and the poor receive the good news. And if that approximates to the Isaiah agenda (and the JPIC agenda!), then surely it is incomplete without the doxological agenda of telling the story of Jesus, and of the triune God whose life he shares with us. We owe the Gospel to every creature!

In the eucharistic community we are enabled by the Spirit to enjoy proleptically that life of communion – with-the-Trinity – which will at the *telos* be ours. We may have grave doubts about an earthly millenium (as certainly I have); yet it is clearly God's will that we should fight violence, injustice and the exploitation of nature wherever we see them. And the very existence of the Church, with all its imperfections yet with all its great joys, is an indication that the earth too can be a happier place than it is today, a place which reflects more perfectly the inner life and love of the Trinity. We are under obligation to seek to make the world reflect the love and care of God.[50] We cannot inaugurate the Kingdom of God.[51] But we can be obedient to the call to evangelize – in word and deed – in Christ's way.

Significant paradigm shifts in Christian theology have always sprung from faith – from a deepened and strengthened understanding of the work of Christ within the life of the Trinity.[52] Such shifts have normally resulted in an increased effectiveness of mission, both within the culture concerned, and in the Church's outreach to people of other cultures. When one looks back at the history of the Church in a particular culture after such a paradigm shift, one can see that features of the culture have been absorbed into the life of the Church: the Church develops its missionary effectiveness in a process of 'Christocentric syncretism'.[53] Thus western Christianity has taken on board Greek philosophy, Roman organisational structure, German music and American business techniques, so that Christians from a variety of cultural milieux can look back at the history of their Church and feel that they 'belong'.

This process of Christocentric syncretism should not be forced to cease, since it is linked to the development of doctrine. For example, as we have seen, a significant 'development of doctrine' in the trinitarian area has been made possible by the Indian concept of Saccidananda. But such development can come only through people who themselves have come to know Christ, and to see him as 'the way' to the trinitarian God. The Marathi poet

Narayan Vaman Tilak testified that he had come to Christ 'over the bridge of Tukaram'.[54] When he came to know Christ, he saw this experience not as a denial of his Hindu faith but as its development.

The people to whom we must look as our guides in this area are not the western 'theologians of world religions' but the theologians based in local eucharistic communities in a variety of cultures who have come to know Christ, and to see in him the completion of a vision of God which without Him was incomplete.

This process must include a firm application of criteria to judge between what is acceptable to the trinitarian schema, and what is not. This is a process familiar in Hindu theology, where the concept of *viveka* – the criterion for choosing between what is real and what is illusory – is essential. A good starting place is Paul's advice in Romans 8:9: 'Anyone who does not have the Spirit of Christ does not belong to him'. This is a criterion which needs to be applied equally rigorously whether one is developing an Asian or European theology: does this new development square with an understanding of God as one who, in Irenaeus' phrase, works with two hands, Christ and the Spirit? In many cases, the answer will be a positive one. As Gavin D'Costa writes, 'The Trinitarian theology of Christianity helps to explain why the presence of God's Spirit in other religions is the presence of Christ. It is only through the guidance of the Holy Spirit that the Christian may discover the presence of Christ ('He will glorify me') both within and outside of the Church ('and declare it to you').[55]

Viable theology does not grow in a sterile environment: it must spring from the warmth and enthusiasm of a living Christian faith-community. The eschatology of interfaith relations will not emerge from an academic attempt to define a neutral pluralism focussed on a neutral God, or a neutral faith, or a neutral 'Real'.[56] It will ultimately emerge from people who hear the story of Jesus of Nazareth, respond to him, and find in the Kingdom of God as he demonstrates it the authentic development and completion of their own homeward journey.[57] Looking back from that arrival point, the road travelled will be seen to lead through their own country: but there will always be a point at which they encountered the unfamiliar yet familiar stranger of the Emmaus road. New life begins from that encounter.

Suppose it had been possible to hold a conference on world religions some time just before 70 AD, perhaps in Athens, with participants from Greece and Rome and from the Jewish and Judaeo-Christian establishments in Jerusalem and Antioch. That high-powered group of delegates might have been able to draw up a report on a soterio-centric, or even theo-centric world faith. But in fact the fertile, growth-producing Christian faith emerged from struggling, persecuted local eucharistic communities in Syria, Turkey, Greece and Rome. Theology has to be earthed, incarnated in specific places. When John wrote 'the Word became flesh', he indicated a paradigm-shift in the meaning of the *logos*: the latent significance of the term was released, and real development took place. There is a world of difference between a sterile theology of world religions and a local Church growing through worship and witness in Christ's way. The local Church may indeed hear and consider the work of the theologians of religion: only if it accepts what they say after applying Christological and trinitarian criteria will that work ultimately prove fruitful.

In the debate on interfaith dialogue today, the most underrated factor is the theology of the local church in areas where Christianity is a minority faith. This is a situation which must be righted, for it is here that authentic, faithful development of doctrine takes place, and the Gospel proves fertile. The colonialism of the 19th century missionary should not be replaced by a neo-colonialism originating from multinational theologians of world religions.

VI

In the long process of interfaith dialogue, in which the Christian partner will share the story of the good news of Jesus of Nazareth, and the non-Christian partner will also share his or her story, both partners will be changed,[58] and different terminologies may well become the vehicles of Christian witness. There will be no aggression or triumphalism; evangelism will witness to God by telling the story of Jesus – in all his humility – in the power of the Spirit. The Gospel will be shared with those who do not know it, and the result left in the hands of God. But Christians cannot rest until they have shared the story with all those who are entitled to hear it, and to whom they owe it.

The eschatological scenario envisaged here is a combination of an inclusivism which gladly accepts from the other faiths features consistent with trinitarian and incarnational criteria, and of an exclusivism which insists on the tri-unity of God and on Christ's simultaneous divinity and humanity. Pluralism is, however, rejected, whether it be of a 'God at the centre', 'faith at the centre', or 'the "Real" at the centre' type. Rejected also is a 're-alised' creation eschatology, which would hold that the *telos* is already here; we just have to realise our existing unity with the whole creation and its creator.[59] We cannot envisage a *telos* in which God ceases to be triune,[60] for 'being as communion' is part of God's nature, as is God's involvement in humanity through Jesus.

What activity will characterise the end-point, our *telos*, when the lines of all our different quests – for peace, for justice, for integrity of creation, for unity of Christians, for the unity of humankind – converge in that omega-point which we would see as Christ-within-the-Trinity?[61] The answer must be 'worship', as the whole creation is caught up into the life and communion of the triune God. It will be 'eucharist' in the widest sense of the sheer thanksgiving of the whole of creation – the 'hymn of the universe'.

Yet, in distinction from all other visions of the end, secular or religious, this eschatology will be marked with the humanity and the suffering of God-in-Christ. The doxology will always reiterate 'Worthy is the Lamb that was slain to receive power and wealth and wisdom and might and honour and glory and blessing'. As all creation unites in giving worship to 'the one seated on the throne' there is no way in which the praise can omit the literally crucial words 'and to the Lamb'.

That is the eschatological vision of interfaith dialogue: not the triumphalism of any institution – certainly not of the Church – but the suffering, loving penetration of all creation by the Spirit of the Lamb that was slain. And in fear and trembling the Church, the eucharistic community which here and now briefly and intermittently anticipates that glory, must accept the responsibility of being the crucial (again literally!) agent on earth of God's own mission leading to his *telos*.

David Bosch points out that Mt 24:14 – 'this good news of the

Kingdom will be proclaimed in the whole *oikoumene* for a witness to all ethnic groups, and then the *telos* will come' – has often been to used to support the idea that the return of Christ is dependent on the completion of the proclamation of the Gospel to people worldwide.[62] The text has therefore been a favourite of premillennialists and their successors, working to complete the task in order that the Lord may return quickly and bring all things to their *telos*. On the other hand, followers of the social Gospel (and, later, those committed to JPIC) have been keener on Jn 10:10, 'I came that they might have life, and have it in all its fullness'.

As we have seen, there is really no contradiction here. My revered teacher, William Manson, in a paper written in 1952 drew attention to two apocalyptic passages: 2 Thessalonians 2, and Mark 13:63. Both warn against premature excitement about the *parousia*, and both inculcate patience: one saying in effect, 'Go on with your work!', and the other 'First must the gospel be preached to all the nations'. The work of justice and peace and the work of evangelism must proceed together. We do not know when God will decide that his *telos* is accomplished. But meantime we engage in mission: the mission to establish justice and peace, and also the mission to enable people of every culture to know that they are 'home' in the triune communion of God, Creator, Redeemer, Helper: Father, Son and Spirit. In Manson's words: 'The sign of the last Advent carries us beyond any world-events that can be imagined. The Morning Star stands directly over the path of the Christian mission to the world, but it refuses to be caught up with until the mission is completed. In this manner New Testament evangelism leaves the door open to history as the province of the working out of God's purpose of redemption for the world. And it will not do for our theology to close it'. Nor will it do for us to deny that history will one day end, and people of every cultural background be caught up into the glory of the triune God whose being is communion, and who, through Jesus the Jew, is also one of us.

Notes

1   e.g. *Baptism, Eucharist and Ministry*, (Geneva, 1982), and the
        ARCIC agreements. See also *Confessing the One Faith*, (Geneva,
        1991), which brings together various theological traditions in a
        common exposition of the Niceno-Constantinopolitan Creed
        (381), but refers to interfaith questions only in a brief reference to
        the work of the Holy Spirit outside the Church (pp.75-6). The
        document – as is seen especially in its glossary –is strictly limited
        to Eastern Orthodox and Western terminology, and takes no
        account of theological insights from churches witnessing e.g. in
        Hindu, Buddhist or animist cultures.

2   *Church and World: the Unity of the Church and the Renewal of Human
        Community*, (Geneva, 1990). This report also, excellent as it is,
        does not specifically deal with questions of interfaith relations:
        indeed it seems to imply that humanity consists of Christians,
        post-Christians and secular humanists, and ignores the fact that
        the majority of the human race follows other faiths. Given this
        limitation, the report is very helpful on the Church as prophetic
        sign, and as communion. The eschatological perspective is not
        avoided. Both the Church and the whole of humanity have their
        goal in the Kingdom of God (p.22). Already the Church as the
        body of Christ participates in the Trinitarian life of communion
        and love. The eucharist enables each local community 'to live
        and witness as a sign and instrument of reconciliation in the
        world'(p.34). The Church is a sign pointing to the coming
        Kingdom; but this is possible only if the Church is directly con-
        nected with the 'mystery' of Christ 'among the gentiles' (cf.Col.
        1:26-6), that is, God's saving purpose to unite all things and
        people in Christ through the preaching of the gospel and the
        response to it (p.30). The present essay is to some extent an effort
        to 'complete' *Church and World* by extending its scope to interfaith
        dialogue.

3   This watchword was adopted by the Student Movement in the
        USA in 1888.

4   The saying is by Troeltsch. Quoted in David Bosch, *Transforming
        Mission*, New York, 1991, p. 498.

5   David Bosch, ibid p. 509. cf. Leslie Newbigin, *Truth to Tell*,
        (Geneva, 1991), p. 24, 'If there is no public doctrine about human
        destiny, there can be no basis for rational discussion in the public
        forum about what are and what are not proper ends of human
        endeavour'.

6   cf. John Hick on 'God at the centre', *God and the Universe of Faiths*,
       (London, 1977), p. 131; on 'The Real' in *An Interpretation of
       Religion*, (Washington Press 1989), p. 248; and Wilfred Cantwell
       Smith on faith in *The Meaning and End of Religion*, (London, 1978),
       p. 191

7   The phrase is John Zizioulas',cf. *Being as Communion*, (New York,
       1985).

8   T.S. Eliot, *Choruses from The Rock*, VII, in *Collected Poems*, (London,
       1946), p. 173

9   Buddhism, Jainism and some forms of Hinduism being techni-
       cally atheistic, their *telos* does not envisage unity with the abso-
       lute so much as release from the bonds of particularity. The 'full-
       ness' may seem to be 'emptiness', *sunyata*. Yet even this release
       into nothingness is in a sense an entry into unity.

10   Zechariah 8:23

11   e.g. Revelation 21:1 - 22:5

12   Compare Gandhi's concept of *Rama rajya*. See also David Bosch,
       Transforming Mission, p. 197 on 'the cosmic expectation of "a new
       heaven and a new earth"'.

13   G.B. Caird, *Commentary on Revelation*, (London,1966), p. 266, on
       21:6

14   ibid.

15   Bosch, *Transforming Mission*, p. 196

16   See, e.g. R.H.S. Boyd, *Introduction to Indian Christian Theology*,
       (Madras, 1975), pp. 19,26; M.M. Thomas. *The Acknowledged Christ
       of the Indian Renaissance*, (London, 1969), passim. The simultane-
       ous Arian controversy in Irish Presbyterianism was another
       example of a widespread phenomenon.

17   e.g. Karl Rahner, Raymond Panikkar.

18   See, e.g., the section IV report of the Canberra World Council of
       Churches Assembly: 'The Holy Spirit is at work among all
       peoples and faiths, and throughout the universe, in *Signs of the
       Spirit*, (Geneva,1991), p. 116. Compare also the WCC's Baar
       Statement of 1990: 'Further we affirm that it is within the realm of
       the Spirit that we may be able to interpret the truth and goodness
       of other religions and distinguish the 'things that differ', so that
       our 'love may abound more and more, with knowledge and all
       discernment'. (Phil. 1:9-10)

19   *The Forgotten Trinity*, British Council of Churches, (Study
       Commission on Trinitarian Doctrine Today), 1989, pp. 40-41

20   Zizioulas, *Being as Communion*, p. 88.

21   ibid p. 107. See also Newbigin, *Truth to Tell*, p.75, where he con-
        trasts 'The Trinitarian faith which sees all reality in terms of
        relatedness' with the individualism which becomes idolatrous.

22   Zizioulas, *Being as Communion*, p. 50

23   *The Forgotten Trinity*, p. 44

24   ibid. We cannot, however, ignore the fact that advaitin Hindus
        do not share the conviction that personal relationships represent
        the highest form of being. For them it is a limitation, indicating a
        lower form of divine existence than the impersonal *(nirguna,*
        without attributes) Brahman. Brahmabandhab Upadhyaya,
        however, believed that Indian Christians could affirm God at the
        supreme level of Brahman, provided they associated this with
        the understanding of Christ as the *Nara-hari* (man-God), linking
        divinity and humanity. See my *Indian Christian Theology*,
        (Madras, 1975), pp. 63-5

25   Jacques Dupuis, *Jesus Christ at the Encounter of World Religions*,
        (New York, 1991), p. 110

26   cf. Charles Sherlock, *God on the Inside: Trinitarian Spirituality*,
        (Canberra, 1991).

27   Zizioulas, *Being as Communion*, p. 83

28   cf. David Lochhead, *The Dialogical Imperative*, (London, 1988), p.
        93, 'The theological agenda for Christians who are concerned
        with our relation with other religious traditions needs to focus
        on a theology of dialogue, not on a new doctrine of God, or a new
        doctrine of Christ, or a new doctrine of salvation'.

29   See e.g. Abhishiktananda, *Saccidananda: a Christian Approach to
        Advaitic Experience*, (Delhi, 1974).

30   Abhishiktananda, *Hindu-Christian Meeting Point within the Cave of
        the Heart*, (Bombay, 1969).

31   Dupuis, *Jesus Christ at the Encounter of World Religions*, p. 76

32   e.g from the *Hymn of the Incarnation*:
        The transcendent Image of Brahman,
        Blossomed and mirrored in the full-to-overflowing
        Eternal Intelligence
        Victory to God, the Man.
And from the *Hymn to the Trinity*:
        I bow to him who is Being, Consciousness and Bliss …
        … Three-fold relation, pure, unrelated,
        Knowledge beyond knowledge.

33   The word 'Hindu' has originally no religious connotation, and
      means simply '(around the) river Indus'.

34   *Bhakti-marga* (way of devotion) and *jnana-marga* (way of knowl-
      edge).

35   For a more extended treatment of this point, see my *India and the
      Latin Captivity of the Church*, (Cambridge, 1974), pp. 96-8

36   See also Dhanjibhai Fakirbhai, *The Philosophy of Love*, (Delhi,
      1966), p. 1. I have been helped here by Hick – with whom I would
      seldom otherwise agree – in his use of the concept *homo-agape*
      for *homoousia*: 'I wish tentatively to suggest that the continuity-
      of-agapeing formulation may today be more intelligible than the
      oneness-of-substance formulation.' John Hick, *God and the
      Universe of Faiths*, (London, 1977), p. 164

37   T.F. Torrance in David W. Torrance (ed.), *The Witness of the Jews
to   God*, (Edinburgh, 1982), p.96

38   *Mission and Evangelism: An Ecumenical affirmation*, (Geneva, 1982),
      para 41, my italics.

39   Lesslie Newbigin, *Mission in Christ's Way*, (Geneva, 1987).

40   Newbigin, *Mission in Christ's Way*, p. 27. cf. Stanley Samartha,
      One Christ Many Religions (New York 1991), p. 136, 'Only the
      renouncers, not the possessors, can truly become the bearers of
      the gospel to the poor and weak. Only this kind of Christology
      can truly become a Christology in and for Asia. The 'conquering'
      Christ has no place in the religions of Asia'.

41   ibid, p. 30

42   ibid, p. 31

43   Lesslie Newbigin, *Truth to Tell*, p. 33

44   ibid p. 35

45   This implies, of course, that the Christian partner in dialogue has
      to take seriously the story of the other partner: the exegesis can-
      not be limited to the Christian tradition.

46   The agenda – from Isaiah 65: 20-23 is (i) that children do not die,
      (ii) that old people live in dignity, (iii) that those who build houses
      live in them, (iv) that those who plant vineyards eat the fruit.
      Raymond Fung, *The Isaiah Vision: an Ecumenical Strategy for
      Congregational Evangelism*, (Geneva, 1992), p. 2

47   John Zizioulas, *Being as Communion*, p. 122

48   Newbigin, *Truth to Tell*, p. 85

49   The different beliefs of pre and post millenialism are excellently
      documented in David Bosch, *The Transforming Mission*, (New
      York, 1991), pp. 313-27

50 An interesting insight from Indian Christian theology here is the
    concept of the world as the body of God, found in the 11th century
    Hindu thinker Ramanuja. It is a concept with a strong appeal for
    creation theologians who see the whole world as already divine,
    and deserving of respect amounting to worship, to a degree
    which relativizes the significance of Christ. The concept does not
    – to my mind – appear in the Bible. Nevertheless it could perhaps
    be helpful as an illustration of our argument here if it were expressed
    in the form, 'The Church is now the body of Christ, in order that
    eventually – when God wills – the world may become the body
    of God, i.e. be completely conformed to His will'. For a fuller
    development of the idea, see my *Introduction to Indian Christian
    Theology*, (Madras, revised edition 1975), pp. 142-3; and
    Khristadavaita (Madras, 1977), p. 315

51 In my Student Christian Movement days in the 1940s a favourite
    (Barthian!) parody of William Pierson Merrill's well known
    hymn 'Rise up, O men of God' was:
    Sit down, O men of God,
    His Kingdom he will bring
    Whenever he desireth it: You cannot do a thing.

52 See Newbigin, *Truth to Tell*, p. 18, for an assessment of how
    Augustine 'made it possible for the western Church to carry over
    into a new culture much of what was good in the old. His life-
    work illustrates the power which the Gospel has shown over and
    over again to transcend human cultures without destroying them'.

53 The phrase comes from M.M. Thomas. For a recent discussion of
    syncretism see Peter Schineller S.J., 'Syncretism: Good? Bad?
    Inevitable?' in *International Bulletin of Missionary Research*, vol. 16,
    No.2, April 1992 pp. 50-3. Syncretism – *pace* Newbigin – does not
    have to be 'negative'.

54 N. Macnicol, *India in the Dark Wood*, (London, 1930), p. 128

55 Gavin D'Costa, *Theology and Religious Pluralism*, (Oxford, 1986),
    p.135

56 cf. Gavin D'Costa, 'In this process of indigenisation those
    elements rightly valued within other traditions are affirmed and
    employed within a narrow structure, one that tells of a
    Trinitarian God', in Gavin D'Costa (ed.), *Christian Uniqueness
    Reconsidered*, (New York, 1990), p. 26

57 For example, given the increasing influence of secular humanism
    in India, it may well be that only a new beginning of the Indian

tradition as transformed by Christ can preserve all that is most valuable in Hinduism. See Newbigin on the results of the Enlightenment in western society: 'We are offering the only basis on which the true fruits of the last 300 years can be saved from the new barbarians'. *Truth to Tell* p. 39.

58   The Indian theologian Brahmabandhab Upadhyaya distinguished between *sadhan dharma* (religion) and *samaj dharma* (culture) in Hinduism. He believed that Christ would be the centre of a Hindu *sadhan dharma*, which would still retain a great deal of the Hindu *samaj dharma* or culture. To give another example, European culture is strongly marked by classical Greek and Roman religion in literature, art, music and even psychology and theology (Oedipus, Prometheus, Dionysius!). Many people today are happy to let the Christian tradition recede into such a purely cultural role in western society, but provide no eschatological projection of what might take its place.

59   The creation theology of Matthew Fox, for example, leads to an eschatological unitarianism of the creator God (Father/Mother), in which the Christian faith gratefully finds accommodation within the cosmic religion followed, in more or less sophisticated forms, by large sections of the human race.

60   While insisting on the tri-unity of God, we do not believe the western term 'Trinity' to be sacrosanct, any more than the many Greek and Latin theological terms such as *ousia, hypostasis, substantia* and *persona* which still characterise Roman Catholic, Eastern Orthodox, Anglican and Protestant theology. The Trinity (*trias, trinitas*) is the home or matrix to which all humankind will come, but the term used to describe her – the Greek and Latin terms are both incontestably feminine – is less important than the Trinity's inner personal being-as-communion: a communion in which the Word made flesh in Jesus of Nazareth will always be central, the only sure bridge between God and humankind. 'Christ will provide the link by which the different religions will be brought into a deep and mutually enriching relationship with each other'. (Bishop David Brown, quoted in *Towards a Theology for Interfaith Dialogue*, (London, 1984), p. 35.).

61   The Alpha and Omega terminology is applied in Revelation to both the Father and the Son. (Rev. 1:8; 21:6; 22:13).

62   Bosch, *Transforming Mission*, pp. 316-7.

63   Bosch, ibid. p. 340, quoting Newbigin, *The Open Secret*, (Eerdmans, 1978), p. 103.

64   William Manson, 'Eschatology in the New Testament'
      Eschatology, Scottish Journal of Theology Occasional Papers No.2,
      (Edinburgh, c. 1952), pp. 15-6.

The Search for the Jewish Jesus

Franklin Sherman

It was Rudolf Otto, in his classic study of *Das Heilige,* who pointed out that the holy or the numinous is at once attractive and re-pelling. It draws us to itself, as Moses was drawn to the burning bush; yet at the same time it resists a too immediate encroach-ment. The same seems to be true of the 'historical Jesus' as an object of modern scholarly research. He has proved to be elusive, yet still alluring; alluring, yet still elusive.

The search for the 'historical Jesus', which continues undaunted after more than a century, can be said to have had three phases. The first, according to this reckoning, was the nineteenth-century quest chronicled by Albert Schweitzer. This ended quite nega-tively, either with a general scepticism about arriving at any 'as-sured results' about the historical Jesus in view of the faith-based and faith-biased nature of the sources, or with an apocalyptical-ly-minded Jesus whose eschatological expectations were doomed to disappointment, and whose religio-cultural horizons were unbridgeably distant from our own.

The second phase, i.e., 'the new quest for the historical Jesus' (as it was called at the time), dated from after the Second World War and was pursued by post-Bultmannian scholars such as Günther Bornkamm in Europe and James Robinson in the U.S.A. The main problem with this phase of the quest was, in the present writer's judgement, that its results were so banal. In a book like Bornkamm's *Jesus of Nazareth,* one had neither the shockingly minimalistic Jesus of a Dibelius or Bultmann nor the grandeur of the old dogmatic portrait. Bornkamm's Jesus seemed to be a very middle-of-the-road and commonsensical figure, garbed in an es-chatological 'already/not yet' scheme that had become a com-monplace in New Testament scholarship.

The third phase of the search, in contrast, has been filled with a sense of novelty, indeed with astonishment at the plethora of methods and hypotheses and interpretative schemata that have

201

been employed to develop not just one new Jesus portrait but many new portraits. Daniel Harrington, S.J., in his presidential address to the Catholic Biblical Association of America in 1986, listed several such portraits or images that have been set forth in recent years. Each of these, he shrewdly notes, locates Jesus against the backdrop of a different strand in the total complex of Jewish life, thought, and socio-political reality in Jesus' time. There is Jesus as political revolutionary (S.G.F. Brandon), as magician (Morton Smith), as Galilean charismatic (Geza Vermes), as rabbi (Bruce Chilton), as proto-Pharisee or Essene (Harvey Falk); and as eschatological prophet (E.P. Sanders).[1]

To these we can add Jesus as partisan of nonviolent social revolution (Richard Horsley), Jesus as founder of a Jewish revitalization movement (Marcus Borg); Jesus as a Mediterranean Jewish peasant (J.D. Crossan); and Jesus as 'marginal Jew' (J.P. Meier).[2]

The common thread, as Harrington noted in his article, and as these more recent volumes confirm, is the emphasis on the Jewishness of Jesus, so much so that we would be justified in calling this third phase of the quest 'The Search for the Jewish Jesus.' Not that this is the only motif of the current quest, nor that it was completely absent earlier; but it has certainly been a major emphasis in recent studies.

Within this general framework, my particular concern in the present essay is to review some of the contributions to the quest that have been made by Jewish scholars. The upsurge of such studies in recent years has been remarkable, but, interestingly, it was prefigured earlier in this century, particularly in Britain, with the publication of a number of works that, although widely noted at the time, did not receive the continuing attention they deserved. Among these were C.G. Montefiore's *Commentary on the Synoptic Gospels*, published in 1909; G. Friedlander's *The Jewish Sources of the Sermon on the Mount* (1911); I. Abrahams' *Studies in Pharisaism and the Gospels* (two vols., 1917/1924); and the English translation by Canon Herbert Danby of Joseph Klausner's classic *Jesus of Nazareth* (1929; the Hebrew original was published in 1922).

My own interest in these matters is not that of a New Testament scholar, but that of one who is interested, in a very practical way, in how such a re-placing of Jesus in his Jewish context may both contribute to Christian self-understanding, and at the same time, by penetrating to the point of convergence (more precisely, pre-divergence) of these two great traditions, may contribute to strengthening the bonds between them. My presupposition, growing out of my work as director of a campus- and-community-based Institute devoted to this theme, is that even among those who are disposed to be open and tolerant toward the other faith, there is a pervasive sense of 'strangeness' that Jews have about Christianity, and that Christians have about Judaism. This is true, to my observation, even of those who have taken the trouble to learn something of the other faith.

I

To Jews, their Christian friends – who otherwise seem so rational, and whom in daily life they experience as common citizens of the contemporary world – when it comes to their religious faith, seem to make a virtue of 'believing six impossible things before breakfast'. To Christians, Jews – with whom, likewise, they feel they in other respects have so much in common – when it comes to their faith, are seen either as persons caught in a net of rigid and irrational religious practices (Orthodoxy), or as people practising such a low-temperature religion (Liberal or Reform Judaism) that it is hard to see what they get out of it apart from a sense of communal identity; or perhaps some mixture of the two.

To Christians, it is mind-expanding and bond-creating to realize how wildly variegated were the religious options within the Judaism of the time of Jesus, and to be able to see Jesus and his disciples as creatively manoeuvring among those options – which, as we now know, go well beyond the usual list of Pharisees, Sadduccees, etc. To Jews, it is similarly mind-expanding and bond-creating to realize that some of those things that seem strangest about Christianity – its metaphysical bent, its focus on a saviour figure, its sense of sin, its ruminations about the world to come – all have their parallels in Judaism, whether in the Second Temple period or subsequently.

What lies behind all the recent interest in the Jewishness of Jesus? Insofar as even scholars have 'interests,' including religious interests, I would say that it results from a convergence of two complementary motivations. On the part of Christians, a desire to root Jesus back in his Jewish environment, so as thereby more deeply to understand his message and mission, as well as his person. On the part of Jews, a desire to reclaim the figure of Jesus, so long a symbol of hostility and heresy, as a legitimate part of the Jewish religious heritage, and to add early Christianity, as it were, to the panoply of creative expressions of the Jewish spirit.

I have sometimes compared this development to the change in the Roman Catholic view of Luther that has accompanied the Protestant-Catholic *rapprochement* in recent decades. At one time either vilified or ignored, Luther has now become the subject of serious studies by Catholic scholars, who contribute to journals of Reformation studies and participate in scholarly congresses devoted to his thought. He is now viewed, by most such scholars, as a faithful son of the Church, one who drew attention to problems that did indeed cry out for reform, and many of whose proposals, such as celebrating Mass in the vernacular and encouraging lay study of Scripture, are now seen as merely a bit ahead of their time. Protestants, in turn, and especially Lutherans, have learned to appreciate more deeply the manifold ways in which Luther was indebted to his medieval background and stood in solid continuity with it. Just so, Jesus is coming to be viewed by Jews (presently only by a scholarly elite, to be sure) as a legitimate son of the Jewish tradition, while Christians learn to appreciate his continuity with and deep indebtedness to his Judaic heritage.

One thing that will determine the 'success' of this new phase of the search, both in a scholarly sense and in terms of its impact on the Christian and Jewish consciousness, is whether it can avoid the reductionistic tendencies that characterized much of the earlier quests. Modern scholars in general, and liberal Protestant scholars in particular, found a great deal in the Jesus story that was simply unassimilable. Anything that smacked of the supernatural could not be fitted into the *Weltanschauung* within which they were working. I am thinking here not only of the traditional sticking points such as the Virgin Birth and the Resurrection, but also of the mystical/theurgical dimensions of Jesus' life and teaching as a whole. However, now that we have reached the post-modern era, we seem to have left many of these empiricist presuppositions behind us. Contemporary studies of religion are full of references to mysticism and religious ecstasy, to shamanistic figures and charismatic individuals. And these are spoken of not as subjects for demythologization, but as operative religious factors that have to be understood in their own terms. The Jesus of whom it was said, 'He saw the heavens opened' (Mk 1:10) and who cried out, 'I saw Satan fall like lightning from heaven' (Lk 10:18) suddenly seems more comprehensible.

The Jewish scholars who played a role in the earlier search shared of course in its general presuppositions, reflecting the culture of the time. They also – like liberal Protestants or Catholic modernists – were affected by their own particular religious sensibilities. The great Joseph Klausner was a clear example of this. Indeed, the concluding thoughts of his Jesus of Nazareth may be taken as a prime example of what might be called 'respectful reductionism'. His final chapter is entitled, quite directly, 'What is Jesus to the Jews?' In answering his own question, Klausner writes, with a passion that reflects his own commitments:

> To the Jewish nation he [Jesus] can be neither God nor the Son of God, in the sense conveyed by belief in the Trinity. Either conception is to the Jew not only impious and blasphemous, but incomprehensible. Neither can he, to the Jewish nation, be the Messiah: the kingdom of heaven (the 'Days of the Messiah') is not yet come. Neither can they regard him as a Prophet: he lacks the Prophet's political perception and the Prophet's sense of national consolation ... Neither can they regard him as a lawgiver or the founder of a new religion: he did not even desire to be such. Neither is he a 'Tanna,' or Pharisaic rabbi: he nearly always ranged himself in opposition to the Pharisees and did not apprehend the positive side of their work, the endeavour to take within their scope the entire national life and to strengthen the national existence.[3]

This last statement of Klausner's would have to be severely qualified in light of subsequent studies of Pharisaism and Jesus' relation thereto. What is of interest here, however, is not only the way in which Klausner dissociates Jesus from the Jewish tradition, but also the way in which he, at the same time, associates him with it. Jesus, he states, is for the Jews pre-eminently to be seen as 'a great teacher of morality and an artist in parable'.

In his ethical code there is a sublimity, distinctiveness and originality in form unparalleled in any other Hebrew ethical code; neither is there any parallel to the remarkable art of his parables. The shrewdness and sharpness of his proverbs and his forceful epigrams serve, in an exceptional degree, to make ethical ideas a popular possession. If ever the day should come and this ethical code be stripped of its wrappings of miracles and mysticism, the Book of the Ethics of Jesus will be one of the choicest treasures in the literature of Israel for all time.[4]

Here is the voice of one who appreciates Jesus for what he was, is very clear about what he was not, and, above all, judges him by his significance for the people of Israel, in a very tangible and corporate sense. Here is the voice of one who himself had made the commitment of *aliyah* (emigration to the Holy Land). Klausner, by birth a Lithuanian, was writing from his position as professor at the new Hebrew University in Jerusalem.

II

In sampling this material, let us move ahead to the work of the American Jewish scholar Samuel Sandmel, professor for many years at Hebrew Union College-Jewish Institute of Religion in Cincinnati, Ohio. Here we find a much broader interpretation of the diverse ways in which Jesus expressed an authentic Jewishness. Perhaps the researches of Gershom Scholem on Jewish mysticism in the meantime had made the difference. In Sandmel's book *We Jews and Jesus*, (New York. 2nd ed. 1973) he reviews the major 'titles' of Jesus, i.e., those appellations by which a special status in the divine scheme of things, or perhaps divinity itself, was ascribed to him: Son of Man, Son of God, Lord, *Logos*. He tests each of them with regard to its compatibility with Jewish thought.

'Son of Man', he points out, is clearly derived from Jewish apocalyptic, and as such must be allowed to have its transcendent and apocalyptic overtones. It would be reductionistic, Sandmel maintains, to suggest that it merely means 'a human one'. Moreover, the apocalyptic Son of Man was conceived as one 'whose abode … was in heaven, and who was destined to 'come in the clouds'.[5]

THE SEARCH FOR THE JEWISH JESUS

Sandmel sees this as the source of the New Testament image of a Jesus who, having been taken up on a cloud into heaven, would return precisely in the same manner. We may add that this notion of a pre-existent Son of Man in fact provides the descent/ascent scheme within which the whole Christian doctrine of the Incarnation takes shape. As such, it makes the idea comprehensible from a Jewish viewpoint – which, however, is not the same as acceptable.

Sandmel's way of putting this distinction between comprehensibility and acceptability is as follows:

> That Jesus was viewed as the 'supernatural' Son of Man ... was an assertion that was expressed fully within the framework of segments of Judaism, and was in no way, in itself, a product of Gentile thinking. We may summarize this aspect of our discussion in this way: once the followers of Jesus were convinced that he was resurrected, there was nothing inconsistent with their Judaism in conceiving of him as the heavenly Son of Man. On the other hand, those who did not believe that he was resurrected denied that he was the Son of Man, not so much because they disbelieved in the idea, but because they did not believe in this particular identification.[6]

Note that Sandmel refers to 'segments' of Judaism as providing the grounding for this notion. He takes the same tack in dealing with the term *Logos*, in this case referring particularly to Hellenistic Judaism. He interprets this idea or this term, which of course had a philosophic provenance, as an effort to deal with the perennial problem of the relation between transcendence and immanence. Palestinian Judaism 'solved' this problem, he writes, by envisaging angels as the bridge between man and the remote God. Hellenistic Judaism, however, being rationalistic in its mode of thought, employed a ready-to-hand philosophical category for this purpose. '*Logos*', Sandmel writes, 'was the device whereby Greek Jews solved the dilemma of a God who was both transcendent and immanent'.[7]

What then of the idea of the *Logos* Incarnate? Again, Sandmel is very bold: 'My opinion is this, that a Greek Jew would not have denied the possibility of the incarnation, but would have either

agreed or disagreed on whether the possible incarnation of the
Logos as Jesus had actually taken place.'[8] The contemporary
Israeli scholar Pinchas Lapide, a prolific contributor to the 'search
for the Jewish Jesus,' also takes a remarkably open and sympathetic approach to the Christological claims and categories. In his
book *The Resurrection of Jesus: A Jewish Perspective*,[9] he speaks of
Jesus' resurrection as 'a Jewish faith experience'. Resurrection, he
notes, was a Jewish expectation, at least in the Pharisaic tradition;
and hence, *ipso facto*, was intelligible within Judaism. The only
question is, did it actually happen? Did Jesus of Nazareth indeed
have a proleptic experience of that resurrection that was confidently expected for all believers in God's good time? That is
where we have a dividing of the ways; but the point is that the
question is a Jewish one.

In a volume co-authored with the Christian New Testament scholar
Ulrich Luz, *Jesus in Two Perspectives: A Jewish-Christian Dialogue*,[10]
Lapide states the case against reductionistic tendencies quite
vividly:

> Any Jewish scholar who examines the New Testament will
> find that Jesus was undoubtedly a Jew – not just a marginal
> Jew, nor a lukewarm, *pro forma* Jew, but a true Jew, whose
> spiritual roots rose out of the prophetic core of Israel's
> faith, that he was closely related to the Pharisees, that he
> was a Galilean, and that, on top of everything else, he was
> a master of the art of telling parables. But to maintain that
> he was only a Jew, or only a Pharisee, or nothing but a
> wandering preacher, would be the height of unbiblical ar-
> rogance.[11]

There is an echo here of the famous statement about Jesus by
Martin Buber, the Jewish thinker who is generally acknowledged
to have had the greatest impact on twentieth century Christian
thought. In the Foreword to his classic work *Two Types of Faith*,[12]
Buber wrote these memorable words:

> From my youth onward I have found in Jesus my great
> brother. That Christianity has regarded and does regard
> him as God and Saviour has always appeared to me a fact
> of the highest importance which, for his sake and my own,
> I must endeavour to understand … My own fraternally

open relationship to him has grown ever stronger and clearer, and today I see him more strongly and clearly than ever before. I am more than ever certain that a great place belongs to him in Israel's history of faith and that this place cannot be described by any of the usual categories'.[13]

III

The fact is that the Jewish scholars whose work we have reviewed are so far from being reductionistic in their view of Jesus that one would have to invent another term for it; 'expansionistic' might be apt. For the present writer, the work that has had the greatest such mind-expanding effect is the brief but pregnant volume by Prof. Ellis Rivkin, also of Hebrew Union College-Jewish Institute of Religion in Cincinnati, *What Crucified Jesus?* (New York, 1984). Its subtitle is significant: 'The Political Execution of a Charismatic.' Rivkin takes his clue from his predecessor, Solomon Zeitlin, who some forty years earlier had published his book *Who Crucified Jesus?* (New York, 1942). It was Zeitlin who, in discussing the question of culpability for Jesus' death, referred to the distinction between the two Sanhedrins that, as he maintained, existed in Jesus' day: a religious Sanhedrin and a political one. It was only the latter, he claimed, that could have conducted a trial such as is described in the Gospels. Thus it was not Judaism as a religion that condemned him.

Rivkin's question is slightly, but significantly, different from Zeitlin's: 'What crucified Jesus?' His answer: it was 'the Roman imperial system' that was responsible, 'not the system of Judaism'. Rivkin is eloquent in describing what that Roman system was and what impact it made upon the Jewish people. He evokes the mood of that extraordinary moment in words that are worth quoting at some length:

> The times were no ordinary times; the tempests, no ordinary tempests; the bedlam, no ordinary bedlam; the derangements, no ordinary derangements. The chaos that gave birth to a charismatic like Jesus was the very chaos that rendered clarity of judgment impossible ... Thrashing about in a world gone berserk, and in abysmal ignorance of the outcome of any decision or action, one did what, in

one's human frailty, one thought was the right thing to do.
The emperor sought to govern an empire; the procurator
sought to hold anarchy in check; the high priest sought to
hold on to his office; the members of the high priest's
Sanhedrin sought to spare the people the dangerous consequences of a charismatic's innocent visions of the kingdom of God ... the Scribes-Pharisees [a special term of
Rivkin's] sought to lift up the eyes of the people from the
sufferings of this world to the peace of life eternal; the followers of Jesus sought to make sense of the confusion and
terror which enveloped the last days of the life of their
Master and Teacher.[14]

It was in this 'maelstrom of time, place, and circumstance,' writes
Rivkin, 'in tandem with impulse-ridden, tempest-tossed, and
blinded sons of men, that the tragedy of Jesus' crucifixion is to be
found'. Thus it was not the Jewish people who crucified Jesus,
nor was it the Roman people – it was 'the imperial system, a system which victimized the Jews, victimized the Romans, and victimized the Spirit of God'.[15]

Powerful as this conclusion is, equally impressive is the portrait
of Jesus that Rivkin develops in the course of the argument. In
what seems like a throwback to an earlier scholarly age, he bases
his work squarely on the writings of Josephus, although other
contemporary Jewish literature is also used. He uses these to
build what he calls 'an objective framework of time, place, structure, and circumstance' within which the emergence of 'a Jesus-
like figure' would be credible. In other words, Rivkin uses his
sources to outline the role that could plausibly have been played
by a figure comparable to the one that the Gospels portray Jesus
as playing. He paints a portrait of a Christ-surrogate with a blank
face, as it were, and then fills in the features, one by one, out of his
knowledge of the religious, intellectual and social context of the
time. The search is guided by the question of what someone
would have to have been like to arouse the kind of expectations
that Jesus aroused, and who met the fate that he met.

Rivkin is clear about the broad category within which Jesus belongs – that of the 'charismatics' of the time (a category basic also
to the work of Geza Vermes).[16] Some of these were 'wandering'
charismatics, some not; many, though not all, were centred in

Galilee. For his purposes, Rivkin lays special emphasis on the distinction between 'political' and 'religious' charismatics. The former are those who call the people to specific action against the imperial authorities; the latter, those who call only for an inward repentance and renewal in preparation for God's action to restore the Kingdom to Israel. These latter are preachers, not revolutionaries – but the authorities made no such fine distinction. Anyone who gathers a popular following is a potential revolutionary, even if, for the moment, he preaches a non-violent gospel. Rivkin, however, is in search of not just an ordinary charismatic, so to speak, but one whom he calls, in a nicely Hebraic phrase, 'the charismatic of charismatics'. Of such a one, however, Josephus does not explicitly speak.

> We scan the writings of Josephus in vain [Rivkin writes] for that charismatic of charismatics whom we would have anticipated finding there – a charismatic so compassionate, so loving, so eloquent, and so filled with the Spirit of God that his disciples would refuse to accept his death as real. But Josephus shares with us only the charismatic John the Baptist. Yet, for all his charisma, John the Baptist failed to arouse in his disciples a love intense enough or a faith secure enough to evoke his death as but a prelude to life.[17]

As he further depicts the object of his search, Rivkin draws deeply on the prophetic heritage, depicting a figure in which a multitude of expectations coincide:

> For an individual to succeed in winning so devoted a following, he must have fused within himself the wonder working charisma of an Elijah, the visionary power of an Isaiah, the didactive persuasion of a Pharisaic sage. But he must have been more than a mere fusion of such guiding spirits. To outlive death itself, he would have had to feel the sufferings of the poor, experience the humiliation of the degraded, sense the loneliness of the outcast, taste the despair of the sinner, and envelop all those who came within his shadow with his graciousness, compassion, and undemanding love.[18]

It is striking how history and eschatology are intertwined in Rivkin's portrait. The Christ-surrogate whom he depicts is one who moves about on the historical scene and works within it to achieve his purposes; yet his dimensions are grander and more mysterious than merely historical terms can convey. He is one who brings about a *Zeitwende* – in Tillich's terms, 'a new state of things'. Though one might think that nothing could be added to exalt this figure further, and though it might seem anticlimactic, Rivkin adds that his charismatic of charismatics also resembles the 'Scribe-Pharisee' of New Testament times. This is a category that Rivkin has devised or adopted to indicate the essential synonymity, in his judgment, of the terms 'Scribes' and 'Pharisees' as used in the Gospels. The resemblance of the two – as well as their resemblance to his Christ-figure – extends to both the method and the content of their teaching.

As to method, Rivkin describes the Scribe-Pharisee's *modus operandi* as follows:

> The Scribe-Pharisee was pre-eminently a teacher, around whom disciples flocked and at whose feet they sat. Like the Stoic sage, the Scribe-Pharisee walked about with his disciples and freely discoursed on the oral and written Law and on the oral and written lore. Legal opinions mingled freely with reflections on God, Torah, Israel, and the struggle of the individual to subdue the power of sin so as to gain the bliss of the world to come.[19]

As to content, the teaching of such a one would focus on what Rivkin has elsewhere[20] identified as the core of Pharisaic faith: 'He would proclaim God's Oneness; call on the people to love God with all their heart and being; urge his listeners to love their neighbours as themselves; acknowledge the legitimacy of Caesar's realm; and trumpet the good news of eternal life and resurrection'.[21]

It will surely seem to the Christian reader that what we have in Rivkin's portrait of the unknown charismatic of charismatics is astonishingly close to the portrait of the one who, in the New Testament, is called the Christ. It also remains clear, however, that the latter is a faith affirmation, and obviously not one that Rivkin or any Jewish scholar is prepared to make. Rivkin writes purely as an historian, specifically, an historian of Judaism. As such, he is depicting only the empty framework that, for

Christians, is filled with the countenance of Jesus of Nazareth. Within these limits, however, we can only marvel at the service that Rivkin performs for Christian readers in helping them to understand the 'time, place, and circumstance' in which the Gospel story is set, and to appreciate the scope and grandeur of the figure who is at the centre of their faith.

IV

We have reviewed some of the literature of what we have called 'the search for the Jewish Jesus', selecting for emphasis the work of certain Jewish scholars. Many others, both Christian and Jewish, have contributed to the search. As we have already noted, this quest is anything but reductionistic. Indeed, for Christians, it can be deeply enriching for their faith, and for Jews, deeply enriching for their understanding of the spiritual history of the Jewish people. The search for the Jewish Jesus, we can say in summary, is illuminating ever more clearly the profound kinship between Judaism and Christianity, even while, paradoxically, it defines ever more precisely the nature of their divergence.

Notes

1   Daniel J. Harrington, 'The Jewishness of Jesus,' *Bible Review* 3 (1987),pp. 33-41. The key works of the authors mentioned are the following: S.G.F. Brandon, *Jesus and the Zealots: A Study of the Political Factor in Primitive Christianity*, (New York, 1967); Morton Smith, *Jesus the Magician*, (New York, 1978); Geza Vermes, *Jesus the Jew: A Historian's Reading of the Gospels*, (New York, 1973 rev. ed. 1981); Bruce D. Chilton, *A Galilean Rabbi and His Bible: Jesus' Use of the Interpreted Scripture of His Time*, (Wilmington, 1984); Harvey Falk, *Jesus the Pharisee: A New Look at the Jewishness of Jesus*, (New York, 1985); E.P. Sanders, *Jesus and Judaism*, (Philadelphia, 1985).

2   Richard A. Horseley and J.S. Hanson, *Bandits, Prophets and Messiahs*, (Minneapolis, 1985); Horseley, *Jesus and the Spiral of Violence: Popular Jewish Resistance in Roman Palestine*, (New York, 1987); Marcus Borg, *Jesus: A New Vision*, (New York, 1987); John Dominic Crossan, *The Historical Jesus: The Life of a Mediterranean Jewish Peasant*, (New York, 1991); John P. Meier, *A Marginal Jew: Rethinking the Historical Jesus*, (New York, 1991).

3   Joseph Klausner, *Jesus of Nazareth: His Life, Times, and Teaching,*
        (E.T., London, 1929), pp. 413f.
4   ibid.
5   Sandmel, *We Jews and Jesus*, p. 34f
6   ibid. p. 35
7   ibid. p. 38
8   ibid. p. 42
9   Trans. by Wilhelm C. Linss, (Minneapolis, 1983).
10   Trans. by Lawrence W. Denef, (Minneapolis, 1985).
11   Lapide and Luz, *Jesus in Two Perspectives*, p. 114
12   Trans. by Norman P. Goldhawk, (New York, 1950).
13   ibid. pp. 12f
14   Rivkin, *What Crucified Jesus?*, pp. 123f
15   ibid. p. 124
16   cf. Vermes, *Jesus the Jew.*
17   *What Crucified Jesus?*, p. 70
18   ibid. p. 71
19   ibid. pp. 76f
20   cf. Ellis Rivkin, *A Hidden Revolution: The Pharisees' Search for the
        Kingdom Within*, (New York, 1978).
21   Rivkin, *What Crucified Jesus?*, p. 78

PART III

Reconciling Memories

The Jesuits and the Reformation

John Bossy

The date conventionally given for the foundation of the Society of Jesus is September 27 1540. It will come as no surprise to some if I begin this essay by drawing attention to several incidents which happened six years earlier, in 1534. Our first scene is Paris, in the milieu of the University, which was still, for all its failings, the most important intellectual institution in Latin Christendom. On August 15, the Feast of the Assumption of Our Lady, Ignatius Loyola and six companions from the University went up the hill to Montmartre and took vows of poverty and chastity, and a third vow to go to the Holy Land and missionise among the Muslims or, if this proved impossible, to put themselves at the disposal of the Pope for some alternative good work.[1] On October 18, an underground group of Protestant students and teachers, including John Calvin, organised the posting up on the doors of the Royal Chapel in the Louvre of posters or 'placards' denouncing the Mass as idolatrous. With a little stretching in either case, we may regard the first event as the beginning of the Society of Jesus, the second as the beginning of Reformed, or Calvinist, Christianity.

Two other things happened in 1534, one in France, one in England. In France, Master François Rabelais published *The Great and Inestimable Deeds of the Giant Gargantua*, the first part of his comic masterpiece, the *Histories of Gargantua and Pantagruel*; it was actually the second part to be published, the first having been condemned by the theological faculty of Paris as obscene.

It portrayed the amiable giant engaged in a dispute with the city of Paris, stealing the bells of Notre Dame and sitting on its twin towers drowning both city and university in a deluge of urine.[2] In England, Parliament passed a statute declaring King Henry VIII's marriage to Queen Katherine of Aragon invalid and his marriage to Queen Anne Boleyn legal.

All these events were probably examples of the penchant of an expansive age for largeness of design and drama in execution. The first three of them were more intimately connected.

Rabelais's satire spoke, among other things, for a powerful current of humanistic evangelicalism; by which I mean a reliance on the text of the New Testament as against the authority of the Church, and a conviction that that text must be expounded and interpreted by scholars learned in, at least, the two classical languages. This was the spontaneous intellectual mode of the time; in France, in England and elsewhere it seemed quite inevitably to be leading serious scholars in the direction already taken by Martin Luther and the new Protestant Churches of Germany and Switzerland. Although Rabelais, who was a serious scholar underneath, did not in fact go that way in the end, his farcical treatment of the University establishment, its intellectual tradition and its persecution of dissenters, suggested that he would.[3]

I

Ignatius was not one of those students carried away by the tide. He was not young: in this year he took his M.A. probably at the age of 43, and may count as a patron saint of mature students and of what is called continuing education. We may think of him as irritated, like others, that he had climbed the mountain of learning only to find that what he had laboured to learn was despised as rubbish by his younger and trendier fellow-students. He was not a scholar; his notion of a university education was vocational. He needed a qualification to give him authority to pursue his favourite occupations, which were talking to people about their salvation and teaching Christian doctrine to the ignorant. He was, as everybody knows, a gentleman with a military background. He was a late-comer to devotion who had undergone a religious conversion a dozen years before after he had had his leg smashed by a cannon-ball in a siege. Finally, by his family connections and early life he was a follower of the House of Spain. He had grown up in the household of Queen Joanna, the Emperor Charles V's mother, and had perhaps had a crush on the emperor's sister. Charles was now the principal opponent of Luther and the Reformation in Europe, and also the nephew of Henry VIII's discarded queen.

For all these reasons Ignatius was a most unlikely figure to be swept away in the direction either of Luther or of evangelical humanism. More than this, he had made it his business to convert others as he had himself been converted; and a good deal of his time in Paris had been spent converting students and masters away from intellectual careers, which had got him into trouble with the University.[4]

Mostly, he had been converting them away from humanism and the influence of the *lecteurs royaux* of what eventually became the *Collége de France,* erected in 1530: with two of his more celebrated targets, Francis Xavier and Jerome Nadal, he was successful in the first case and not in the second. Behind all this lay a fairly deep antipathy to the father of evangelical humanism – by now, indeed, a chastened and dying father – Erasmus. He complained of Erasmus's book of spiritual advice, the *Enchiridion militis Christiani,* that he had felt less devout when he finished with it than when he started.[5] 'Devotion', precisely, was what he was defending against Erasmus's updated 'piety': the taking of vows was a very anti-humanist form of devotion, as well as a demonstration against Luther.

So far, we have been seeing Ignatius more as an enemy of evangelical humanism in general, than of the Reformation in particular. When we look at the question directly we notice, as has often been noticed, that this was not an early concern of his. Until his late thirties he was simply on a different wavelength, and the bulk of his instrument of conversion, the *Spiritual Exercises,* had probably been written before he had heard of Luther at all. There is, for example, no sign that the meditation on the Two Standards, or the Rules for the Discernment of Spirits, which opposed the forces of Christ and Lucifer, of God and the Enemy of the Human Race, were meant to have anything to do with Luther or the Reformers when Ignatius composed them. I should indeed go farther than this: Ignatius was, to put the point very crudely, really a fifteenth-century man rather than a sixteenth-century man: by which I mean something different from the traditional 'medieval' man, whatever he may be. His preoccupation with the Devil, which was something he shared with Luther, was perhaps a sign of this. Otherwise one may think of all sorts of characteristics of his spiritual posture as evidence of a fifteenth-century background. There is his tendency to use in spiritual matters the language of chivalry, and his concern, one might say obsession, with systems of meditative devotion and examination of conscience. The tradition of meditations on the life of Christ, Thomas a Kempis's *Imitation*, memory systems and a great deal else went into the *Spiritual Exercises*, but outside of his own mystical experience I cannot think of any contribution to them which was not well established before 1500. I should add to the fifteenth-century input his feeling for visualisation and the mental image; the doctrine of frequent confession and communion; and the devotion to the name Jesus which inspired the title of the Society. The latinate 'Society' may give a less faithful impression of Ignatius than the original 'Company'. Not only the Reformation, but the whole of sixteenth-century culture, seem more or less irrelevant to all this.

Nevertheless, the *Spiritual Exercises* were a weapon against the Reformation. They were so, in the first place, in a way of which I do not think Ignatius was aware. Systematic examination of conscience, the struggle with individual sins, entailed the kind of attitude to sin and repentance which Luther, while still a Catholic Augustinian, had rejected as a form of torture: he had been partly condemned by Rome for denouncing it.[6] In quite a strong sense it was what, pastorally speaking, the doctrine of justification by faith alone was intended to do away with; in his mature judgement Luther would have dismissed it as Pelagian. In the end, though only in the end, the *Spiritual Exercises* were also a conscious weapon against the Reformation. The last thing to be added to them were the celebrated Rules for Thinking with the Church, which were the result of his experience in Paris and date from the early 1530s.[7] The Rules say that those who do the Exercises should: (i) submit their own opinions to those of 'the hierarchical Church'; (ii) speak favourably of the whole range of Catholic devotional practices, such as indulgences, which was now under intense criticism; (iii) speak well of superiors of all kinds; (iv) speak well of scholastic theology and not make heroes of contemporary writers; and (v) 'believe that the white object I see is black if that should be the decision of the hierarchical Church'. Whether the Rules amount to a system of reactionary brainwashing is a matter of opinion: they are clearly intended to produce people who are rigorously hostile to the Reformation and to anything connected with it, as they did when the Jesuits arrived in Italy and found themselves surrounded by churchmen who were not as rigorously hostile as Ignatius thought they ought to have been. But I find myself surprised to notice how much, in 1534 or so, the enemy still seems to be evangelical humanism in general rather than the Reformation as such. The black-and-white point appears to be specifically directed against Erasmus,[8] and several of the others could and probably should be construed as directed against Rabelais and the frame of mind he represented.

Hence there may possibly be something significant about the relative mildness of the remarks directed against Reformation theology as such at the end of the Rules. Ignatius begins: 'Whilst it is absolutely true that no man can be saved without being predestined, and without faith and grace, great care is called for in the way in which we (meaning, I think, people in universities) talk and argue about these matters'. One should not talk publicly about predestination, for reasons which became widely accepted among Protestants in the course of the seventeenth century; one should not emphasise faith without charity; one should not emphasise grace against human freedom of choice and action, 'especially in times like these which are full of dangers'. The ecumenically minded may want to read into this the chance that Ignatius recognised in Luther's doctrine an expression of genuine Christian religion, and in the man himself ultimately an ally against the sapping of Christianity as such which he may have associated with humanist culture. Perhaps that is what Ignatius ought to have thought; and Luther said much the same about predestination, which became a bone of fierce contention between his followers and those of Calvin.[9] But this was not where the question stood in 1534, when 'Calvinism' did not exist.

I should think that in composing this text, apart from wishing to exemplify the doctrine of submission to the hierarchical Church and by that token to dismiss Luther out of hand, Ignatius had three particular motives in mind. These were: the need to defer to St Augustine; a faith in the spiritual guidance of the *Imitation of Christ*; and the wish, after a good deal of fairly transparent carping at him, to make a sympathetic reference to Erasmus's stand against Luther in the *Freedom of the Will* of ten years before. Our glimpse of an ecumenical Ignatius is a mirage.

II

I turn from Ignatius's individual relations with the Reformation to those of the Society of Jesus. These two questions, even if one confines oneself to the sixteenth century as I propose to do, are not necessarily the same. If, as I have said, Ignatius seems a fifteenth-century sort of person, the Society, which already possessed thousands of members shortly after Ignatius died in Rome in 1556, was composed of sixteenth-century persons. By this I mean: people who had had a fairly intensive classical education; who had a strong view that the true virtues were the active virtues, and liked to see them embodied in heroic enterprises; who were in favour of unfettered monarchical government; who regarded the traditions of the Church as somewhat less sacrosanct than Ignatius had; and who were mostly Italians. Hence they were more likely than Ignatius had been to adopt notions and practices which were generally in the air, and might be shared by them and by Protestants.

Under this heading I think there are various topics which need to be ventilated. The first is the influence of Jerome Nadal on the development of the Society after his belated conversion in Rome. Nadal, whom Ignatius probably intended to succeed him, was an example of all the characteristics mentioned except that he was not Italian. For some twenty-five years after Ignatius's death he became the guardian of Ignatian spiritual and organizational doctrine as he understood it, and this he conveyed vigorously to the growing Society in the capacity of visitor of Jesuit houses and colleges in which successive Generals of the Society employed him. One of the doctrines with which he became most identified was that of 'finding God in all things'. It implied a degree of dismantling of traditional boundaries between the sacred and the profane in the activities which Jesuits were to undertake and the way in which they were to undertake them.[10] In Nadal's intention, which I do not think was quite the same as Ignatius's, this dismantling was probably fairly radical, but if so he did not really carry the Society with him. By the time of his death in 1580 it had become clear that the Jesuits' redrawing of such boundaries was going to be very relative. It did not remotely approach the general demolition of boundaries made by Luther in the doctrine of the priesthood of all believers. The lay sodalities launched on a grand scale during the early decades of the Society were, it seems to me, actually much more respectful of the boundary between lay and clerical roles than fraternities which had been inherited from the Middle Ages like the *Sculoe* of Venice. The most interesting recent book on the long-term influence of the Jesuits in Europe, Louis Chatellier's *The Europe of the Devout*, seems to show that the so-dalities and congregations which had been founded under the aegis of the Society only began to act as automonous forces in the countries where they operated after the Society itself had been suppressed in 1773.[11]

There is, to be sure, a very serious question whether the doctrine of the priesthood of all believers was ever actually practised by mainstream Protestants, whether Lutheran or Calvinist; and it may well be that Luther never really intended that it should be. Still, ideal for ideal, there seems to be a difference between a spirit-ual doctrine to be practised, as it were, professionally by people specially dedicated to it, and a theological principle applicable universally: I do not think Jesuits ever showed any sympathy for the second.[12]

We can probably find a more fundamental resemblance in the notion (if that is not too explicit a word) that charity to one's neighbour is less importantly realised in immediate human rela-tions than in what we should now call social work. This instinct seems to transcend all denominations in early modern Europe, if one excepts a fringe of spiritual radicals. It had some unfortu-nate, as well as a lot of beneficial consequences. I do not think it was quite what Ignatius had originally had in mind: as Thomas Clancy says, his *forte* was individual 'spiritual conversation'. But it was what the Society became identified with, and the identifica-tion had a lot to do with the enormous prestige which it acquired during its first century: it was tapping a generally available source in a way which Protestants could only marginally object to and in some fields would have to strive belatedly to emulate.[13]

Then there are simple borrowings, like the adoption by German Jesuits such as Canisius and later by others such as Bellarmine, of Luther's form of the catechism as the way to instruct children and the ignorant. Not that the Jesuits borrowed the idea: simple cate-chising was one of Ignatius's first and most persistent ambitions. But they borrowed a good deal of the method, and their use of it testifies to the presence of unspoken axioms transcending the confessional divisions which the actual contents of catechisms were increasingly devoted to reinforcing.[14]

Finally there are some rather unclassifiable resemblances, mainly with Reformed or Calvinist Christianity, of which the most obvious is a difficulty in getting on with bishops. There are some, notably Cardinal Manning, who have regarded Jesuits as presbyterians. There must be something in the idea, otherwise it would be hard to account for the doctrine of the Church of Trent: viz, that the Church required episcopacy, but that it was perfectly possible for the entire episcopal office to be exercised by the Bishop of Rome.[15] Looked at a little more closely, I think the resemblance falls down, since the followers of Calvin's way thought that the Church had a God-given structure which happened to be non-episcopal, while Laínez and some other Jesuits (though clearly not Ignatius) may have thought that God-given structures were an obstacle to getting on with large-scale works of charity, or to the operations of what nowadays is called the 'church managerial'.

Altogether, if we look at these resemblances, which I once thought rather far-reaching, they seem to come down, except for the classical education and the works of charity, to not all that much. There was certainly one general sixteenth-century culture, shared by both or all parties; but there were also two or more different cultures, inspired (even among the Jesuits, who were rarely distinguished theologians) by different theological positions. So we come in the end to the *loci* of opposition between the Society and the Reformation, which there is no point in disguising. I shall mention two: one an opposition of type, and one of actual conflict.

III

The first is missionary work. As a historical body, and in the conception of Ignatius, the Jesuits are probably best characterised as a missionary order. True, at any given time the majority of Jesuits have probably been doing relatively humdrum things like teaching schoolboys in securely Catholic countries or regions. But from the beginning the urge to go on 'missions' outside such areas was characteristic: which meant either going to the Indies,

east or west, or going to parts of Europe where the Reformation
was strong and in control. Everybody knows about the distinguished Jesuit missionaries in China, like Matteo Ricci,[16] in India
and Japan, and in the rather different circumstances of Paraguay;
everybody also knows that this was a field which for various reasons Protestant Europe failed to cultivate before about 1700. The
opposition of type is very marked. It was also, in so far as the missions were to the Protestant countries of northern Europe, an
opposition of actual conflict. Jesuits went to rescue benighted
Europeans from the drastic consequences to their chances of salvation which followed from their or their governments' adoption
of Protestantism. The most bizarre of these was surely the Swedish
mission of 1576-1580, where a Norwegian Jesuit, with the con-
nivance of King John III, succeeded in setting up an apparently
Lutheran seminary in Stockholm and using it for the training of
Catholic missionaries.

It could be argued that the scheme, which was not a success, testifies to a degree of theological convergence between Catholics
and Lutherans during the late sixteenth century; but I do not
think that was how the Jesuits viewed it. At least for those in
charge of the Society, it was a particularly bold move in an enterprise of reconquest, which has left a permanent mark on Protestant
sensibilities in the alarming notion of the Jesuit in disguise.[17]

As the Swedish case indicates, the boundaries between Jesuit
missionising and Jesuit politics were, in Europe at least, rather
thin: as the wars of religion heated up during the later sixteenth
century the matter became of intense concern, not only to Protestants and Protestant governments, but to the Jesuits themselves.

The question was whether, among the missions for the help of
souls which a Jesuit might engage in, political missions were to
be included; and in particular whether Jesuits might be employed in political missions or activities designed to secure the
overthrow of Protestant governments or of Catholic governments thought to be conniving with them. As far as one can see,
Ignatius had no objection to such missions: it seems to have been
a consequence of his principle of finding God in all things that
one might find God in politics, if the politics were directly intended to advance the cause of Catholicism. Sweden apart, the
idea was, I think, put into practice in the early days of the English

mission, which was roughly contemporary; it was of particular relevance to the Jesuits in France.[18]

In 1581 the policy, if that was what it was, was altered by one of Ignatius's more distinguished successors, Claudio Acquaviva. Acquaviva held that Jesuits were not permitted to engage in political activity; or, to be more precise, he held that Jesuits were not permitted to participate in movements intended to overthrow existing governments, Protestant or Catholic. Acquaviva was a very powerful influence in the Society, and except in some doubtful cases, like the overthrow of Protestant Bohemia in 1620, where it could be doubted whether the Protestant government was actually the government, I think the principle was observed pretty well thereafter.

Its most important effect was in France, where Acquaviva managed to extract the Jesuits sufficiently from the anti-government (or 'revolutionary') Catholic League to secure, after twenty years of ups and downs, the successful re-settlement of the Society in the country by King Henry IV in 1604. It also had consequences in England, where Acquaviva achieved, with a good deal of difficulty, the transition from the missionary régime conducted by Robert Parsons, who did believe in finding God in politics, to that conducted by Henry Garnet, who did not. It was a nasty joke of history that Garnet should have been the one who was executed for political conspiracy: that is, for the Gunpowder Plot. Much the same thing happened also in Ireland.[19] The early exploratory missions, of which the first happened as early as 1541, were probably as much political as missionary in intention; the permanent Jesuit 'mission', as finally established by a follower of Henry Garnet, Christopher Holywood, was certainly not. Until the Restoration at least, the Irish Jesuits were a model of non-interference in politics, or, from the opposite point of view, a shocking example of political loyalism. Whether Ignatius would have sympathised with them I find it very hard to say. Possibly not.

IV

From the title of this essay it may have been supposed that I intended to say that in the sixteenth century there were two Reformations, a Protestant one and a Catholic one, and that the

Society of Jesus, in contributing to a Catholic Reformation, was doing the same kind of thing as Luther or Calvin. It will be clear that that is not what I want to say. If we wish to use the word 'Reformation' of one of these events, we cannot use it in the same sense of the other, and I should personally be happy to stick to customary usage, and use it only of Luther and Calvin.

If we use the word like this, and then ask, 'What is the relation between the Jesuits and the (Protestant) Reformation?', the answer is simple. They were against it. I have said that there were respects in which what you might call cultural similarities or family resemblances might be detected. There were some family resemblances between Ignatius and Luther, such as their dislike of Erasmus. There were some family resemblances, in the age of the wars of religion, between the Society of Jesus and what has been called the Calvinist international: perhaps the closest of these was something to do with the allegedly Protestant ethic. They do not now seem to me to be very fundamental, or even really to approach the degree to which the C.I.A. is bound to be rather like the K.G.B. It is true that, from a professional historian's point of view, they will loom larger or smaller according to the kind of history we may want to do. If we are doing what the French call the history of mentalities, the family resemblances are likely to seem the things that matter.[20] If we are doing traditional history, we shall be struck by the differences. What I have been doing here is fairly traditional history. Only the members of the Society can really decide what sort of a history, at this interesting juncture, their very distincitve institution requires.

Notes

1.   Thanks to the Institute of Jesuit Sources in St Louis, Missouri, there are three valuable guides to Jesuit history available in English: William V. Bangert, *A History of the Society of Jesus* (1972); Joseph de Guibert, *The Jesuits, their Spiritual Doctrine and Practice* (1964, 1972); and Thomas H. Clancy, *An Introduction to Jesuit Life* (1976) – a real breath of fresh air which ought to be reprinted. The most serious attempt at a strictly historical reflection on the earlier history of the Society is H.O. Evennett, *The Spirit of the Counter-Reformation*, ed. with a postscript by myself (Cambridge, 1968).

2.   English translation by J.M. Cohen, *Gargantua and Pantagruel* (London, 1955), book Vol I, ch. 17. The two classic books on Rabelais are Lucien Febvre, *Le problème de l'incroyance au XVIe siècle: la réligion de Rabelais* (Paris, 1942; repr. 1962); and M.A. Screech, *Rabelais* (London, 1979).

3   Georg Schurhammer, *Francis Xavier:* Vol. I 1506-1541 (Rome, 1973), pp. 75-273, is a very comprehensive account of the state of affairs in the university at the time.

4   *The Autobiography of St Ignatius Loyola,* (ed.), J.C. Olin and J. F. O'Callaghan (New York, 1974), pp. 75 ff

5   De Guibert, *Spiritual Doctrine,* pp. 165f; Marcel Bataillon, 'D'Erasme a la Compagnie de Jesus', *Archives de sociologie des religions,* no. 24 (1967), pp. 57-81, is a learned rebuttal of this traditional view, which does not seem to have commanded general agreement.

6   Evennett, *Spirit of the Counter-Reformation,* pp. 28-42; cf. Luther's letter to Johan von Staupitz, 30-5-1518, and the Bull *Exsurge Domine,* in E.G. Rupp and B. Drewery, *Martin Luther* (London, 1970), pp. 10, 37 f

7   I use the translation by Thomas Corbishley, *The Spiritual Exercises of St Ignatius* (Wheathampstead, Herts, 1973), pp. 120-124 (nos. 352-370). Bataillon (above, n. 5) takes the view that the 'Rules' were added later, in Italy, and under pressure.

8   cf. Schurhammer, *Francis Xavier,* I, p.132 and n. 198, quoting Erasmus's *Supputationes errorum in censuris Bedae* (1527): 'Neque enim nigrum esset album, si ita pronunciaret Romanus Pontifex ...'

9   *Spiritual Exercises,* pp. 122-3 (nos. 366-9); Luther, *Table Talk,* (ed.), T.G. Tappert (Luther's Works, vol. 54; Philadelphia, 1967), p.249.

10   Clancy, *Introduction,* pp. 87, 110 f; Bangert, *History,* pp.43, 48 etc; Evennett, *Spirit of the Counter-Reformation,* p.47

11   Louis Chatellier, *The Europe of the Devout: the Catholic Reformation and the Foundation of a New Society* (Cambridge/Paris, 1989), especially part IV.

12   This an important theme in Euan Cameron's masterly *The European Reformation* (London, 1991); Salmerón on the priesthood of believers at Trent, in H. Jedin, *Geschichte des Konzils von Trient,* III (Reiburg, 1970), pp. 350f, 523

13   cf. my *Christianity in the West,* 1400-1700 (Oxford, 1985), pp. 143-52; Clancy, *Introduction,* p.36

14   *Christianity in the West,* pp. 118-121; Gerald Strauss, *Luther's*

House of Learning (Baltimore/London, 1975) is fundamental on this subject.

15   Expounded, rather radically, in my 'Postscript' to Evennett, *Spirit of the Counter-Reformation*, pp. 135-7

16   On whom see now Jonathan D. Spence's wonderful *The Memory Palace of Matteo Ricci*, (London/Boston, 1985).

17   Oscar Garstein, *Rome and the Counter-Reformation in Scandinavia*, (?Oslo, 1963): there was probably some divergence on this point between the two Jesuits mainly concerned, the Norwegian Laurentius Norvegus and the Italian Antonio Possevino.

18   I refer here to my own piece, 'The Society of Jesus and the Wars of Religion', *Monastic Studies* (Bangor), I (1991), pp. 229-44, discussing a mostly unpublished correspondence between Acquaviva and Robert Parsons, 1581-1585.

19   The Irish mission is discussed in my 'The Counter-Reformation and the People of Catholic Ireland, 1596-1641', in T. D. Williams (ed.), *Historical Studies* VIII (Dublin, 1971), which is based on Edmund Hogan, *Ibernia Ignatiana*, I (Dublin, 1980). The non-latinate can consult J.J. Corboy, 'The Jesuit Mission to Ireland, 1596-1626' (University College, Dublin, M.A. thesis, 1941).

20   So the more recent work of Jean Delumeau, e.g. *Le peche et la peur: la culpabilisation en Occident, XIIIe-XVIIIe siecles*, (Paris, 1983); but not noticeably in A. Lynn Martin, *The Jesuit Mind: the Mentality of an Elite in Early Modern France*, (Ithaca and London, 1988).

The European Context of William of Orange's Expedition to Ireland:

A Reconsideration on the Occasion of the Tercentenary of the Battle of the Boyne[1]

Patrick Kelly

The year 1990 marked the third centenary of the Battle of the Boyne, a battle that, however perfunctory an engagement in military terms, was of momentous consequence for the subsequent history of Ireland. Although Williamite propagandists may have been premature in issuing a medal with the legend *Liberata Hibernia*,[2] both sides recognised that the Boyne spelt the inevitability of the eventual loss of Ireland to the Jacobite cause, short of a successful French invasion of England or long-term defeat for the Allied Cause on the Continent. Early in 1689, however, things had seemed very different. Given adequate French support James could have hoped to control the whole of Ireland and thus been in a position to move his forces to mainland Britain and attempt to regain England and Scotland by arms. The outcome of such an expedition might well have been in James's favour, since a crucial factor in the Glorious Revolution in 1688 had been the absence of military conflict in England. Indeed many of James's former subjects might have proven reluctant actually to take arms against their former sovereign.

What this points to is the importance of the fact that the conflict for the sovereignty of the three kingdoms of England, Ireland and Scotland between James II and his son-in-law William of Orange in 1689-91 was not just an internal dynastic struggle in the British Isles. It also formed part of a wider European contest between France and an alliance of other European states notably the Holy Roman Empire, Spain and the United Provinces of the Netherlands, with James as the satellite of France and the Protestant kingdoms of mainland Britain as part of the Grand Alliance. The European dimension of the Jacobite War is of course well known. Less well appreciated is the significance for

Ireland of this wider context in terms of the origin of the war, the course of the conflict between 1689 and 1691, the nature of the settlement at Limerick and the way in which the settlement was subsequently implemented.

II

Historians are not always sufficiently aware that William's expedition in late 1688 that led to the expulsion of James II from the English throne was only made possible by a remarkable series of chances. We also tend to forget how close James came to his objective of changing the religious establishment in England in the three years following his accession in February 1685. By the summer of 1688, given James's substantial army and his success in preparing for a compliant parliament to reverse the religious settlement, the capacity of the Anglican majority for internal resistance was but slight – as the signatories of the letter requesting William to come to England starkly recognised.[3] Had William not been able to intervene, James's policies might have triumphed and the subsequent history of Britain and Ireland been very different. In fact it was only as a result of the complex way in which a series of hitherto distantly connected crises in different parts of Europe came together in the autumn of 1688 that the opportunity presented itself for making an expedition to England, an opportunity that neither James, nor his French ally and would-be protector, was in a position to resist.

The common factor in these crises was the involvement of France. It was the aggressive, brutal and largely pointless policies pursued by Louis XIV and his chief advisers, the war minister Louvois and foreign minister Croissy, which brought together the Grand Coalition that was to fight the Nine Years War. The immediate provocation for the war was a pre-emptive strike by French into the Rhineland Palatinate. This incursion was intended to carry out a policy of deliberate devastation that would deter the German Princes from joining with the Spaniards and the Holy Roman Emperor in resisting further French expansion. Although French action precipitated the war in the autumn of 1688, there was no intention on the part of Louis and his advisers to embark on a major European campaign. Indeed France was singularly ill-prepared for war, as her showing in 1689 made clear, and though by 1690 she was in a somewhat better position vis-à-vis the Allies, this initial unpreparedness crucially influenced the development of the Irish war. To understand why this should have been so, we need to look at international relations in the decade prior to 1688, with some general attention to developments going back to the beginning of Louis XIV's personal rule in 1661.

From the conclusion of the war with Hapsburg Spain in 1659 France was undoubtedly the major power on the European Continent, having already triumphed over the Austrian Hapsburgs in the settlement of the Thirty Years War in 1648. In 1661 following the death of Cardinal Mazarin, Louis decided to act as his own chief minister. He embarked on a series of reforms devised by Colbert to strengthen the internal position of the French monarchy and to complete the system of absolutist rule which had been initiated by Richelieu in the late 1620s.[4] As a result of these reforms France by the end of the 1660s was rich, well-governed and internally at peace. The reverse side of this achievement was the gearing of the State exclusively for war and international domination at a time when there were no obvious goals which France needed to achieve. Given the lack of proper objectives the energies mobilised by Colbert's reforms could only be released in a pointless and aggressive fashion. The brief (and intrinsically trivial) episodes of war against the Spaniards in 1662 and the affray in Rome in 1663 clearly indicated Louis's determination to make himself respected, regardless of the interests and feelings of other States. Contemporaries interpreted these events as signs that the French king aspired to what they called an universal monarchy, a phrase that was to echo as a description of French foreign policy well into the Nine Years War.[5]

The most pressing issue affecting real French interests in the 1660s was the question of the succession in Spain, where Philip IV's death in 1665 left as successor only the sickly four-year-old Carlos II. The prospect of the failure of the Hapsburg male line in Spain brought out in naked form the dynastic rivalry between Louis and the Holy Roman Emperor, Leopold I, head of the Austrian branch of the Hapsburgs. What was at stake was not merely the possession of metropolitan Spain and her vast possessions in the non-European world, but also a number of key strategic territories on the European mainland. These included the Spanish Netherlands and possessions in Northern Italy controlling movement over the Alps, as well as Naples and Sicily. However, despite the brief War of Devolutions in 1667-8 after which the victorious Louis showed himself surprisingly reluctant to annex the territories he had occupied, Carlos II did survive into manhood and the question of the Spanish succession faded into the background till the later 1680s. Then his deteriorating health and the by now obvious fact that he would not father children made the succession once more an important issue.

No such reservations inhibited the French king's next round of military activity in the 1670s, when in conjunction with his cousin Charles II of England Louis launched a surprise attack on the Dutch in the summer of 1672. After two decades of Stadtholderless rule, the oligarchic republic of the deWitts was prepared to concede humiliating terms for immediate peace.[6] But Louis's demands rose even higher, and a popular uprising brought to power the heir of the House of Orange, Prince William-Henry the future William III. William-Henry represented a broad national will to resist, and despite a faltering start succeeded in recreating both an effective Dutch army and an alliance first with the Spaniards and later with the Emperor. Though heir to the House of Orange, and a sovereign prince by virtue of his tiny hereditary territory on the Rhone, William-Henry's international importance largely derived from the fact that he was also the nephew of Charles II and the king's next male heir after his brother, the future James II. Since James's daughters were thought to be sickly, there was already a strong possibility that William would some day occupy the throne of Britain.

Rather more significant than the course of the Franco-Dutch war were the terms of the Treaty of Nijmegen (1689) which followed. French diplomatic skill and the break up of the coalition against them allowed Louis to emerge considerably stronger than the showing of his armies suggested. In particular the defection of the Dutch left their former allies, especially the Emperor, highly mistrustful for the future. More importantly Louis had also succeeded in isolating William of Orange at home by making him appear a contender for the sovereignty of the Netherlands, in a way that confirmed three decades of anti-Orange propaganda. Furthermore, French territorial gains considerably reduced William's personal income. Louis and his ministers also drew strategic lessons from the Dutch War – not least regarding the need to consolidate their North Eastern frontier, by extending France's territories in Alsace and Lorraine, and gaining control over the middle Rhine.

The means to which the French resorted for the expansion of their frontiers was the policy of *réunions*. This involved the use of the decisions of French courts in the frontier zones to confirm Louis' claims to towns and territories feudally dependent on his acquisitions under the Treaties of Westphalia and Nijmegen. Such partial decisions were then backed by forcible seizure of territories belonging to the Spaniards, the German Princes and the Emperor. French occupation of the fortress of Luxemburg provoked the Spanish into war in December 1683, wrongly calculating that the Emperor and the German Princes could not afford to allow France to acquire further territories at Spain's expense. Although William tried to put together an anti-French alliance, the Spanish war ended in August 1684 with the Emperor and the German Diet agreeing to the twenty-year Truce of Ratisbon, which allowed Louis to retain most of his post-Nijmegen acquisitions. This surprising climb down brings into consideration the other side of European politics in the 1680s, namely what was happening in the East on the frontier with the Turks, where the possibility had suddenly opened up of recovering the parts of greater Hungary that had been lost a century and a half before.

In 1682 the Sultan and his Grand Vizier, Kara Mustapha, embarked on a period of westward expansion which, in the summer of 1683, carried them to the gates of Vienna. The choice of Austria rather than Poland or the Ukraine as the target for attacks was influenced by French diplomacy; however, the European powers (with the notable exception of France) responded to Leopold's call to save Vienna, and the siege was raised in early September by a joint Imperial and Polish force. The collapse of the Turks initiated a period of expansion eastwards in which the Hapsburgs, aided by an army of the German Princes and financed by the Pope, regained lost territories in Hungary, culminating in the great victory at Mohacs in 1687.[7] These gains were, however, only acquired at the price of bowing to French aggression in the West, and debates in the Imperial Council as to which sphere was more important had been finely balanced. It was recognised that what had passed to France would not be easily disgorged again, but the Emperor and his advisers perceived that the army which the German Princes provided for service in Hungary might in time be used in the West.

In the period following the Truce of Ratisbon in 1684 Louis's policies grew increasingly aggressive and contemptuous. One notable instance was the humiliation of the Genoese republic for its assistance to Spain in the war of 1683-4, while the Papacy found itself another victim of Louis's aggression.[8] At home the Huguenots were finally deprived of what remained of the protection of the Edict of Nantes in the culmination of a brutal policy of persecution and forced conversions that horrified Protestants and scandalised the Pope and Catholic Princes. Although the Revocation of the Edict and the persecution which had preceded it helped turn a significant part of European opinion against Louis, not least in losing the support of the Elector of Brandenburg and other anti-Imperial German Princes, it was the policy which Louis adopted towards the Pope which probably did most to bring about the outbreak of the Nine Years War. Louis's reign in France had been marked by considerable religious upheaval, the most recent episode of which had been the conflict with the Papacy over the *régale* issue in the 1670s.[9] Resistance from Rome led to the summoning of an Assembly of the French clergy in 1682, intended to blackmail Innocent XI by asserting the superiority of General Councils to the Pope. Innocent refused to submit, and continued to refuse recognition to new French bishops. When Louis subsequently revoked the Edict of Nantes, Innocent made no secret of his disapproval of forced conversions and of the hollowness of Louis's actions in the face of his disobedience over the Gallican articles and the *régale*. He was further aggrieved by the French King's refusal to support the crusade against the Turks.

Unfortunately for Louis, developments in Germany at this point suddenly made it essential for him to obtain papal support. The main issue was the succession to the Archbishop-Electorate of Cologne, the most important of three Rhenish ecclesiastical electorates. Louis was determined to preserve the long-established French influence in the Electorate through securing the election of his client Cardinal Furstenburg. But when the current elector died in June 1688, the Pope made clear that he favoured the claims of the rival candidate, Clement-Joseph, brother of the Elector of Bavaria. The Bavarian Elector was the Emperor's son-in-law and commander of his army in the East.

Other complicating factors for the French in 1688 were the danger that the Turks might be forced to concede peace in the East and the question of England. Since succeeding his brother Charles II in 1685, James II had increasingly alienated his Anglican Protestant subjects by his determination to remove the penal laws and political disabilities imposed on Catholic and Protestant dissenters. While his successor remained his daughter Mary, wife of William of Orange, the majority of James's subjects were prepared to put up with him. However, with the birth of a Catholic heir in June 1688 the position radically changed. Discontent was transformed into the will to armed resistance under the leadership of William of Orange, who received an invitation to intervene signed by leading Whigs and Tories. Given the risk to his long-expected inheritance William was willing to respond. Opinions differ as to when the Dutch ruler had made up his mind to intervene in England. On balance it seems unlikely that he had decided to act before the beginning of 1688.[10] But now, faced with the threatened loss of his wife's inheritance on which he had counted for the final humbling of Louis XIV and for the safeguarding of what he called the 'common cause' of the liberty of Europe, William did not hesitate. Notwithstanding the public proclamation of his intentions and private assurances to the emperor and the Elector of Brandenburg, it is hard to believe that William would have risked an invasion of England without intending to remain in control there.

In the United Provinces Louis had concentrated since 1684 on undermining William's position largely through the actions of his ambassador, the Comte d'Avaux, the man subsequently chosen to accompany James as ambassador to Ireland in 1689. D'Avaux played on the anti-Orange fears of the Dutch regent party and on the reluctance of the Amsterdam merchants for further war with France. The initial success of these policies was, however, nullified by the treatment of Dutch nationals in France after the Revocation of the Edict of Nantes. By then the eyes of even the most rabidly anti-Orange magistrates were opened by the punitive anti-Dutch tariffs France introduced in 1686. The perennial nightmare for the Dutch remained a repeat of the sudden French attack of 1672, and they regarded the French threat to the Electorate of Cologne in the summer of 1688 with considerable alarm. With the States General's consent William proceeded to establish a base on the Rhine at Nijmegen, where he collected troops, arms and naval supplies. As early as July reports informed Versailles that these preparations were for an invasion of England, but as a result of earlier misunderstandings with James there was no French fleet available to assist in the interception of an invasion from Holland. French policy-makers now thought in terms of a pre-emptive strike across the middle Rhine at a series of targets in the Palatinate, where Louis's sister-in-law, the Duchess of Orleans, had claims on the personal estate of the previous elector. The invasion of the Palatinate was also undertaken with the intention of frightening the German princes into abandoning support for the Emperor and forcing the latter to transform the Truce of Ratisbon into a permanent settlement. On 21 September news came that the Pope had decided in favour of Clement-Joseph at Cologne, and four days later the French launched their attack. The French concentration on the middle Rhine gave William the opportunity for which he had been waiting to embark for England. By French calculations it was already too late to risk a fleet with soldiers and above all horses in the Channel, and even should William reach England there seemed every likelihood that James's army would fight a prolonged civil war. In the event, this calculation too turned out to be false. On William's arrival James lost his nerve; his carefully cherished forces deserted, and on Christmas Day 1688 he reached France as a fugitive. French efforts to prevent the formation of an alliance against them by pre-emptive action had failed. Despite the deposition of James, the Emperor, after long debate with his conscience found it possible to ally with the heretic William and expand the League of Augsburg, founded in 1686, into a full-scale coalition against France.

III

The common objective of the Grand Alliance which came into existence in May 1689 was the reduction of French power through the disgorging of all the territorial conquests of Louis's personal reign since 1661. William's political interest in preserving the Dutch Republic in the Franco-Dutch War of the 1670s was now transformed into a personal crusade against Louis XIV by the gratuitous seizure of his patrimony of Orange in 1681. The war was a matter of preserving the liberties of Europe and the future of Protestantism against the French tyrant. But for Leopold of Austria the objectives were very different. He had extreme reservations as to the lawfulness of allying with heretics against a fellow Catholic sovereign.[11] Like Louis, the Emperor also believed that the final solution to the European war should involve a Stuart restoration in England. Having failed to understand the nature of the parliamentary settlement of the throne at the Revolution, Leopold thought that James's son might succeed William as a Catholic ruler of the British kingdoms. These divergent views did not directly impinge on the war in Ireland because contingents of Imperial or Spanish troops were not involved, but as a Catholic sovereign Leopold felt obliged both during the war and after to intervene with William in the interests of his correligionists in Ireland. However, the effectiveness of the Emperor's protests was compromised by the continuing persecution of Calvinists in Hungary.[12] Finally relations between William and the Emperor became hopelessly strained as a result of the obstructiveness of the Imperial envoys in the peace negotiations at Ryswick in 1697. As a result Leopold's protests against the penal legislation of the Irish parliament in 1697 and the truncated ratification of the Treaty of Limerick were simply ignored.

To say all this is very much to anticipate. It was by no means inevitable that war would break out in Ireland following James's flight from England. Undeniably the Catholic resurgence in Ireland under Tyrconnell had been seen as a blueprint for what James wished to achieve in England. In both the army and the civil administration Protestants had been replaced by Catholics, and preparations were underway to summon a parliament to amend the Restoration land settlement. However, Tyrconnell's new Catholic army was by no means well organised or equipped, and from December 1688 to February 1689 it seemed possible that Tyrconnell might make terms with the new régime in England. The uncertainty ended with James's acceptance of Tyrconnell's invitation to come to Ireland and use it as a base from which to recover his other two kingdoms.[13]

James's acceptance was only made possible by the French decision to support him with arms, supplies and a small number of troops, a project sponsored by Seignelay, the Minister of Marine, but opposed by the powerful war minister Louvois. Discussion of French commitment to the war in Ireland has overlooked the fundamental fact of France's general unpreparedness for war at the beginning of 1689. Even had French statesmen taken a more favourable assessment of the potential of the Irish conflict, France was desperately short of both men and material in the first year of war. But the French decision to back James, however inadequately, made it necessary for the English to undertake the military reduction of Ireland. From the very start those who expelled James had seen Ireland as one of the four major issues with which William would have to deal.

Despite this, English commitment to regaining control of Ireland in 1689 was far from impressive. The relief of Derry was badly bungled, and the major expedition under Schomberg in the late summer was delayed by difficulties in equipping and transporting the force. Once in Ireland Schomberg proved excessively cautious, and failed to advance further south than Dundalk, where an ill-sited camp led to heavy losses through sickness particularly amongst English troops. The original objective of taking Dublin by the end of 1689 was abandoned, and Jacobite morale, which had completely collapsed in the face of Schomberg's arrival, was once more buoyant. James even wrote to his ambassador at Versailles of driving Schomberg back to England and of 'break(ing) that formidable league against France and lay(ing) the corner stone of a lasting peace in Christendom'.[14]

A number of reasons can be suggested for William's failure to act decisively with regard to Ireland in 1689. Most obvious was the need to regain control of mainland Britain before committing forces across the Irish Sea. After all it was only the fortuitous death of Dundee at Killiekrankie in late July that allowed William to avoid a major campaign in Scotland in 1689. Funds were short, as William became increasingly locked in conflict with the Whig-dominated Convention parliament. Troops were also lacking, despite the clamour of Protestant refugees from Ireland for military employment. But probably most significant was the far greater importance which William attached to the campaign in Flanders. This area, intersected with rivers and canals and controlled by fortified cities, was and remained the main theatre of the Nine Years War. It was a terrain in which victory was difficult to achieve but where defeat would largely determine the outcome of the war. A useful comparison in this respect can be drawn with the Western Front in the 1914-18 war. Both in 1689 and the 1690s, as letters to the Elector of Brandenburg and to the Elector of Bavaria show, the king saw the Irish war primarily as an impediment to his proper involvement in the campaign in Flanders.[15]

In the light of these priorities the decision to come to Ireland to conduct the campaign of 1690 in person was not one that William reached easily. A further problem had arisen in the winter of 1689-90 in relation to the United Provinces, where William's absence was being urged as an excuse by Amsterdam for not contributing its fair share to the war. A combination of the increased fiscal burden and the long-standing distrust of the House of Orange, fanned by clandestine peace-feelers from France, led to a refusal to accept William's orders through the intermediacy of his closest political associate, Hans Willem Bentinck, who had been created an English earl with the title of Portland in the coronation honours of 1689. William's tact eventually brought about a compromise. Nonetheless it was a fresh indicator of the dangers of remaining away from Holland, and of the fragility of the alliance against France even in his native country. Even more uncertain was the continuing commitment of the Emperor. Leopold was plagued by a successful Turkish revival in the East and by ever increasing financial weaknesses, particularly as the new Pope was no longer prepared to finance the war against the Turks. However, lesser members of the alliance were prepared to offer troops for Ireland. Protracted negotiations with Denmark in 1689 had produced a force of six thousand infantry and one thousand cavalry under the command of the Duke of Wurtemberg. These would prove most valuable in both the current year's campaign as well as 1691.

William's arrival in Ireland was delayed by the opening of the new parliament elected in the spring of 1690, which meant abandoning his original intention of going to Ireland via Scotland. Jacobite sources were well informed about his intentions. In February Tyrconnell had written to James's Queen Mary Beatrice, 'this confounded Prince of Orange's coming over to us with such a power this spring ... will set us hard considering how little (help) we are to expect from (France)'.[16] The solution was to mount a simultaneous Jacobite expedition to England, which Tyrconnell was confident was only waiting for William's absence to rise against him. French reaction to this proposal was not enthusiastic; the war minister Louvois conveyed Louis's personal prohibition in mid June. The minister stressed that the Jacobites must avoid battle at all costs, and rely on the Irish climate to exhaust the expedition by disease, just as Schomberg's English forces had been affected the previous autumn.

The desire to avoid battle was also shared by Tyrconnell. Writing again to Mary Beatrice in late June about the superiority of William's forces and the general opinion as to the impossibility of defeating him, 'for as it is his business to force us to a battle, so it is ours to avoid it all we can...'[17] Tyrconnell also put his faith in delay and disease. He predicted that if William failed to conquer Ireland by November it would not merely finish his cause in an England seething with discontent and xenophobia, but also put an end to the Grand Alliance. This cautious approach was not shared by James. The king clamoured for action, as he had done against Schomberg at Dundalk. However, the size of his army was only two thirds of the thirty-six thousand men William was able to dispose of on his march south at the end of June.

The crucial engagement between James and William took place at the Boyne on 1 July. Here there finally occurred the personal confrontation between the two claimants for the British throne. This engagement was to give William the nearest thing which he was ever to achieve to personal triumph on the field of battle. However, what matters for present purposes is not the details of the battle but the reactions which followed. It must also not be forgotten that the Williamite victory at the Boyne coincided with major reverses for the Grand Alliance on land and sea. On the very day of the battle William's commander in the Netherlands,

Prince Waldeck, was defeated by the French at the Battle of Fleurus, though the Dutch army was able to reform almost immediately. Rather more seriously, on the previous day the combined Anglo-Dutch fleets were defeated by the French at the Battle of Beachy Head, thus opening the way for an invasion of England and provoking panic in the absence of the King. In Irish terms the immediate consequence of Beachy Head was William's uncertainty whether to return at once to England. Although no invasion actually took place he was forced to remain on the east coast for four crucial weeks that allowed the Irish army to regather at Limerick.

William's initial impression that the Jacobites were incapable of resisting his better-equipped forces was shared by James, who fled the country together with d'Avaux and other members of his suite. The Jacobite abandonment of Dublin reinforced William's conviction of imminent success. A peace initiative was proposed in the Declaration of Finglas that was little short of a demand for an immediate Jacobite submission. It offered terms to the lower ranks while holding out no hope to the officers and gentry. Though not unexpected in view of James's conduct, Finglas was a mistake that would cost the Grand Alliance dear, as the immediate inclination of the Irish leaders would have been to surrender had anything like reasonable terms been offered. Furthermore by allowing the desire of maximising land confiscation to prevail, at the expense of his true priority of freeing his hands to concentrate on Europe, William awoke expectations amongst Irish Protestants that the Jacobites would be entirely expropriated at the end of the war. When in the end substantial concessions had to be made to Jacobites at Limerick in the interests of the continental alliance, the Irish Protestants were left feeling abandoned and betrayed.

Although the failure to take Limerick in 1690 was somewhat offset by Marlborough's recapture of Cork and Kinsale, the Williamite position in the autumn was one in which a negotiated settlement once more appeared essential. The Grand Alliance was increasingly in difficulties; the Emperor and even more so the Spanish Netherlands were short of money. Austrian advisers alarmed by a Turkish revival in the East were keen to make terms with France. Leopold had also lost his most able general with the

death of the Duke of Lorraine. The assessment of conditions in
Ireland which Tyrconnell drew up for the French in late 1690
spoke confidently of the difficulty that William would have in
reducing the country in 1691.[18] He estimated that this would require a force of 30-40,000 men who could thus not be used for the
Allied Cause in Flanders. Thanks to what Tyrconnell called the
'happy successes' of the Turks in Hungary, Imperial forces had
to be withdrawn from the Rhineland to the East following the
catastrophic Turkish recapture of Belgrade.

On the plus side, first Spain and then, more unexpectedly, Savoy
had joined the Grand Alliance. Meanwhile the French naval victory at Beachy Head had not resulted in the feared invasion of
England. France, however, had by now made good its unpreparedness of 1689. In general it retained the military advantage
in the Netherlands and the Rhineland, while opening up a new
front in Catalonia – an advantage Louis would keep till 1693.
Some of the lesser German States were showing an inclination to
be won away from the Grand Alliance, and the position in
Europe was by no means promising. In these circumstances ending the Irish war became a major priority. Negotiations went on
into the spring of 1691 till blocked by the hawks amongst the
Irish military, notably Sarsfield. In order to put fresh life into
what seemed an alliance on the verge of collapse William visited
the Continent for the first time since the Revolution to preside
over a major diplomatic congress at the Hague.[19]

In William's absence the discussions for a settlement in Ireland in
the autumn and winter of 1690-91 were carried on through the intermediacy of a lawyer, named O'Grady, who was forwarded by
the Williamite government in Ireland to London to hold talks
with Portland. The key issues were the retention of Jacobite land
and the status of Catholicism. Portland was at first hesitant, but
things opened up with William's intervention from Holland.
William's letters both to Portland and to his commander-in-chief
in Ireland, Godart van Ginkel, betray an increasing urgency to
save the 'common cause'. On 24 December Portland informed
Ginkel that William was 'so persuaded of the need to employ his
forces (in Ireland) elsewhere that he would grant the Irish
Jacobites a general pardon with the exception of some few...'[20]
By the middle of January Portland was writing that 'it would be

better to lose all confiscations in Ireland so as to be able to use the troops (there) directly in France next campaigning season ...'[21] Interestingly the question of guarantees for an Irish settlement was raised. The Irish had hopes that William's Spanish and Imperial allies could be persuaded to underwrite the Treaty and so convince the waverers who argued that the English could not be trusted to observe the terms which would be negotiated.

French attitudes also radically changed during the winter of 1690-1. In 1690 even Louvois conceded the diversionary value of the Irish campaign, and considerably more supplies and munitions could now be spared for Ireland. However, even in 1690 there was still great reluctance to commit larger numbers of French troops in Ireland, especially as several experienced officers had been lost to little advantage in the siege of Derry. Following the defeat at the Boyne a substantial part of the French army was withdrawn under the influence of the view held by James, Tyrconnell and Lauzun that the Jacobite cause in Ireland was finished. In the winter of 1690-91 French attitudes changed yet again, and the undeniable value of the Irish campaign was recognised as well as the obligations of Louis's promise to restore James. The resistance at Limerick greatly impressed the French officers in Ireland. They thought that with an experienced French commander and adequate equipment the Irish campaign might be effectively sustained at least into 1692. Louis himself was persuaded of the importance of the 1691 campaign and the experienced St Ruth despatched to command in Ireland. Supplies, however, did not match the needs of the Irish and it was not till the autumn of 1691 that a major supply fleet set sail. It did not reach the Shannon until three weeks after the surrender of Limerick. The French delay in the early summer astonished the Danish commander, the Duke of Wurtemburg, who informed Christian V that if sufficient French troops arrived the war could easily be prolonged till 1692.

William's correspondence with his commander in Ireland, the Dutch general Ginkel, between May and September 1691 harped on endlessly about the necessity of ending the Irish war as soon as possible for the sake of 'the common cause' in Europe. At the beginning of May William wrote that 'all Europe which opposes France is concerned that Ireland be reduced this campaign', and urged Ginkel 'to act with all possible vigour'.[22] Ten days later in response to news that the Irish were again seeking terms, Portland assured Ginkel that there was no need to haggle over conditions, 'for nothing could be more advantageous to us than to see the end of the war in Ireland'.[23] Though the Williamite armies were slow in taking the field in 1691, success came rapidly in July. On 1st July Athlone fell; on the 11th the Irish lost the major battle of Aughrim, and by the 21st Galway had surrendered. In August the Williamites re-invested Limerick. However, as late as mid-September the senior French officers d'Usson and de Tessé were reassuring Louis that the city was capable of holding out till the winter, despite the shortage of supplies. The rapidity with which the will to resist was eroded in late September astonished Ginkel and his subordinates. Irish commentators could only argue that treachery had changed the minds of the Irish commanders, especially Sarsfield.[24] Yet the terms of the surrender make clear that the objective of the Irish command and the French officers had now become the transport of James's army to fight on the Continent. So desperate was William to disengage that he made no difficulty on this point, even agreeing to a *douceur* to Sarsfield in recognition of his role in the surrender (a quite normal practice in late seventeenth-century warfare).

IV

We have thus seen how crucial developments in Europe were for the origin of the revolution in 1688, the course of the Irish war, and the way in which it ended. In the long run it may be argued that despite the French commitment to sustaining his campaign in Ireland, James had little reason to be grateful for the role which Louis XIV played in his affairs. The Revocation of the Edict of Nantes made James's religious policy far more menacing to his subjects in England than might otherwise have been the case. His domestic policies came close to achieving the objective of a packed parliament intended to destroy the Anglican political monopoly by repealing the penal laws and the Test Act. What provided the opportunity for William's invasion was the mistaken pre-emptive strike by France in the Palatinate in the autumn of 1688. This in itself was the culmination of nearly three decades of brutal self-aggrandisement and it brought together the very unnatural alliance of traditional, Catholic, land-locked Austria and the progressive, Protestant, maritime powers of Holland and Britain. Once the Revolution took place and James was expelled from England, it was the French decision to back James in Ireland that transformed our country for the first and only time into a theatre of European war. William's interest in the Irish war was primarily in terms of ending an irritating side-show that distracted attention from the main campaign in Europe. His concern for the welfare of Ireland was minimal. When he scented victory prematurely after the Boyne in 1690 his chief interest was in maximising the land available for confiscation. Once it became clear that victory was not just around the corner, he reverted to his original objective of ending the Irish war as quickly as possible with little thought for how the terms granted would affect the country's future. The Treaty of Limerick was clearly viewed by both sides in 1691 primarily as a military cessation intended to facilitate the withdrawal of their armies to the Continent. The Civil Articles, despite the ambiguous references to preserving the position enjoyed by Catholicism under Charles II, were exclusively directed to safeguarding the interests of the surrendering garrison and those under their immediate protection.

As so frequently happens, an *ad hoc* solution turned into a substitute for the more definitive settlement originally envisaged. The Irish question was not directly raised in the negotiations at Ryswick which brought the Nine Years War to an end in 1697, even though the final treaty dealt with a broad range of issues in minor territories and dependencies. The Ryswick settlement did, however, force Louis to recognise William as King of Great Britain and to abandon his commitment to James, as well as his support for the restoration of Jacobite estates. In the event the 1697 Treaty turned out to be merely a breathing space. Within four years France was once more at war with the coalition of Austria and the Maritime Powers, this time over the issue of the Spanish Succession. With Louis's recognition of James II's son as James III of England on the former's death in 1701, this new war also came to be fought for the defence of the Protestant Succession in England, as was accepted by the other allies in the *Pretensus* clause of the renewed Treaty of Grand Alliance of May 1702. Victory for the French in this war would also have meant a Jacobite restoration and presumably a reversal of the land and

Church settlements in Ireland. For the eighteenth century the unfortunate legacy of these wars of Grand Alliance in Ireland was the spectre of Jacobitism, represented by the acceptance by the Catholic Church of the Stuarts' continued right of provision to Irish bishoprics.[25] Arguably it was this link between the Irish Catholic hierarchy and the Stuart court that was responsible for the Irish Protestants' fears and for their refusal to accept the terms of the Treaty of Limerick as binding. The European dimension continued to bedevil relations between the descendants of the victors and of the conquerors in the War of the Two Kings. At a time when, under the aegis of the European Community, hopes are emerging of a solution to the business left over from the Williamite-Jacobite conflict in Ireland, it is worth keeping in mind the European background of the original conflict. We must hope that the consequences of European involvement will be happier today than they were in the seventeenth century.

Notes

1   This paper represents the text of a lecture delivered at the
     Columbanus Community of Reconciliation, Belfast, on 13 February
     1990. A somewhat different earlier version was delivered to the
     Merriman Summer School at Lahinch, on 21 August 1989, under
     the title *'The Common Cause': Ireland and the European
     Backgound to the Jacobite War*. Dates are Old Style unless indicated otherwise.
2   The Boyne medal is reproduced in Walter Harris, *The History of
     the Life and Reign of William-Henry, Prince of Nassau… King of
     England, Scotland, France and Ireland, &c.* (Dublin, 1749), plate 3,
     item 1.
3   '… we do much doubt whether this present state of things will
     not yet be much changed to the worse … by a great alteration
     which will probably be made both in the officers and soldiers of
     the army, and by such other changes as are to be expected from a
     packed parliament… as will prevent all possible ways of relieving ourselves': letter of invitation to Prince of Orange from the
     Earls of Shrewsbury, Devonshire, and Danby, &c., 30 June 1688,

English Historical Documents, 1660-1714, (ed.), Andrew Browning (London, 1953), pp. 120-2

4   The reforms included restoration of internal order, stabilisation of state finances, expansion of commerce and reorginisation of the army, see Pierre Goubert, *Louis XIV and Twenty Million Frenchman* (London, 1970), ch. 6; John B. Wolf, *Louis XIV* (London, 1968), chs. 12-13

5   Wolfe, *Louis XIV*, 242-4. Cf. Henry Slingesby, Master of the Mint, to Sir Paule Neile, 22 Mar. 1665/6: *Historical Manuscripts Commission*, 6th Report, app., 338. The claim that Louis aspired to 'an universal monarchy' was asserted by the Speaker of the House of Commons in a speech requesting William to intervene in Ireland, 1 May 1689. *Journals of the House of Lords*, xiv, 298. For the use of the term in 1695, see H.M.C. Buccleuch MSS., vol ii. pp. 205-6

6   The concessions offered by the Dutch included the cession of all territories outside the original Seven Provinces, together with an indemnity of 1.0 m. livres. The French counter-demand was for even more territory; restoration of Catholicism in all provinces; extensive trade privileges, and the annual presentation of a commemorative medal; Goubert, *Louis XIV*, pp. 129-30; Wolf, *Louis XIV*, pp. 287-8

7   The total sum which Innocent XI (1676-89) paid towards towards the Turkish war amounted to between six and seven million Austrian florins, of which five million went to the Emperor and the rest to Poland and Venice. Only token sums were given by Alexander VIII (1689-91) and Innocent XII (1691-1700); L. von Pastor, *History of Popes*, trans. E.Graf (40 vols), vol. 32 (1940), ch. iii passim, and pp. 549, 659-61. Two highly important articles for the background to the outbreak of the Nine Years War are Richard Place, 'The self-deception of the strong', *French Historical Studies* iv (1970), pp. 459-73; Geoffrey Symcox, 'Louis XIV and the Outbreak of the Nine Years War' in *Louis XIV and Europe*, (ed.), R. Hatton (1976).

8   Following the bombardment by the French navy, the Doge of Genoa was forced to come in person to Versailles to sue for forgiveness: Wolf, *Louis XIV*, pp. 516-7. In the affair of the franchises in 1685-8, the French alone resisted pleas to reduce diplomatic privileges in Rome which protected criminals. When the new French ambassador, Lavardin, arrived in 1687 with what amounted to a miniature army, Innocent XI complained that he

was treated like the Huguenots: Pastor, *History of Popes*, vol. 32, pp. 342-74, 397-405

9   The *régale* controversy involved two distinct rights claimed by Louis XIV during an episcopal interregnum, namely administration of the temporal possessions of the see (*régale temporelle*), and the right to appoint to vacant benefices (*régale spirituelle*). Starting in 1673 the dispute with the papacy dragged on till 1692. See further *New Cambridge Modern History*, vol. v (Cambridge, 1961), pp 135-8.

10   Stephen Baxter, *William III* (London, 1966), pp. 231-2; W.A. Speck, *Reluctant Revolutionaries* (Oxford, 1988), pp.74-5.

11   J.B. Spielman, *Leopold I of Austria* (London, 1977),p.146; see further the list of questions posed by Leopold to his confessor Menegatti on the question of lawfulness of entering into alliance with heretics against France: Otto Klopp, *Der Fall des Hauses Stuart* (14 vols, 1875-88), vol. iv, appendix 6.

12   J.G. Simms, 'The bishops' banishment act of 1697' in *War and Politics in Ireland, 1649-1730*, (ed.), D.W. Hayton and G.O'Brien (London, 1986), pp. 237-47; for the impact of Hungarian persecution, see Blathwayt to Shrewsbury, 15 July 1695; H.M.C. Buccleuch MSS., vol. ii. p. 494.

13   Tyrconnell to James II, 29 January 1688-9: Marquise E. Campana de Cavelli (ed.), *Les Derniers Stuarts à Saint-Germain-en-Laye* (2 vols, Paris, 1871), ii. p.530.

14   James II to Lord Waldergrave, Sept. 1689: J. MacPherson, (ed.), *Original Papers; Containing the Secret History of Great Britain ... (1660-1714)* (2 vols, London, 1775), i. p.315.

15   William to Duke of Brandenburg, 8 Nov. 1689; same to Elector of Bavaria, 14 Mar. 1690: N. Japiske, (ed.), *Correspondentie van Willem III en Hans Willem Bentinck, eersten Graaf van Portland*, 2nd ser. vol. iii (The Hague, 1937), pp. 130, 157-8.

16   Tyrconnell to Queen Mary Beatrice, 20 Feb. 1689-90, 'The Letterbook of Richard Talbot', *Analecta Hibernica* iv (1932), p. 108.

17   Same to same, 24 June 1690, ibid., p.132.

18   *Franco-Irish Correspondence*, (ed) Sheila Mulloy, (Irish Manuscripts Commission). 3 vols., 1983-4), iii. pp. 184-5.

19   Also present in person were the Electors of Brandenburg and Bavaria, two Dukes of Brunswick, together with representatives of the Emperor, the Duke of Savoy, the United Provinces of the Netherlands, &c: Baxter, *William III*, p.293.

20   Japiske, *Correspondentie*, iii. p.199. The identity of those to be
        excluded from pardon is not revealed.
21   Same to same, 13/23 Jan. 1991, ibid., pp.201-2
22   Same to same, 1/11 May 1691, ibid., p.235
23   Same to same, 11/21 May, ibid., p.236
24   Ginkel to Lords Justices of Ireland, 23 Sept 1691: J.G. Simms,
        Jacobite Ireland, 1685-91 (London, 1969), p.249; Charles O'Kelly,
        Macariae Excidium or, the Destruction of Cyprus, (ed.), J.C.
        O'Callaghan (Irish Archaeological Society, Dublin, 1853),
        pp.154-5; J.T. Gilbert, (ed.), *A Jacobite Narrative of the War in Ireland*,
        1688-91 (London, 1971 reprint), pp.168-75
25   Cathaldus Giblin, OFM, 'The Stuart Nomination of the Irish
        Bishops, 1687-1765', *Irish Eccleciastical Record*, 105 (1966), pp. 35-
        47. Last exercised in 1765, the Stuart right of nomination to Irish
        bishoprics ceased with the Papacy's refusal to recognise Charles
        Edward as King of Great Britain on his father's death in 1766.

Gladstone and the disestablishment of the Church of Ireland

An Overview

Oliver Rafferty

By the end of his days Ireland had in a real sense become Gladstone's consuming passion.[1] It was the question which had come to dominate his four administrations, and despite the fact that he visited the country only once, he had perhaps more direct impact on the affairs of that nation than any other British statesman in the nineteenth or twentieth century.[2] Yet for all this, when he came to form his first government he had, in Sir Philip Magnus' eccentric phrase 'no experience and no real knowledge of the Irish people, and his ignorance was shared by the whole of his cabinet and by the mass of the British people'.[3]

In fact even at a relatively early stage in his public life Gladstone was not unaware of the importance of the Irish question in British politics. He had written to his wife in October 1845, at a time when he had no special interest in the country, that Ireland was a cloud in the west, 'that coming storm, the minister of God's retribution upon but half-atoned injustice!'[4] The beginnings of Gladstone's attempts to atone for the injustice of England's historic treatment of Ireland was to deal with the Church question.[5] Even Disraeli as a young man characterised the Irish establishment as 'an alien church.' Yet the process of disestablishment was surrounded by controversy, not simply because of the understandable opposition of members of the Irish Church, but because it involved so many diverse elements, charges of inconsistency on Gladstone's part, the displeasure of the Queen, Roman Catholic intrigue, and a parliamentary and constitutional crisis of the first order.

Gladstone's disestablishment of the Anglican church in Ireland can be variously estimated. It can be seen as either a pragmatic

step as part of the process of the pacification of Ireland in the face
of the Fenian threat, or as the culmination of the grand old man's
personal political and theological odyssey, which begun with the
publication of *The Church in its Relations with the State*, 1838, and
ended with the appearance thirty years later of *A Chapter of
Autobiography*.

For those inclined to cynicism it can be argued that Gladstone
acted decisively to unite and secure the fortunes of the Liberals at
a time when that party was in disarray and propping up a minority Tory administration. The Irish Church question was the
one issue which commanded widespread agreement on the
Liberal benches in parliament.[6] Gladstone saw his opportunity
and seized it for party political motives as well as for fear that
Disraeli might decide to act on the Irish Church question and so
once again, as over the Reform Act, out-manoeuvre the Liberals.[7]

However Gladstone liked to present the measure, perhaps it was
Lord Stanley who best penetrated to the heart of the matter,
when he had clause five of the Act of Union read at the beginning
of the debate on Gladstone's famous resolutions of March 1868.
There it was stated that 'the Churches of England and Ireland, as
by law established, be united into one Protestant Episcopal
Church, to be called "The United Church of England and Ireland",
and that the doctrine, worship, discipline and government of the
said church shall be, and shall remain in full force forever.'
Strong words. The significance of disestablishment then, lay in
the fact that it demonstrated the possibility of altering the Union.
Gladstone's Act of 1869 was the essential key which opened the
way ultimately for the radical modification of the Union that occurred in 1922. Already in 1865 W.J. O'Neill Daunt had written to
Archbishop MacHale of Tuam indicating that Irish disestablishment would facilitate repeal of the Union by removing 'a most
potent cause of the denationalisation of Irish Protestants.'[8]
During the passage of the Bill through Parliament Archbishop
Tait of Canterbury took a similar line, saying that the measure
would encourage Irish ultramontanists to press for repeal.[9] This
is not to imply that Gladstone in any sense saw Irish disestablishment as a first step towards 'Home Rule'. His conversion to that
cause came at a later date and even then he did not regard Home
Rule as altering the Union. The vital point about the 1869 dises-

tablishment was that the British parliament of its own volition, admittedly under pressure from Ireland, amended the terms of the Act of Union. It was a lesson that both Irish radicals and reactionaries were to note for the future.

Gladstone's penchant for popular causes, amounting to crusades, was for the most part modified by his instincts for knowing when popular agitation would be to his own advantage, hence Disraeli's charge that the pretext for the resolutions was but a 'monstrous invention of a crisis got up by the right honourable gentleman opposite for the advantage of his party'. Nonetheless the election of November 1868 was fought largely on the 'Church question'. Gladstone hoped to capitalize on the 'rainbow coalition' of Scottish Presbyterians, English non-conformists, radical politicians and Irish Catholics, on this single issue of Irish disestablishment. Although he had cultivated English non-conformists since the mid-1860s his dealing with them scarcely amonted to a meeting of minds.[10] It was by no means certain that such an amalgam would win the day.[11] Indeed Disraeli was equally hopeful that a blast of 'no-popery' would have the usual effect on the British electorate, to the advantage of the Conservative party.[12] On this occasion Disraeli had seriously miscalculated and the Liberals were returned with a majority of 112 in the House of Commons, half of that number being provided by Ireland. It was perhaps the first truly party political government in modern history. Gladstone immediately set upon his mission to pacify Ireland with a religious enthusiasm. But were the charges of intellectual inconsistency merely party political barbs, or had the new Prime Minister sold his conscience for the sake of a Commons majority?

I

In April 1865 Gladstone had told his brother-in-law that after the Maynooth grant episode of 1845 he no longer had any 'resistance in principle' to the idea of the disestablishment of the Church of Ireland. 'But', he told Lord Lyttleton, 'I held this embryo opinion in mind as there was no cause to precipitate it into life, and waited to fortify or alter or invalidate it by the teachings of experience'.[13] This was to be consistent with the statement he made in the

Commons during the debate on his resolutions in March 1868. Against the charges of a recent intellectual conversion on the Church question Gladstone observed that 'a change of mind which extends itself over a quarter of a century ... is hardly to be esteemed a sudden change'.[14]

Even as Prime Minister Gladstone was to react swiftly to any suggestion that his policies on Ireland were simply the product of expediency or designed to deal with contingent political problems. In response to Earl Grey's speech in the House of Lords on 26 April 1869 accusing Gladstone and his supporters of bringing forward the Church measure because their eyes had been opened 'to the urgency of the Fenian conspiracy', Gladstone would admit only that Fenian outrages had an influence merely on the timing and not the principles of his Irish policy.[15] On the other hand the Prime Minister candidly wrote to the Queen's secretary, General Grey, that the government's 'purpose and duty is to endeavour to draw a line between the Fenians & the people of Ireland, & to make the people of Ireland indisposed to cross it'.[16]

Previous attempts to raise the disestablishment issue in parliament had been dismissed by Gladstone as not 'practical politics', and this is a line he took as late as the summer of 1865 when writing to the warden of Trinity College, Glenalmond. Nor indeed before the November 1868 election was he entirely sure of the exact nature of what the settlement of the Church question ought to be. There is some evidence which suggests that he may have considered the possibility of 'a levelling up' of all the Churches in Ireland, in other words a concurrent endowment. Such a policy was however anathema to the non-conformists and to the Irish Roman Catholic bishops, who had rejected such a suggestion in October 1867. However it seems clear that the principle of the Irish establishment was one which Gladstone had long since felt to be untenable.

Gladstone was able to justify his change of principle by pointing out that at the very least it was the lesser of two evils. Despite the popular perception of his position on State religion Gladstone had never in fact taught that *simpliciter* the State ought to maintain the establishment. Indeed he approvingly quoted Macaulay's review of his 1838 work to the effect that Gladstone's theory rested on the fundamental proposition, 'that the propagation of religious truth is one of the principal ends of government as government. If Mr. Gladstone has not proved this proposition, his system vanishes at once.'[17] Rather frustratingly Gladstone does not address himself to this substantive issue in his 1868 work; he almost seems content to maintain that it is impossible to give a theoretical blueprint of the relation between Church and State which is valid for all time. By then he simply argues the pragmatic case that the Irish Church cannot profess to be the Church of the nation, nor was it even the Church of the poor, and thus its claim to establishment must fail. In the circumstances of Ireland in the late 1860s 'the attempt to maintain an establishment becomes an error fatal to the peace, dangerous perhaps even to the life of civil society', given this the Church is no longer 'the temple of civil society, but its cemetery'.[18] This then becomes the mark of authenticity for the Church in its relations with the State. It is by a practical rather than a theoretical test that establishment ought to be measured.

There can be little doubt that Gladstone had in fact abandoned his position on Church-State relations as he had expounded them in 1838. The important point, however, is that this was not purely opportunistic, a simply pragmatic departure to gain electoral advantage. Almost as soon as he had outlined his principles he came to see, in Alec Vidler's words, that their application to the conditions of social and political life in the United Kingdom was 'anachronistic.'[19] The difficulty for Gladstone's opponents was that too often his evolution of principle looked as if it was determined by popularity at the hustings rather than moral conviction. Equally, however, one might argue that in sponsoring the disestablishment of the Irish Church, Gladstone exposed himself to the wrath of the Tory establishment, a wrath which could easily have prematurely ended his political career. As we shall see he came perilously close, because of the opposition of the House of Lords, to abandoning the whole project, a move that would have precipitated the fall of his government.

II

That parliamentary opposition in the Lords was to be expected Gladstone took for granted. Neither did he expect that the Church of Ireland itself would surrender without a fight. There is however something refreshingly innocent, or especially crafty, about Gladstone's letter to Archbishop Richard Trench of Dublin in December 1868 inviting the opinions of the Irish Churchmen on how best to proceed with his government's legislative proposal.[20] 'All views and wishes' he told Trench, 'which may be entertained by the Primate and the Irish Bishops and by the other leading clergy in general, will at all times have my most respectful attention'.[21] Such respectful dispositions did not prevent the Prime Minister refusing the Irish bishops' request to meet in Convocation on the disestablishment issue. Gladstone did not see why the government should provide them with such a forum from which to attack the legislative proposal. However, had the meeting been designed to come to terms with the Bill, then Gladstone would have recommended to the Crown that Convocation be summoned. By mid-January 1869 however he appears to have amended his position somewhat. Then he told Samuel Wilberforce, Bishop of Oxford, that 'Trench seems to be a dreamer of dreams: and talks of negotiating at a time when all negotiation will have gone by'.[22]

The refusal of Church of Ireland co-operation had serious repercussions on the attitude of the English Church. By and large it must be said that the English clergy took a more detached view of the proceedings. Archbishop Tait, following his meeting with Gladstone on 19 February, came to the conclusion that it was best to concede the principle of disestablishment and concentrate on getting the most favourable financial terms possible for the Church. To this end both the archbishops of Canterbury and York abstained in the crucial second reading in the Lords on 19 June 1869, and the bishop of St David's, Connop Thirwall, actually voted in favour of the measure. On the whole the English clergy were filled with as little enthusiasm for the measure as were their Irish colleagues. One factor in this for the English churchmen was that the fate of the Irish Church today might be that of the English Church tomorrow.[23]

That said, not all Irish opposition was equally hostile. The Bishop of Down was the only Irish prelate who took (in Gladstone's terms) a 'rational' attitude to the legislation, urging his diocesan synod to moderation in its opposition to the proposal. Down was very much the exception. The Archbishop of Armagh, Dr Marcus Beresford, warned that if the Bill became law it would cause Protestants to leave the country, and, worse still, it would be the death blow to Irish Protestantism. He also voiced the opinion of many Anglicans by declaring that he condemned the proposal from first to last, and looked upon it as nothing more than a confiscation. Gladstone told Earl Spencer, the Lord Lieutenant of Ireland, on 6 February 1869 that he felt such opposition to be lamentable and that the Irish bishops had 'spurned a great responsibility at a time when a man like the Archbishop of Canterbury advised moderation… I think they overestimate their resources. We shall see'.[24]

Most of the Irish Anglican arguments against the disestablishment were sectarian in nature, emphasizing that the abolition of the State Church would leave the country in a condition where Roman Catholicism would be religiously and politically supreme.[25] But a number of technical arguments were also advanced to the effect that disestablishment was a violation of the Acts of Settlement and Union, and a repudiation of the spirit of the Catholic Emancipation Act, in which it had been solemnly declared that the established Church would not be interfered with.

Even the avuncular former Dean of Cork, William Connor Magee, whom Disraeli had made Bishop of Peterborough at Queen Victoria's suggestion in the dying days of his administration, initially resolved in March 1868 in the face of Gladstone's proposals that 'there was nothing for it but to fight the battle to the bitter end.'[26] However when the lower house of the Convocation of Canterbury drew up an address to the Queen asking her help in preventing the disestablishment, Magee dismissed it as 'preposterous'.

After the massive majority for the Bill's first reading in the Common's on 24 March, Gladstone again made overtures to the Church of Ireland bishops in the hope of arriving at some understanding with them. The intention here was tactical in view of the impending battle in the Upper House. It would have been an enormous fillip to the government's position had they been able to rely on some semblance of support from the Irish Church. But the approach was once again spurned, the Irish bishops declaring the bill to be 'offensive to God and the greatest national sin ever committed'.[27]

In Ireland the opposition was not confined to the established Church. Clearly there was some overlap of interest between

Catholics and Presbyterians in the matter, but this very fact led other Presbyterians to voice outright opposition to the measure. The former moderator of the Ulster Synod, Henry Cooke, was concerned that the disestablishment would further weaken pan-Protestant hegemony in the face of Romanism.[28] The Presbyterian General Assembly in the summer of 1868 voted in favour of 'concurrent endowment' but the majority was a narrow one, 182 ministers and 28 elders in favour, as opposed to 134 ministers and 46 elders who favoured complete disendowment.[29] This to some extent reflected Presbyterian concern for the limited State support which they received through the *Regium Donum*. In the event the Bill proposed the abolition of the grant, but successful negotiation on the part of the Irish Presbyterian authorities secured in excess of £1,000,000 compensation for the Church. Charles Morell, the moderator of the General Assembly, had pleaded with Gladstone to be generous in compensating the Presbyterians for the loss of the revenues to their seminary in Belfast, especially given the 'princely' endowments which would remain after disestablishment at the disposal of Trinity College Dublin for the training of Church of Ireland clergy.[30]

The opposition of the Irish bishops, although at times vociferous, could not compete with the realities of Irish political and religious life. The 1861 census had revealed that Irish Anglicanism represented only one eighth of the total population of the country, less than 700,000 people. There were some parishes where despite the fact that a minister was paid for the performance of religious duties there were no members to minister to. At the very least the Church was in serious need of reform. It was to meet precisely this problem that Lord Russell had been instrumental in setting up the Royal Commission on the Irish Church temporalities in 1867. However the time for reform was long past and whilst Gladstone's administration could see off the posturing of a Church about to face abolition as a State body, the real test lay in the passage of the Bill through Parliament. With such an overwhelming majority on the government benches in the Commons, the major obstacle was obviously the Tory-dominated House of Lords.

III

The first and most serious opposition Gladstone encountered

was from Queen Victoria. Although not an intensely religious person, in contrast it may be said to Gladstone, she was nonetheless concerned to uphold the prerogatives of the Crown in both State and Church. Gladstone wrote to Lord Granville as early as April 1868 stating that he was aware of the Queen's 'displeasure' at his having introduced the resolutions in the Commons. At that time the leader of the opposition was inclined to blame the Queen's advisers for what Gladstone took to be Victoria's implacable hostility. In fact as the Queen wrote to Granville, reports of her anger were inaccurate. She was, however, expressing her fear that the whole enterprise would become mixed up with 'a party movement', which would make a settlement more difficult.[31]

When Gladstone became Prime Minister in early December 1868, Victoria made her position clear. Her secretary gave Gladstone a memo on 4 December in which it was stated that the Queen entertained 'a very strong opinion in favour of the Irish Church.' When Gladstone saw Victoria two days later she expressed her hope for the Irish Church that 'some connection however slender with the Crown should be maintained'.[32] Although she freely admitted that she did not understand Gladstone's proposals, in many ways she fought a rearguard action to have whatever change the government envisaged kept to a minimum. In a letter of 31 January 1869 Victoria set forth her views in no uncertain terms:

> Mr Gladstone knows that the Queen has always regretted that he should have thought himself compelled to raise this question as he has done; and still more that he should have committed himself to so sweeping a measure. Regret, however, is now useless, and the Queen can only hope that it may all end in the passing of a measure satisfactory to the country, and to which she can conscientiously assent.[33]

The Queen disliked the principle of disestablishment, and could not see why even if the Church were disestablished it should not keep all its endowments. Victoria also hoped that even after disestablishment the Church of Ireland would still maintain some form of organic and organizational unity with the Church of England, a point which Gladstone confessed he did not at all understand.[34] She had various additional fears, that the Church of Ireland would fall into schism, and that internal difficulties would result in rival candidates competing for vacant bishoprics as was then happening in the Cape. At the very least she was insistent that more time was needed to deal with such an important question; on this however the Prime Minister made clear that it was in the best interests of the Irish Church to proceed with the matter as expeditiously as possible. Her greatest fear was the possibility of a constitutional crisis, and when this loomed in the summer of 1869 she worked assiduously to avert it.

Gladstone introduced the disestablishment Bill in the House of Commons on 1 March in a speech which lasted three and a half hours, and of which, according to Disraeli, not a word was wasted. The second reading was carried on 24 March by a majority of 118. Gladstone immediately informed the Queen, convinced as he then was that the large Commons majority would cause the Lords to think twice about rejecting the measure. Roundell Palmer, a Liberal who had turned down Glastone's offer of the Lord Chancellorship because he could not in conscience support the measure, gave the most effective speech against the bill in the Commons. His main argument was against disendowment and this proved to be the issue on which the two houses of parliament were to clash.

This bill's most difficult moment in the Lower House came over the question of Maynooth College. It too was to be disendowed but fourteen years worth of its grant was to be given in a lump sum as compensation, amounting to £309,040, and in addition a further £12,704 of debt which the College owed to the Board of Works was to be remitted. The Commons in committee considered this question on 5 May, and spent longer debating this clause than any other in the Bill. Gladstone was especially anxious lest there might be substantial non-conformist opposition to this proposal. In the event, as he confided to his diary, 'The final division on the prickly point of 107 was the most creditable I think I have ever known'.[35] The third reading in the Commons took place on the 31st of May, and was carried with a majority of 114. It then passed to the Lords.

The stormy passage of the Bill in that place had long been expected. Disraeli, having had no possiblity of obstructing the Bill in the lower house, tried to use the Lords to block the measure. His motives here, as in the general election, were purely tactical. He thought that the recently found Liberal unity would simply not hold and that the party might once again fall apart, giving the Tories yet another opportunity for government.[36] However he soon saw that this was impossible and changed tack, asking the Archbishop of Canterbury to lead the opposition in the Lords. Thus he was trying to give the impression that the Tories had the best interests of the Church at heart.[37]

However before this politicking took place sundry attempts had been made to try and work out some compromise. The Queen had written in February to Lord Granville, the Colonial Secretary and the Liberal leader in the Lords, suggesting an agreement which had the backing of Magee of Peterborough, and which would have been acceptable to most of the Church of England bishops. Granville replied however that Magee's proposed compromise seemed too much like concurrent endowment. This would have no support from the cabinet, and would be unacceptable to the more radical Liberals. Such a course was politically impossible and flew in the face of the Government's election promises.[38]

When it became clear in June that a number of the Tory peers were determined to throw out the Church Bill at its second reading[39] the Queen again intervened, this time with the former Prime Minister, Lord Derby. She wrote to Derby on 7 June that:

> The Queen has never concealed her opinion as to this measure - which remains unaltered; but after the Dissolution last autumn, and the large majorities with which the Bill has been passed in the House of Commons, for the House of Lords to throw it out, and place itself in collision with the House of Commons would be most dangerous, if not disastrous ... Most earnestly does the Queen appeal to Lord Derby to try and prevent this dangerous course from being pursued. She would ask him to show this letter in confidence to Lord Cairns (the Conservative leader in the Lords.) [40]

Derby still refused to use his influence to ensure the second reading. Cairns however proved more amenable to royal persuasion, although he himself was an Ulsterman and ardent champion of the Irish Church. However, perhaps some attention was also paid to Gladstone's veiled threat that if the Lords rejected the second reading then the tolerance of the country 'in the dignity, efficiency and permanence of that Assembly' might begin to wear perilously thin.

There were a number of important speeches both for and against the second reading which deserve some note. Magee of Peterborough, although convinced that the Bill ought to pass its second reading, gave a thunderous speech in defence of the endowments of the Irish Church. Archbishop Trench of Dublin 'made a melancholy and almost inaudible "keen"' to which no one listened. Lord Clarendon, the Foreign Secretary, drawing on his own experience of having been Lord Lieutenant of Ireland said that the Bill was both just and necessary. Like Gladstone he also warned of the danger for the Lords as an institution if the Bill were rejected. The bishop of St David's speech was so long winded and off the point that Wilberforce of Oxford remarked that he now knew why Thirwall's history of Greece was in ten volumes.[41] William Alexander, the bishop of Derry gave, in Lord Kimberley's words, 'A powerful but coarse and slightly vulgar declamation … (he) evidently forgot he was not on a platform at a meeting of Orangemen'.[42] The Bill was given its second reading at 3am on 19 June by a margin of 179 to 146 votes, a government majority of thirty-three. Thirty-two Tories voted with the government, and two Liberals against. Sixty Conservative peers and ten Liberals who were in a position to vote simply stayed away, and there were eighteen pairings.

The best explanation for the strength of Tory resistance to the measure is that given by the bishop of Peterborough. In a letter to the Reverend John MacDonnell on 7 June 1869 he remarked that the peers dilemma was that:

> they must fight on the land question, in which they have a deep personal interest; they could not & ought not to begin by yielding on the church question, in which they have less personal interest, lest it should be said that they sacrificed their convictions when it cost them little so to do, and maintained them only when sacrifice would cost them much.[43]

The Bill, having now passed its second reading, became subject to the Lords amendments, which in fact completely distorted the will of the Commons. The preamble was changed to allow for the financial surplus remaining after compensation was paid for disendowment to be applied for religious purposes. Somewhat inauspiciously on 12 July the Lords also approved of concurrent endowment by a majority of seven. After having been given its third reading in the Upper House, the Bill was returned to the Commons, which promptly disposed of the more offensive amendments on 16 July. Parliament was thrown into a state of crisis.

Meanwhile Henry Edward Manning, the Archbishop of Westminster, had written to Gladstone to assure him that the Lords had made 'no impression on the mind of the country by their amendments. They are too transparently the work of the ascendancy party'.[44] This was a critical period and Gladstone claimed that he felt himself sustained only by the prayers of non-conformists and Catholics.[45] Despite his 'prayerful support' at this stage in the great work, Gladstone's nerve began to fail. The cabinet met on 17 July and asked the Prime Minister to see the Queen again. Victoria suggested negotiations with the Archbishop of Canterbury and advised that the Dean of Windsor might be used as an intermediary. Gladstone told the Dean that the cabinet would sanction £170,000-£180,000 further compensation being added to the sum that was already on offer, amounting to more than eight million pounds.

At this stage Disraeli proposed a compromise which would have given the Church of Ireland an extra £900,000 to £1,000,000. The government declared that such a sum was unacceptable, Gladstone in particular felt that they had made all the reasonable concessions that were possible. By 19 July, he seems to indicate in his diary that he was prepared once again to go to the country on the matter. Two days later he warned the Archbishop of Canterbury that if the Lords finally rejected the Bill, the Commons would not be as generous in the future in considering Church of Ireland claims to compensation. The real crisis for Gladstone seems to have occurred on 20th July when the Bill, again before the Lords, was further amended by the Upper House to their Lordships previous specifications. The Prime Minister, fearing all was lost, decided to let the Bill drop. He was, however, outvoted in cabinet and Granville made it clear that if the Bill were dropped he would resign.[46] Granville then persuaded the cabinet to go for an adjournment in the debate.

On 22 July Gladstone had 'taken to his sofa', emotionally exhausted from the strain of the whole business. Granville was thus left to negotiate with Lord Cairns and by 5pm a settlement had been arrived at. Cairns had agreed to an improved settlement for the clergy, but less than he wanted, and he agreed to drop the Lords' amendment on concurrent endowment. The preamble, however, was to be accepted by the government as per the Lords' amendment, since it was sufficiently ambiguous whether or not the surplus could be used for religious purposes, and in any event it would be for parliament to decide how it should be spent. The Bill then passed through the Lords and the Commons on the government's recommendation, and received the Royal assent on 31 July. Of some £16 million involved in the disendowment about £9 million was to go to the new Church of Ireland, approximately one and a half million to the Catholics and Presbyterians and the rest to charitable purposes to be determined by Parliament.

On 24 July Archbishop Manning wrote to Gladstone commenting on the successful passage of the Bill:

> I can find no exaggeration in saying that this is the greatest act of the legislature towards Ireland in our history. The act of Union, and the Repeal of the Penal laws alone approach it ... I believe that in its bearing upon Ireland, and upon the British Empire it will have inaugurated a new period of legislation and government, vital to our safety.[47]

In reply Gladstone thanked Manning for his constant support throughout the passage of the Bill, and asked that his thanks be conveyed also to Cardinal Cullen in Dublin.[48] Such exchanges were by no means unusual. The extent of Roman Catholic agitation and pressure on Gladstone for the dismantling of the Church of Ireland is a matter to which we must now turn our attention.[49]

IV

Shane Leslie has advanced the surprising thesis that the persistent influence of Archbishop Manning and Cardinal Paul Cullen had more direct impact on persuading Gladstone of the need for disestablishment than had the threat of Fenianism.[50] According to Leslie, Gladstone raised the issue of the Fenian crisis as an artifice to deflect any suspicion of an undue influence from the two Roman prelates.[51] There is certainly some suggestion that many of the arguments Gladstone advanced on his 'resolutions' speech in March 1868 were taken from Manning's pro-disestablishment *Letter to Earl Grey*, published in early March.[52] It has even been suggested that Manning's influence on Gladstone against the Irish establishment predated his conversion to Catholicism.[53]

Cullen's *animus* against the Church of Ireland was of a long-standing nature. As Archbishop of Armagh in 1850 he described it as 'effete and bearing all the marks of the decrepitude of age and of approaching inevitable dissolution'.[54] He had lent his formidable authority to the foundation of the National Association in December 1864 because one of the chief issues the Association was pledged to campaign on was the Church question. Like Gladstone he had come to see a link between ending Fenian agitation and the disestablishment and disendowment of the Irish Church. He regarded the position of the Anglican Church in Ireland as both a badge of oppression and 'an insult'.[55]

In July 1867 Cullen asked Sir John Gray, the Protestant owner of *The Freeman's Journal* and Liberal M.P. for Kilkenny, to find out Gladstone's position on the disestablishment issue. At this stage Gladstone seems to have been quite open, according to Gray, either to disestablishment or concurrent endowment. Several months later, writing to Gray, Gladstone declared that in fact his leanings in the matter were towards concurrent endowment, but added that he would not let his personal feelings interfere with 'whatever may be seen to be the most hopeful mode of delivering (Ireland) from a great mischief and a great scandal'.[56] The following month the Catholic bishops issued their declaration against concurrent endowment, and this seems to have tipped the balance against that proposal, since it could clearly not be 'practical politics' to proceed with such a policy against the wishes of the Catholic Church in Ireland. Both Cullen and Manning sent to Gladstone copies of the bishops' resolutions, which, among other things, declared that it was the establishment 'to which as to their fountain-head, are to be traced the waters of bitterness which poison the relations of life in Ireland and estrange from one another Protestants and Catholics, who ought to be an united people'.

Such sentiments were re-echoed in a letter of Manning to Gladstone on 28 March, as the leader of the opposition was preparing his speech on his Common's resolution. Then Manning declared:

> The Irish Establishment is a great wrong. It is the cause of division in Ireland, & alienation between Ireland and England. It embitters every other question. Even the land question is exasperated by it … The fatal ascendency of race over race is unspeakably aggravated by this ascendency of religion over religion… I say this, not as a Catholic, but as an Englishman & a good subject who desires to see the union of the two countries confirmed by a complete reconciliation.[57]

It would perhaps be inaccurate to say that Cullen and Manning kept up a relentless campaign against the Church of Ireland, but equally one must not underestimate the encouragement and support they gave Gladstone in prosecuting disestablishment. Manning had not only told Gladstone that he was the only man who could gain Ireland's confidence in such a way as to prevent it becoming republican,[58] he had also pledged himself, on Gladstone becoming Prime Minister, to work with him 'in a case in which my whole heart can go with you'.

It was Manning who urged Gladstone of the need to consolidate the 'victory' of the resolutions vote and to follow it up by turning the majority thereby surprisingly gained to 'practical purposes'. And it was Manning who assured Gladstone that the extraordinary coalition of interests could only have held together if disestablishment and disendowment were pursued with full vigour.[59] In a subsequent letter on 24 July 1869 Gladstone also remarked 'Your last note was of much value, and shewed me at once with what an accurate eye you had measured the situation'.

The two prelates had strongly advised Gladstone to overturn the amendments which the Lords had introduced into his Bill. Cullen, on the 14 July, assured the Prime Minister that the amended Bill would do no good in Ireland. 'The Fenians alone will be gratified by the adoption of the amended Bill, as it will give them an opportunity of proclaiming that Ireland can expect nothing good from British legislation'.[60] For his part, Manning, on the day after the Bill's third reading in the Lords, wrote that in the interests of peace in Ireland their amendments would have to be revoked. He was even of the opinion that it would be better to lose the Bill than have it enacted in its amended form.[61] Gladstone assured both men that the government had no intention of allowing the Lords to have their way on either the endowment question or the disposal of the residue.

Not all Catholics were as equally convinced of the evils of concurrent endowment. Aubrey de Vere, the convert and Liberal M.P., favoured that arrangement, as did, at an earlier stage, Bishop David Moriarty of Kerry, Lord Gormanston and John Henry Newman.[62] But the internal debate among Catholics in the United Kingdom was also influenced by thinking from Rome. The Vatican Secretary of State, Cardinal Giacomo Antonelli, assured the British Minister at Rome that the Holy See would not approve of such an arrangement. At the same time he made it clear to Odo Russell that papal policy could not approve of disestablishment either. Such a proposal smacked too much of the European radical idea of a 'free Church in a free State'.

On the other hand Pius IX indicated that in broad terms he was pleased with Gladstone's Bill [63], as were the Irish clergy in Rome, but not, it seems, the English clergy in the eternal city.[64] Ireland was very much the exception in Roman thought on the relationship between Church and State. For the most part it was Manning who directed the Holy See's policy on the matter, rather than Cullen. The Foreign Office had made clear its distrust of the Cardinal and this did make the Vatican wary of at least some of his pronouncements on this issue.[65]

There can be no doubt however that Gladstone relied on both Cullen and Manning as the chief exponents of Catholic attitudes on the disestablishment and disendowment question. He was grateful for their support and advice. When the measure was finally passed he wrote to Manning, 'I am much indebted to you on behalf of the Government for the firm, constant and discriminating support which you have afforded to our Bill during the arduous conflict now happily concluded. Should you happen to write to Cardinal Cullen, pray be kind enough to ask him to accept a similar tribute of acknowledgement'.[66]

V

Gladstone's purpose was not simply to keep at bay the competing influences upon him as he tried to grapple with the intricacies of Irish and British political life. His stand on the Irish Church question was principled but tempered with the harsh realities of public life. Some commentators have treated too lightly the difficulties of enacting this particular piece of legislation. It is surely a mistake to believe, in the light of what we have seen, that the passage of the disestablishment Bill was 'one of the smoothest political operations ever carried through the British Parliament'.[67]

One might variously estimate the purpose and effect of the measure on Irish social and political life. It might be seen as the decisive point in the formation of party affiliation in British politics,[68] or as 'an exercise in the constitutional dismantling of a great and complicated vested interest'.[69] Alternately one might think that Gladstone saw in the measure 'the whole answer to Fenianism',[70] or see it as the final triumph of Roman Catholic ultramontanism and so rejoice with Cullen that 'The poor Protestants are all very irritated. They never did imagine that England would have abandoned their cause'. One might feel with Queen Victoria that Gladstone had dreamed the whole thing up on the basis of personal ambition,[71] or think that he merely saw it as an end in itself, as a means of cutting down the Establishment.[72] Beyond doubt the Church of Ireland under the 1869 Act was able to preserve a much greater sense of corporate identity, and a greater share of its wealth, than it would have done had it been disestablished in 1922 rather than in 1871.[73] The passing of the measure was undoubtedly a staging post in the modernization of the Irish State.[74]

However one estimates Gladstone's position, and it is not without some ambiguity, it is an error to think that 'the fundamental source of (his) interest in Ireland at this time was neither moral conviction, nor Fenianism, but votes'.[75] In the early months of 1868 there was no certainty that the disestablishment issue would arouse such popular support. Equally Gladstone's championing of the Church question might have, in his own words, led 'the Liberal Party to Martyrdom'.[76] At least in the short term the Church Bill and the subsequent Land Act enabled Ireland, as Manning observed, to have 'a revised confidence in Parliament'. 'You', he told Gladstone, 'have fairly earned this', i.e. the trust of the Irish people, 'which no other English statesman has yet deserved.'[77]

From a political perspective Gladstone was convinced that the Church measure was one step on the road of giving justice to Ireland. But his political dispositions were hedged around with religious convictions. We must never overlook the fact that in the first flourish of victory for his parliamentary measure Gladstone did not forget his deeply held religious principles, and wrote to the Archbishop of Dublin, offering any help he could as a private individual to the newly freed church.[78]

Notes

1   On 23 September 1897, he wrote of his first cabinet, that it was Ireland 'which mainly and almost entirely filled the political horizon.' cf. *Autobiographica I*, ed. by John Brooke and Mary Sorensen, (London, 1971), p. 97

2   It must be said however that scholars are divided on Gladstone's attitude to Ireland. Professor H.C.G. Matthew is of the opinion that Ireland was for Gladstone at best a preoccupation, not an interest or an intellectual attraction. cf. *Gladstone: 1809-1874*, (Oxford, 1986) p. 192. J.L. Hammond, *Gladstone and the Irish Nation*, (London, New Impression 1964), p. 70, says that Gladstone threw himself into the Irish problem as the main task of his life.

3   Philip Magnus, *Gladstone: A Biography*. (reprinted with corrections) (London, 1960), p. 196. This typically forthright assertion is not accurate. Two members of Gladstone's first cabinet were former Lords Lieutenant of Ireland, and John Bright, president of the Board of Trade, had made an important fact-finding visit to the country in November 1866, during which he developed a keen interest in the welfare of Fenian prisoners.

4   Cf. A. Tilney Bassett, *Gladstone to His Wife*. (London, 1936), p. 64. In an address to the British Academy Professor John Vincent sought to demythologize this letter by explaining that it was written a time of great emotional stress, and that the letter as a

whole was not concerned with Ireland. Whatever the strength of Vincent's other arguments about Gladstone's lack of interest in Irish affairs on this point, his case here is both weak and unconvincing. cf. 'Gladstone and Ireland' in *Proceedings of the British Academy* Vol. LXII 1977.

5   'In the removal of this Establishment I see the discharge of a debt of civil justice, the disappearance of a national, almost a world-wide reproach, a condition to the success of every effort to secure the peace and contentment of that country...' *W.E. Gladstone, Speeches in South-West Lancashire*, (October, 1868), p. v

6   Even on the Tory side there was little sympathy for the Irish Church, at least according to the Foreign Secretary Lord Stanley who recorded in his diary on 15 March 1868 that 'no one not an Irishman had a good word to say for it...' cf. John Vincent (ed), *Disraeli, Derby and the Conservative Party: Journals and Memoirs of Edward Henry Lord Stanley 1849-1869*, (Hassocks, 1978), p. 331

7   cf. Robert Blake, *Disraeli*, (London, 1966) p. 496; J.P. Parry, *Democracy and Religion: Gladstone and the Liberal Party 1867-1875*, (Cambridge, 1986), pp. 261-2, & 265-6 and passim; Vincent, *Gladstone and Ireland*, p. 201, E.D. Steele, 'Gladstone, Irish Violence and Conciliation', in Art Cosgrave and Donal McCartney, *Studies in Irish history presented to R. Dudley Edwards*, (Dublin, 1979), pp. 260f. In fact at a cabinet meeting on 2 March 1868 the government had decided to take no action on the Church question until the next parliament. cf. *Stanley Journals*, pp. 331-2

8   Quoted in Bernard O'Reilly, *John MacHale Archbishop of Tuam: His Life and Correspondence*, (New York and Cincinnati, 1890), Vol. II. p. 543.

9   P.T. Marsh, *The Victorian Church in Decline: Archbishop Tait and the Church of England 1868-1882*, (London, 1969), p. 22

10   As V. Alan McClelland makes clear, 'that the Church and the State were separate alien powers incapable of coalition, the fundamental principle pursued by British non-conformity, he could not endure.' cf. 'Gladstone and Manning: a Question of Authority.' in Peter J. Jagger (ed) *Gladstone, Politics and Religion*, (London, 1985), p. 149

11   The non-conformists quickly became disillusioned with Gladstonian Liberalism over the Education Bill of 1870 and the Licensing Bill of 1871. H.J. Hanham, *Elections and Party Mangagement: Politics in the time of Disraeli and Gladstone*, (London, 1959), pp. 118-9

12   Disraeli had written to the Queen on 23 March 1868, that 'The
        abhorrence of Popery, the dread of Ritualism, and the hatred of
        the Irish, have long been smouldering in the minds of the nation.'
        cf. *The Letters of Queen Victoria*, (second series 1862-78), Vol. I p.
        517. Lord Blake is of the opinion that Disraeli's anti-Catholic
        election addresses with their hard line insistence on the preroga-
        tives of the Irish establishment helped the Tory cause only in
        Lancshire and alienated two groups which traditionally supported
        the Conservatives, English Catholics and Wesleyan Methodists.
        Disraeli, p. 513

13   Quoted in John Morley, *The Life of William Ewart Gladstone*, Vol. II
        (London, 1903), p. 238

14   Hansard's Parliamentary Debates, Third Series, Vol. cxci, 474

15   Gladstone to Grey, B.L. Add.MS. 44536 f. 152

16   Gladstone to Grey 28 March 1869, B.L. Add. MS. 44536 f. 134

17   Gladstone, *A Chapter of Autobiography*, (London, 1868), pp. 21-2

18   *Chapter of Autobiography*, pp. 60-1

19   Alec R. Vidler, *The Orb and the Cross*, (London, 1945), p. 29

20   It is important to stress in this context that although Gladstone
        took advice from Lord Granville, Sir John Acton, and
        Archdeacon Stopford of Meath, the parliamentary Bill which he
        presented to the Commons in March 1869 was very much his
        own handiwork. Lord Clarendon, the Foreign Secretary, writing
        to Odo Russell in Rome on 25 January 1869, still did not know
        what Gladstone's proposals were. By 8 February, after two cabi-
        net meetings on the matter, he was still none the wiser. He told
        Russell, 'I am in a state of confusion about the I(rish) Church
        measure which seems a heap of complications so I can tell you
        nothing about it.' Clarendon Papers Oxford, MS C 475, f. 215-16

21   D.C. Lathbury (ed.), *Correspondence on Church and Religion of
        William Ewart Gladstone*. Vol. II, (London, 1910) p. 156

22   H.C.G. Matthew (ed), *The Gladstone Diaries*, Vol. VII, (Oxford,
        1982), pp. 14-5

23   Donald Akenson, *The Church of Ireland: Ecclesiastical Reform and
        Revolution, 1800-1885*. (New Haven, 1971), p. 250. Marsh,
        Archbishop Tait, p. 22. J.P. Parry, *Democracy and Religion*, p. 132

24   B.L. Add. MS. 44536 f. 111

25   cf. N.D. Emerson, 'The last phase of the Establishment', in W.A.
        Phillips (ed,), *History of the Church of Ireland*, Vol. III, (London,
        1933), pp. 319-20

26   John C. MacDonnell, *The Life and Correspondence of William Connor*

Magee, Vol. II, (London, 1896), p. 175

27   Cf. Morley, *The Life of William Ewart Gladstone*, Vol. II, p. 262

28   Cf. K. Theodore Hoppen, *Elections, Politics and Society in Ireland
       1832-1885.* (Oxford, 1984), p. 266

29   W.D. Killen, *The Ecclesiastical History of Ireland*, (London, 1875)
       Vol. II. pp. 537 ff. cf also R.F.G. Holmes, *Our Presbyterian Heritage*,
       (Belfast, 1985), p. 132. Strangely, Peter Brooke, *Ulster
       Presbyterianism: The Historical Perspective 1610-1970*, (Dublin and
       New York, 1987), does not go into the details of the crucial
       General Assembly debates on the matter, though of course he
       does advert to the divisions in Irish Presbyterianism over the affair.

30   B.L. Add. MS. 44418 f. 243

31   cf. Edmond Fitzmaurice, *The Life of Granville George Leveson
       Gower: Second Earl Granville.* Vol. I, (London, 1905), p. 525

32   Matthew, *Gladstone Diaries*, Vol. VI 1861-1868, (Oxford, 1978), p.
       645

33   *The Letters of Queen Victoria*, (Second Series 1862-1878), Vol I,
       (London, 1926) p. 578

34   *The Letters of Queen Victoria*, (Second Series), Vol. I p. 582

35   Matthew, *The Gladstone Diaries*, Vol. VII, p. 65

36   John D. Fair, *British Interparty Conferences: a study of the procedure
       of conciliation in British politics 1867-1921*, (Oxford, 1980), p. 22

37   J.D. Clayton, *Mr. Gladstone's Leadership of the Parliamentary Liberal
       Party 1868-1874*, (Oxford University, unpublished, D.Phil thesis
       1960), pp. 206-8

38   cf. Fitzmaurice, *The Life of Granville*, Vol. II. p. 7

39   This was a departure from their agreed previous position. Thus
       Lord Cairns told a meeting of the former Tory cabinet in April the
       Conservative peers 'would not throw out the bill on the second
       reading, though they might amend it in detail.' *Stanley Journals*,
       p. 340. Stanley comments 'This is right and wise.' ibid.

40   *The Letters of Queen Victoria*, (Second Series), Vol. I. pp. 604-5

41   R. B. McDowell, *The Church of Ireland 1869-1969*, (London, 1975),
       p. 46

42   Ethel Drus (ed.), *Kimberley Diary*, (London, 1958) p. 5. Kimberley
       was Lord Privy Seal at the time and a former Lord Lieutenant of
       Ireland.

43   MacDonnell, *Life of William Connor Magee*, Vol. II, p. 227

44   B.L. Add. MS. 44419 f. 87.

45   Matthew, *The Gladstone Diaries*, Vol VII, p. 96

46   Fitzmaurice, *Life of Granville*, Vol II, p. 12 note 1

47   B.L. Add. MS. 44419 f. 92.

48   cf Shane Leslie, 'Irish Pages from the Postbags of Manning,
     Cullen and Gladstone'. *Dublin Review*, October 1919, pp. 177-78.

49   Akenson, *The Church of Ireland*, p. 228, is mistaken in his belief
     that apart from minor details relating to Maynooth Gladstone
     had little contact with Catholics over the disestablishment issue.

50   The Protestant Defence Association had protested in January
     1868 that the Catholic clergy were conspiring to have the Church
     of Ireland disestablished as a first step to destroying Protestant-
     ism in Ireland. cf. P.M.H. Bell, *Disestablishment in Ireland and
     Wales*, (London, 1969), p. 70

51   Leslie, *The Dublin Review*, Vol. 165, (October 1919), p. 163

52   cf. Edward Norman, *The Catholic Church in Ireland in the Age of
     Rebellion: 1859-1873*, (London, 1965), p. 339

53   V. A. McClelland, *Cardinal Manning: His Public Life and Influence.
     1865-1892.* (London, 1962), p. 171

54   *Letter to the Catholic Clergy of the Archdiocese of Armagh.*

55   Cullen to Manning 8 August 1867, Cf. Leslie, *The Dublin Review*,
     (October 1919), p. 168

56   Gladstone to Gray 6 September 1867. B.L. Add. MS. 44413 ff. 134-
     5. This is at variance with Professor Matthew's interpretation
     that for Gladstone 'The notion of the State being involved in the
     support of various denominations which were doctrinally
     irreconcilable he profoundly abhorred...' *Gladstone: 1809-1874*,
     p. 193

57   B.L. Add. MS. 44249 f. 34-5

58   B.L. Add. MS 44249 f. 21

59   cf. also Gladstone's response B.L.. MS. 44249 f. 82

60   B.L. Add. MS. 44421 f. 151. The bluster against concurrent
     endowment did not prevent Cullen nor Archbishop Leahy of
     Cashel asking Gladstone for some of the Church of Ireland
     cathedrals, a proposition the Prime Minister strongly rejected.

61   B.L. Add. MS. 44249 f. 80

62   cf. Charles S. Dessain and Thomas Gornall (eds.), *The Letters and
     Diaries of John Henry Newman*. Vol. XXIV, (Oxford, 1973), p. 182

63   Russell to Clarendon 21 April 1869, P.R.O. F.O. 918/4 f. 43

64   P.R.O. F.O. 918/4 f. 52

65   In an ill-tempered letter of 25 January 1869 Clarendon wrote to
     Russell that he had told the Pope that Cullen was 'the bitter and
     pertinacious enemy of the English government and never misses
     an opportunity to do mischief'. He continued 'it is really too bad

that this viper should be permitted to create difficulties (over the Church Bill) in addition to those which already exist....I shall be grateful if in gentle language you could convey to the Cardinal (Antonelli) and to Manning the utter disgust we feel at the conduct of Cullen and Co, who, as I need not say, give the tone to the whole priesthood of Ireland'. Clarendon MS Oxford C 475 ff. 211-3.

66   Gladstone to Manning 24 July 1869. B.L. Add. MS. 44537 f. 11. Manning wrote to Cullen the following day passing on Gladstone's remarks and saying that the Prime Minister had acted with 'great firmness & uprightness'.

67   Gabriel Daly, 'Church Renewal: 1869-1877', in Michael Hurley (ed.), *Irish Anglicanism 1869-1969*, (Dublin, 1970), p. 23

68   Kevin B. Nowlan, 'Disestablishment: 1800-1869', in Hurley (ed.), *Irish Anglicanism*, p. 8

69   W.E. Vaughan, 'Ireland c 1870' in Vaughan (ed.), *A New History of Ireland*, Vol V. Ireland Under the Union 1801-70, (Oxford, 1989), p. 728

70   F.S.L. Lyons, *Ireland Since the Famine*, (Revised edition, London, 1973), p. 143

71   Erich Eych, *Gladstone*, (London, 1938), p. 195

72   Nicholas Mansergh, *The Irish Question 1840-1921*, (London, 1940), p. 299

73   Roy Foster, *Modern Ireland 1600-1972*, (London, 1988), p. 396

74   Joseph Lee, *The Modernisation of Irish Society 1848-1918*, (Dublin, 1973), p. 60

75   R.V. Comerford, 'Gladstone's first Irish Enterprise, 1864-70.' in *A New History of Ireland*, Vol. V. p. 441-2

76   W.E. Williams, *The Rise of Gladstone to the Leadership of the Liberal Party, 1859-68*, (Cambridge, 1934), p. 162-63

77   Leslie, *The Dublin Review*, (October 1919), p. 178

78   B.L. Add. MS. 44537 f. 13

Catholics and Protestants
in Partitioned Ireland

R.F.G. Holmes

Partition was not a solution to the Irish problem which any significant group in Ireland wanted, and it could be said that, far from solving the Irish problem, it only doubled it. Instead of one majority/minority problem there were now two – the problem of a Roman Catholic and nationalist minority in Northern Ireland, and the problem of a Protestant and unionist minority in the Irish Free State.

Partition may not have been what any significant group in Ireland wanted, but there was a considerable difference in different groups of Irish people regarding it. The majority in the six counties of Northern Ireland were determined that it should be permanent, while a majority in Ireland as a whole were equally determined that it should be temporary and they had reason to hope that a Boundary Commission, which Lloyd George the British Prime Minister had promised to determine the precise boundaries between Northern Ireland and the Irish Free State, would reduce the partitioned area to a point which would make it no longer viable politically or economically.

There were influential groups in Britain, particularly among the Liberals and on the left – the T.U.C. at its annual conference in 1920 called for a total British withdrawal from Ireland[1] – and even in the Conservative party there were elements which were sharply critical of what was perceived as the intransigence of the Ulster Unionists.[2] Long before Harold Wilson and the Ulster Workers Council strike of 1974 there were those at Westminister, particulary in the Treasury, who regarded them as 'spongers'.[3] The fact that Northern Ireland came into existence surrounded not only by enemies but by uncertain friends contributed to the development of a siege mentality which came naturally enough to a people for whom the siege of Derry was an emotive symbol. Protestant Unionists were a clear majority in Northern Ireland which, in the perception of their critics, they had contrived to fashion as the largest area of Ireland in which they could enjoy such a majority. But they were always to feel threatened and insecure in a way in which the southern Catholic majority did not.

I

For the minorities on both sides of the border partition represented a traumatic experience. Archbishop Gregg of Dublin expressed the southern Protestant sense of desolation in appropriately biblical terms – he felt like Adam banished from the Garden of Eden.[4] A northern historian has described the reaction of the northern minority as one of 'shock, incredulity and resentment'.[5] When the possibility of some kind of exclusion for Ulster had been canvassed with the northern Catholic bishops in 1916, Cardinal Logue had expressed their unanimous opposition, declaring: 'It would be infinitely better to remain as we are for fifty years to come under English rule than to accept these proposals'.[6]

The situation was exacerbated by continuing violence. Indeed partition, as an affront to militant nationalist feeling, contributed to the continuing violence. The sufferings of the vulnerable minorities in both parts of Ireland were soon being interpreted by their co-religionists as religious persecution. The long-standing identification of religious and political loyalties in Ireland meant that a person's religion was often taken as an indication of his or her political sympathies, exposing Catholics in the north and Protestants in the south to the attacks of violent extremists.

Political and religious antipathies were reinforced by social and economic grievances; this was particularly true in post-war Belfast. Unemployed Catholics were easily tempted to react violently against those whom they believed responsible for their unemployment and poverty, while unemployed Protestant ex-servicemen were easily persuaded that their jobs had been taken by Catholics from the south of Ireland who had 'infiltrated' the shipbuilding and engineering industries during the war. Lurid reports of Republican atrocities in the south, carried by the *Belfast Newsletter*, accompanied by allegations that they were being encouraged by the Catholic Church, fanned anti-Catholic feeling in Belfast.[7] The murder in 1920, shortly after the twelfth of July, of

Colonel G.F.S. Smyth, a County Down man who was Divisional Commander of Police in Munster, and difficulties about bringing his body home for burial, detonated an explosion of anti-Catholic fury in the Belfast shipyards on the day of Smyth's funeral, and Catholic workers were brutally assaulted and driven from their jobs.[8]

When the Catholic hierarchy, meeting in Maynooth, condemned these and other attacks upon Catholics, including evictions from their homes, Protestant church leaders protested in reply that Catholic workers had not been attacked because of their religion but because of their suspected support for 'Republican murder-gangs'.[9] They advised the Catholic bishops, 'instead of making wild and baseless charges, to unite with them in their endeavours to discourage violence by whomsoever committed and urge their people to live quiet and peaceful lives, submitting to the authority of the country to which they belong'.[10] Many Catholics found great difficulty, however, in recognising the legitimacy of Northern Ireland and northern Catholic bishops and clergy served on an advisory committee established by the Irish Free State to explore ways of making it impossible for the northern government to survive.[11] At the same time, many Catholics combined with their Protestant neighbours in Northern Ireland to protect one another and make peace.[12]

Catholic bishops had alleged that 'able-bodied Protestants had been supplied with arms to harrass their Roman Catholic neighbours.'[13] This was indignantly repudiated by Protestant spokesmen. The role of the almost exclusively Protestant Special Constabulary in the northern security situation became a recurring Catholic grievance. Indeed nothing illustrates the different perspectives of Roman Catholic and Protestant churchmen more than their conflicting attitudes to the Ulster Special Constabulary.

One of the problems which the northern authorities had to face was the emergence of unofficial vigilante groups as 'peace-keepers' in their own localities. Thus the Rev John Redmond, rector of St Patrick's, Ballymacarett, organised a group of parishoners under the command of an ex-officer curate to keep order in the riot-torn Lower Newtownards Road in Belfast.[14] It was out of such groups that the Special Constabulary were recruited, but from their beginnings they were regarded by some Catholics as agents of repression, described as 'nothing more or less than the dregs of the Orange Lodges, armed and equipped to overawe nationalists and Catholics'. Liam de Paor has identified them as 'the same people who had been burning out Catholic homes', adding that, 'not unnaturally the creation of such a police force added to the violence, which took the form of a full-scale pogrom against Catholics'.[15]

De Paor is largely repeating the contemporary condemnations of the 'Specials' by Cardinal Logue, described by their historian, Arthur Hezlett, as 'astonishing'.[16] Hezlett claims that, in Belfast, where the pogrom was alleged to have taken place, the Specials were seldom used and then chiefly to protect Catholic public houses in Protestant areas.[17] Significantly, on the other side of the ecclesiastical fence, we find that the Presbyterian General Assembly, in its expression of thanks to Almighty God for the eventual restoration of some kind of peace, paid special tribute to the Special Constabulary's part in the restoration of law and order.[18]

The allegation that an anti-Catholic pogrom took place in Belfast in 1922 is frequently repeated but the official statistics of numbers killed and wounded, horrific though they are, scarcely support the emotive description of the violence as a pogrom. In the period from 6 December to 31 May 1922, the first six months after the Belfast government assumed responsibility for law and order, 73 Protestants and 16 members of the security forces were killed and 143 Protestants and 37 members of the secruity forces were wounded against 147 Catholics killed and 166 wounded.[19] A British civil servant, S.G. Tallents, later Sir Stephen Tallents, who was observing the Northern Ireland situation for the British government, considered that many Catholic casualties were the victims of indiscriminate firing by Catholic gunmen.[20]

II

If Roman Catholic churchmen seem to have been outspoken in condemning violence against Roman Catholics in Northern Ireland, Protestant churchmen, who often attempted to rebut their condemnations, were equally outspoken in condemning violence against Protestants in southern Ireland. The Presbyterian General Assembly's 'State of the Country' committee reported in 1921 that, 'in Sinn Féin Ireland', '... quiet and law abiding people are being put to death in the most inhuman and cold-blooded manner. In some districts the Protestant population is being entirely exterminated'.[21] In 1922 the committee reported that 'many members of our church have been shot or maltreated or deprived of their property and compelled to leave the country'.[22]

Archbishop D'Arcy, opening the General Synod of the Church of Ireland in May 1921, claimed that 'Members of our Church, and others in special parts of the country – quiet defenceless farmers for the most part – have been most cruelly killed'.[23] A particular case which had a considerable impact on Protestant opinion was the murder, after kidnap, of an elderly lady, Mrs J.W. Lindsay of county Cork, together with her chauffeur. Mrs Lindsay had observed an ambush being prepared for the security forces and had warned the police, who arrested the I.R.A. men involved. These were subsequently sentenced to death.[24] Mrs Lindsay was kidnapped by the I.R.A. and murdered when the I.R.A. men were executed. From an I.R.A. point of view, and in the view of the Republican historian, Dorothy Macardle, Mrs Lindsay was being executed as an informer.[25] From a Protestant point of view, her death, and that of her chauffeur, were cold-blooded sectarian murder.

Many southern Protestants, including ex-Servicemen from World War I, regarded the British security forces as legitimate forces of law and order and the I.R.A. as rebels, while, from a Republican point of view, after the establishment of Dáil Éireann by Sinn Féin in December, 1918, the I.R.A. were the rightful forces of the Irish state. Loyalty and disloyalty were therefore ambiguous terms and Protestants tended to see the victims of Republican attacks as loyal British subjects who were being victimised simply because they were Protestants.

A considerable number of southern Protestants found it prudent to leave the country. This was particularly true of the landed gentry, whose homes were targets for Republican attacks. Lady Gregory reported that in Galway, 'furniture vans were engaged nine months ahead taking goods from the country to England'.[26] Not all southern Irish Protestants were landed, however. The *Irish Times* of 16 June 1922 reported that in Ballinasloe,

Mr Salter, manager of Mr Woods' boot establishment received notice to leave the town. Mr Swan ... agent for Messrs Guinness received final notice to leave. Mrs J. Rosen, a widow residing at Clanmore, with her eighteen year old daughter, a linesman named Davidson and Mr W. Crawford, the station-master, all of whom were Protestants, have been warned.[27]

The Presbyterian Home Mission's report to the General Assembly in 1922 showed that between 1915 and 1922 there had been an alarming loss of church members in their southern presbyteries – a loss of 45% in the Cork presbytery, 44% in Munster, 36% in Connaught and 30% in the Athlone presbytery, though in the Dublin presbytery losses were only 16%.[28] Of course these statistics must be seen against a background of falling population numbers since the nineteenth century, and the effects of the 1914-18 war, in which so many potential fathers of families were killed, but they were easily interpreted as evidence that Protestants were being driven out of a Catholic State. Indeed Archbishop Gregg led a deputation from the General Synod of the Church of Ireland to Michael Collins to inquire 'if they were to be permitted to live in Ireland or if it was desired that they should leave the country'.[29]

The truth was, of course, that the Free State government, struggling for survival in a situation of civil war, could no more protect isolated individuals and their property than the British government, with far greater military resources, had been able to do during the so-called war of independence. It ought also to be added that, when the Home Mission report was being debated in the General Assembly, Presbyterian ministers from southern Ireland stated that their people were not being attacked or murdered because they were Presbyterians. But this only provoked the question expressed in the *Belfast Newsletter* of why, then, were they being persecuted?[30]

The restoration of peace in both parts of Ireland provided an opportunity for new beginnings. Both governments expressed benevolent intentions towards their minorities. Sir James Craig, the Northern Ireland Prime Minister, had promised from the beginnings of the State that they would be 'absolutely honest and fair' to all within their boundaries and that 'none need be afraid'.[31]

In the Dail, Kevin O'Higgins assured the southern minority that they were not regarded as 'alien enemies' but were invited to take their share in the life of the new State.[32] There were indications, also, that these were not merely empty words. The first Lord Chief Justice of Northern Ireland and the first permanent secretary at the Ministry of Education, together with the first secretary of the Northern Ireland civil service commission were all Catholics, though they were certainly not regarded by nationalist members of the minority as their representatives. In the south, twenty-four of the sixty members of the first Senate were Protestants. *The Witness*, the Ulster Presbyterian weekly newspaper, expressed the hope that 'the best and most progressive and most prosperous and most loyal and most law-abiding state' would be created and maintained in Northern Ireland.[33] What was created, unfortunately, has been described by an English civil servant who worked in the province for twenty years, Sir Wilfred Spender, as 'a factory of grievances', even if he did add that Northern Ireland had a strong competitor for that unenviable title in the Irish Free State.[34]

III

Whatever suspicions the Protestant Churches may have had about the new Irish Free State they gave it recognition as the lawful government of a legitimate State and encouraged their members, in the words of a Presbyterian General Assembly resolution, 'to co-operate whole-heartedly with their Roman Catholic fellow-countrymen in the best interests of their beloved land'.[35] The bishops of the Church of Ireland also urged their people to accept the new regime, though as J.H. Whyte has commented: 'There was a great difference between acceptance and enthusiastic support'.[36] Some Protestants did give the Irish Free State their enthusiastic support, but they were Protestant nationalists like W.B.Yeats. The moderator of the Presbyterian synod of Dublin struck a positive note when he declared in 1924 that, 'instead of wasting energy in regrets and repinings ... we must concentrate upon the business of building up our country's fortunes on sound lines ... we must give our best in honesty, sincerity, yes, and in love'.[37]

The Roman Catholic hierarchy did not feel able to reciprocate by giving any recognition to the Northern Ireland State. Cardinal Logue, the Catholic Archbishop of Armagh, declined an invitation to attend the formal opening of the northern parliament in 1921 and the Church also held aloof from the Lynn committee on education set up to advise on the divisive question of State education in Northern Ireland.[38] D.H. Akenson, a historian of educational controversies in Ireland before and after partition, and who has many criticisms of the role of the Protestant Churches in determining the character of education in Northern Ireland, considers that the Roman Catholic refusal to participate in the Lynn committee 'was the single most important determinant of the educational history of Northern Ireland from 1920 to the present day' for it 'surrendered their last shred of influence at the very time when the basic character of Ulster's educational development was being determined'.[39]

Perhaps Ulster Protestants failed to appreciate the conscientious objections of many Irish Catholics to the State of Northern Ireland. It was perceived as a monstrous affront to justice, the institutionalisation of militant anti-Catholicism, in which, from the beginning, discrimination against Catholics was built into the very nature of the State. Peter McKevitt, a former professor of Sociology at Maynooth, describing the establishment of Northern Ireland in a survey of the history of Irish Catholicism, commented, 'That the Church cannot be favourable to such flagrant injustice goes without saying'.[40] The notorious statements of the first Northern Ireland Prime Minister, Lord Craigavon, that Stormont was 'a Protestant parliament for a Protestant people' have often been used as evidence of the sectarian character of the northern State. The full context of Craigavon's remarks are not so well known, however. On 24 April 1934, Craigavon was claiming that, on an Orange platform, he had laid down the principle, to which he still adhered, that he was 'Prime Minister, not of one section of the community but of all, and that as far as I possibly could I was going to see fair play was meted out to all classes and creeds...' Interrupted by the question, 'What about your Protestant parliament?', (On 12 July 1932 Craigavon had told an Orange demonstration that 'ours is a Protestant government and I am an Orangeman.'[41]) he replied that 'in the South they boasted of a Catholic State. They still boast of Southern Ireland being a

Catholic State. All I boast of is that we are a Protestant Parliament and a Protestant State'.[42]

IV

If northern Roman Catholics found difficulty in supporting the Northern Irish State, many southern Protestants were equally unable to identify with the new Irish state with its compulsory Irish in schools, its ban on contraceptives and divorce. The 1937 Constitution gave official recognition to the special position of the Roman Catholic Church as the guardian of the faith professed by the large majority of its citizens, though also recognizing the main Protestant Churches. In 1929 the centenary of Catholic Emancipation was celebrated. In 1932, a Eucharistic Congress took place. In 1931, Cardinal McRory declared that the Protestant Churches were 'not even a part of the Church of Christ'.[43] All these were clear and unmistakable, if unwelcome signs of the new order of things. W.B. Yeats declared in the Irish Senate that legislation to outlaw divorce was 'grossly oppressive' to the State's minority[44] and Dr A.A. Luce, the distinguished Trinity College Dublin Berkeleian scholar, agreed that 'compulsory Irish in Protestant schools was a wrong to the religion of Protestants because Irish school text books contained Roman Catholic teaching'.[45] But this was all far from persecution, and the response of most southern Irish Protestants was, in the words of another distinguished Trinity College scholar, W.B. Stanford, 'to lie low and say nothing'.[46]

Their co-religionists in Northern Ireland felt under no compulsion to do likewise, however. Northern churchmen and politicans were only too eager to represent these pressures upon their southern brethren as persecution against Protestants. While acknowledging from time to time the generosity of the Free State government, particularly in the field of education, where the Education Department's requirements in Irish were not always enforced in the case of Protestant teachers, suspicions were expressed by Presbyterians that the Roman Catholic Church was 'putting forth every effort to make Ireland a wholly Roman Catholic country'.[47]

The 1950s were to provide some of the most outstanding examples of possible trends in this direction and the distinguished Catholic political scientist, J.H. Whyte, author of a definitive work on Church and State in modern Ireland, has acknowledged that 'There were a number of signs about this time that the Republic (as it now was) might be moving in the direction of a theocratic state'.[48]

A *cause célèbre* was the Tilson case of 1950. The whole area of inter-church marriages and the *Ne Temere* decree is of course a fruitful source of conflict between Protestants and Roman Catholics in Ireland. In this case, Tilson, a Protestant, had broken his promise to bring up the children of the marriage in his wife's Roman Catholic faith, and had put them in a Protestant children's home.[49] His wife appealed to the courts to have her children returned, and the High Court and Supreme Court both found in her favour. Protestant critics claimed that this meant that Catholic canon law was enforceable by the courts of the Republic, though it has been argued that this was specifically repudiated by the Supreme Court.[50] To those Protestants who did not or could not appreciate the finer points of law involved in the case, it was clear evidence of the Roman Catholic character of the Irish State.

Shortly afterwards the Minister for Health in the Republic's coalition government, Dr Noel Browne, was sacked because his 'Mother and Child' proposals to provide free medical care for expectant mothers had earned the disapproval of the hierarchy. This was used to support the contention of Ulster Protestants that ultimate authority in the Irish State lay with the hierarchy. There is evidence that, in fact, the hierarchy may have been made scapegoats for what was essentially a political decision by a government downing a difficult minister.[51]

Finally, another court case, involving Jehovah's Witness preachers who had been assualted after offering their version of the gospel on the steps of a Roman Catholic church, provided another target for Protestant attack.[52] The District Justice expressed his opinion that 'when men come into an Irish village and provoke people by voicing their views ... they are abusing whatever rights they have under the Constitution which guarantees freedom of religious worship. Such action is bound to bring down the rod of the people whose hospitality they have received'.[53] In the public controversy which followed the case, the Protestants now felt that they must lie low if their persons and property were to be safeguarded.[54]

V

The Government Committee of the Presbyterian Church now began a correspondence with the Taoiseach, Eamon de Valera, to express their Church's 'disquietude' about ' a number of events in the Republic which, cumulatively, have caused serious misgivings'.[55] It appeared that 'constitutional guarantees of religious liberty in the Republic are of little practical value'.[56] Predictably the Taoiseach refused to enter into any discussion of particular cases and reminded the committee of the important principle of non-interference by the Executive in the decisions of the Judiciary.[57] It is to the credit of the committee that this correspondence was not made public at the time.

Earlier they had corresponded with Cardinal D'Alton on the subject of alleged persecution of Protestants in Colombia in Latin America. The Cardinal, having assured them that he would always use his influence to stop presecution wherever it existed, added that that was because 'we Catholics have and are suffering so much in the way of persecution that we should resolutely set our faces against its every form'.[58]

Certainly Catholics in Northern Ireland believed that they were the victims of persistent and institutionalised anti-Catholicism. In his Lenten pastoral of 1938, Dr Daniel Mageean, Bishop of Down and Connor, alleged that the history of the Northern Ireland parliament was 'one long record of partisan and bigoted discrimination in matters of representation, legislation and administration'.[59] But the historian, David Kennedy, has asked the question: 'Were they suffering as Catholics or as nationalists?' and he acknowledged the difficulty of distinguishing the two categories. His own answer was that 'there was no persecution of the Catholic Church in Northern Ireland'.[60] He agreed that in fact the Church enjoyed vigorous and healthy growth in Northern Ireland with some of the most effective modern Catholic institutions, such as the Catholic Truth Society and the Apostolic Work Society, originating in the province.[61]

C.E.B. Brett, scion of an Ulster plantation family but sharp social-ist critic of the Stormont regime and, as an agnostic, impartial as between competing Christians, has judged that 'although the Catholic minority has received less than fair treatment from the Protestant majority they were not actually oppressed' and that their grievances 'certainly did not justify a recourse to force'.[62] That they did, indeed, receive 'less that fair treatment' and were often the victims of discrimination has now been well document-ed by the evidence of historians, social scientists and official in-vestigations, and not only by partisan propagandists.[63]

Why then were so few Protestant voices raised in protest on their behalf? It may be significant that such a sensitive and liberal-minded Presbyterian as J.E. Davey, one of the finest scholars to emerge in Irish Presbyterianism this century, appears to have shared the general view of Ulster Protestants that Catholic com-plaints were largely nationalist propaganda. Davey considered that 'the Roman Catholic harbours a love of grievance which finds imaginary grounds where real ones do not exist and exaggerates them greatly when they do'.[64] The historian A.T.Q. Stewart may be nearer the truth when he observes that 'the Irish, Catholic and Protestant alike, are not prone to underrate a grievance'.[65]

Davey, though active in promoting tolerance and reconciliation in Ireland, shared deep-seated Protestant suspicions of Roman Cathoicism. 'Intolerance is the one thing which cannot be easily tolerated', he wrote on one occasion. 'This is particularly difficult for the Protestant, for if he is intolerant he is being false to his principles, and, regrettably, there have been such cases. For a Roman Catholic, on the contary, in a considerable measure, in-tolerance is an accepted principle'.[66] Davey's view of Protestant tolerance may have reflected his own liberal Protestant outlook. In 1950 the Presbyterian General Assembly's committee on na-tional and international problems, in a report on 'The duties of Christians in relation to political and religious differences in Ireland', described the Roman Catholic Church as:

> a world-wide religious organisation that seeks to gain con-trol of the institutions of mankind and of public life gener-ally; it is not merely a church, it is a political organisation. And, as long as it maintains this position we are inevitably confronted by irreconcilable factors ... thus the Protestant

often fears the dangers of the violation of his freedom and of ecclesiastical power in religious, political and social affairs.[67]

Nevertheless the same report also affirmed that 'it was the duty of a Christian to stand for the spirit of reconciliation ... and against the spirit of suspicion and enmity'. It was recognised that 'a radical change of attitude on both sides, and a more generous spirit of goodwill' were needed if there was to be any hope of healing 'political and religious differences and their consequences in Ireland'.[68]

VI

There was little enough evidence in the 1950s that any radical change of attitude could be anticipated. By and large, Protestant churchmen in Northern Ireland had shown themselves more concerned about alleged discrimination against Protestants in the South of Ireland than in exposing and opposing discrimination against Catholics in Northern Ireland. And Roman Catholic churchmen had manifested less concern about the position of Protestants in southern Ireland than they had about the alleged sufferings of their own people in the north. In 1957, the Catholic population of Fethard on Sea in county Wexford organised a boycott against the small local Protestant community because the Protestant partner in an inter-Church marriage had taken her children away in order to evade her obligations to have them brought up as Catholics. Two Catholic bishops described the boycott as 'a peaceful and reasonable protest'[69] although the Taoiseach, De Valera, was prepared to condemn it unequivocally in the Dáil as 'unjust and cruel'.[70]

It would be unfair, however, to paint a picture of unrelieved gloom. There were always those who, like De Valera on that occasion, were prepared to acknowledge that wrong had been done. The Catholic bishop of Killaloe, Dr Fogarty, in his Lenten pastoral in 1923, condemned the treatment of Protestants in the violence of the early 1920s, though he insisted that they had not suffered because they were Protestants.[71] And in 1956, when the Northen Ireland government proposed to limit the payment of family allowances to the first three children in a family, the

General Assembly of the Presbyterian Church protested that this would discriminate against Catholics, whose families were normally larger than the families of Protestants, and sent a deputation to Stormont to express their protest to the government.[72]

Things began to change dramatically in the 1960s and it is ironic that a decade which began with great promise should have ended in disaster and renewed violence. The pontificate of John XXIII and the second Vatican Council signalled a revolution in Roman Catholic attitudes, and there was a reciprocal response from Protestant churchmen, even in Northern Ireland. In 1961, Dr Austin Fulton, outgoing Moderator of the General Assembly, called upon Presbyterians to reach out to Catholics in Christian charity, seeking, wherever possible, to find ways of co-operation for the common good.[73] Two years later, in 1963, the General Assembly stood in tribute to Pope John, whose death was announced during the Assembly's public opening meeting, and only one voice was raised in protest when the Assembly's business session began on the following day.[74]

The decree on ecumenism of Vatican II was welcomed by the General Assembly in 1965, and a resolution of penitence for Presbyterian uncharitableness in the past was carried.[75] The *Belfast Telegraph* applauded this evidence of a new spirit: 'Against the background of the last half century of Irish history the gesture has considerable significance. It is a public admission by the body most representative of Ulster Protestantism that Presbyterians have behaved in an unchristian manner towards their Roman Catholic neighbours'.[76]

On the other side of the divide, Roman Catholic ecumenists like Michael Hurley, professor of Dogmatic Theology at Milltown Park in Dublin, were reaching out to encourage and foster positive relationships with their 'separated brethren'. In 1963 Michael Hurley edited a handbook of studies, meditations and prayers, entitled *Praying for Unity*, to which the Church of Ireland Archbishop of Dublin, G.O. Simms, the Moderator of the General Assembly, W.A. Montgomery, and the President of the Methodist Conference, F.E. Hill, contributed, and the Roman Catholic Bishop of Down and Connor, William J. Philbin, wrote a foreword.[77] Conferences and groups of Roman Catholics and Protestants meeting at Glenstal Abbey near Limerick (1964) and Greenhills

Presentation Convent, Drogheda (1966) provided opportunities for dialogue.

But there were some who were alarmed by these developments. Letters in the Belfast newspapers and in the *Presbyterian Herald* expressed strident criticism of 'ecumenism', which was perceived as a form of apostasy.[78] In 1966 the opening meeting of the Presbyterian General Assembly in Belfast became a scene of intemperate protest by a mob led by Ian Paisley, a 'Free' Presbyterian who claimed to be the authentic voice of traditional Ulster Protestantism.[79] Paisley, originally an independent Baptist, had become the leader of a small but vociferous protest movement against an alleged 'Romeward trend' in Irish Protestantism.[80] It must never be forgotten that Ulster Protestantism could easily be divided over the perennial tensions between conservatives and liberals in the mainstream Churches, and in Irish Presbyteriansm in particular, with vigorous sects always eager to provide for malcontents.

The revival of sectarian violence in Northern Ireland gave Church leaders, Protestant and Roman Catholic, an opportunity to come together to give Christian leadership to the divided community, to condemn violence and to promote reconciliation. But their response to the situation which has developed and continued since 1969 is another story.[81] However sincere and well-intentioned their efforts since 1969 may have been, it is hard to resist the conclusion that, in spite of the prophetic contribution of individuals and small groups in all the Churches, too little has been done over the years to promote mutual understanding between Catholics and nationalists on the one side and Protestants and unionists on the other. Though they have excelled in the pastoral care of their respective flocks, the Churches in Ireland have been less successful in giving prophetic leadership in a situation of division and conflict. To some extent, therefore, the Ireland of to-day is a terrible judgement upon their failure.

Notes

1   G. Dangerfield, *The Damnable Question*, (London, 1979), p. 386
2   P. Bew, P. Gobbon and H. Patterson, *The State in Northern Ireland.1921-72*, (Manchester, 1979), p. 53
3   ibid
4   G. Seaver, *John Allen Fitzgerald Gregg, Archbishop*, (London, 1963) p. 128
5   B.A. Kennedy, 'Catholicism in Northern Ireland' in *The Years of the Great Test* (ed.), F. MacManus, (Dublin and Cork, 1978), p. 39
6   D.W. Miller, *Church, State and Nation in Ireland,1898-1921*, (Dublin, 1973), p. 337
7   *Belfast Newsletter*, (hereafter B.N.L.) 29 January 1920
8   P. Buckland, *Irish Unionism*, vol. 2, (Dublin, 1973), p. 122
9   *The Witness*, 5 May 1922
10   ibid
11   R. Fanning, *Independent Ireland*, (Dublin, 1983), pp. 27ff
12   H.C. Waddell, *John Waddell*, (Belfast, 1949), p. 72 and T.M. Johnstone, *The Vintage of Memory*, (Belfast, 1943), p. 177
13   Quoted in *The Witness*, 5 May 1922
14   D. Kennedy, 'Aspects of the Northern Situation' in *Irish Anglicanism 1869-1969* (ed.), M. Hurley, (Dublin, 1970), p. 163
15   L. de Paor, *Divided Ulster*, (London, 1970), p. 108
16   Sir Arthur Hezlett, *The 'B' Specials*, (London, 1972), p. 92
17   ibid
18   *General Assembly Reports* (hereafter R.G.A.) 1923, p. 105
19   P. Buckland, *A History of Northern Ireland*, (Dublin, 1981), p. 46
20   Hezlett, *The 'B' Specials*, p. 85
21   R.G.A. 1921, p. 78
22   ibid. 1922, p. 103
23   Proceedings of the Church of Ireland General Synod, 1921 quoted by D.Kennedy, *The Widening Gulf*, (Belfast, 1988), pp. 54-5
24   Kennedy, *Widening Gulf*, pp. 50-2
25   D. Macardle, *The Irish Republic*, (London, 1937) quoted by J. White, *Minority Report, The anatomy of the Southern Irish Protestant*, (Dublin, 1975), p. 85
26   *Journals of Lady Gregory*, (ed.), Lennox Robinson, (London, 1946), p. 13
27   *The Irish Times*, 16 June 1922.
28   *General Assembly Minutes*, 1922, p. 144, afterwards M.G.A.

29   *Irish Times*, 13 May 1922
30   B.N.L. 28 June 1923.
31   *Parliamentary Debates*, Northern Ireland House of Commons,
        Vol. I, pp. 367, 23 June 1921.
32   *Dáil Reports*, 6 January 1922 quoted by White, *Minority Report*, p. 91
33   *The Witness*, 9 December 1920.
34   Sir W. Spender, *Financial Diary*, November 1939 - May 1940, p.
        84. P.R.O.N.I. D. 715
35   M.G.A. 1922, p. 40
36   J.H. Whyte, 'Political Life in the South' in *Irish Anglicanism* 1869-
        1969
37   *The Witness*, 18 April 1924.
38   Buckland, *Northern Ireland*, p. 35
39   D. H. Akenson, *Education and Enmity*, (Newton Abbot and New
        York, 1973), p. 52
40   P. McKevitt, 'Epilogue: Modern Ireland' in *A History of Irish
        Catholicism*, (ed.), P.J. Corish, (Dublin, 1970), Vol.10, p. 27
41   Kennedy, *Widening Gulf*, p. 166
42   *Parliamentary Debates*, N.I.H.C., Vol. XVI, 1095.
43   *Irish News*, 18 December 1931.
44   *Senate Reports*, 11 June 1925.
45   *Irish Times*, 17 November 1926.
46   W.B. Stanford, *A Recognised Church*, (Dublin, 1944), p. 16
47   R.G.A., 1936 p. 5
48   J.H. Whyte, 'Political Life in the South', p. 148
49   ibid. pp. 147-8
50   G.H. Hand, 'Professor Barkely, the Tilson Case and Mr
        Blanshard', *The Newman Review*, I no.2, December, 1969, pp. 35-9
51   J.H. Whyte, *Church and State in Modern Ireland*, (Dublin, 1973),
        pp. 196-273
52   *Irish Times*, 16 November 1958.
53   *The Presbyterian Herald*, December 1958.
54   *Irish Times*, 17 November 1958.
55   Minutes of the Government Committee of the Presbyterian
        Church in Ireland, 17 November 1958.
56   ibid. See also W.E. Davison, 'A Critical analysis of the
        decisions of the General Assembly of the Presbyterian Church
        in Ireland on social issues, 1921-70', Unpublished Ph.D. thesis.
        (Q.U.B., 1977), pp. 465-72
57   ibid

58   R.G.A. 1954, pp. 56-7
59   *The Years of the Great Test*, p. 145
60   ibid. p. 146
61   ibid. pp. 147-8
62   C.E.B. Brett, *Long Shadows cast Before*, (Edinburgh and London, 1978), pp. 98-9 and p. 101
63   R. Rose, *Governing without Consensus*, (London, 1971); P. Buckland, *The Factory of Grievances*, (Dublin, 1979); *Disturbances in Northern Ireland*, Govt. of Northern Ireland Cmd. 512, (Belfast, 1969).
64   A.A. Fulton, *Biography of J. Ernest Davey*, (Belfast, 1970), p. 43
65   A.T.Q. Stewart, *The Narrow Ground*, (London, 1977), p. 178
66   Fulton, *Davey*, p. 150
67   R.G.A., 1950, pp. 87-91
68   ibid
69   *Irish Times*, 23 May; 1 and 8 July, 1957.
70   *Dáil Debates*, clxiii 731; Whyte, *Church and State* pp. 323-5
71   R.G.A., 1923, pp. 103-5
72   M.G.A., 1956, pp. 20 and 43
73   *Northern Whig*, 6 June 1961.
74   M.G.A., 1963, p. 5 and B.N.L. 5 June 1963.
75   ibid. 1965, p. 26
76   *Belfast Telegraph*, 10 June 1965.
77   *Praying for Unity*. (Dublin, 1963), (ed.), M. Hurley.
78   *Presbyterian Herald*, July 1965.
79   M.G.A. , 1963, pp. 33 and 41-2
80   cf. E. Moloney and A. Pollack, *Paisley*, (Dublin, 1986); S. Bruce, *God Save Ulster*, (Oxford, 1986) C. Smyth, *Ian Paisley, Voice of Protestant Ulster*, (Edinburgh, 1987).
81   E. Gallagher and S. Worrall, *Christians in Ulster, 1968-1980*, (Oxford, 1982).

Michael Hurley S.J.

A Bibliography

1948

1   'Francisco Suárez SJ (1548-1948)', *Irish Monthly* 76 (1948), pp. 265-73

2   'The Communist Manifesto 1848-1948', *Irish Monthly* 76 (1948), pp. 532-40

1951

3   'Illumination according to S. Bonaventure', *Gregorianum* 32 (1951), pp. 388-404

1953

4   'Belgian Workers Today', *Social Order* 3 (1953), pp. 109-16

5   'The Belgian Enterprise Councils, 1948-53', *The American Catholic Sociological Review* 14 (1953), pp. 218-29

1960

6   'Scriptura Sola: Wyclif and his Critics', *Traditio* 16 (1960), pp. 275-352

7   'Scriptura Sola: Wicleffus ejusque Interpretes', *Verbum Domini* 38 (1960), pp. 223-9

1961

8   *Towards Christian Unity: An Introduction to the Ecumenical Movement.* (Dublin, 1961), pp. 36

9   'Feast of the Ascension: The Mystery and Its Significance', *The Irish Ecclesiastical Record* 95 (1961), pp. 255-62

10 'Born Incorruptibly: The Third Canon of the Lateran Council (AD 649)', *The Heythrop Journal* 2 (1961), pp. 216-36

11 'The New Delhi Programme of the World Council of Churches I', *The Irish Theological Quarterly* 28 (1961) pp. 303-17

12   'Christian Unity', *Doctrine and Life* 11 (1961), pp. 532-42

13   'The World Council of Churches and its Forthcoming
        Assembly', *Studies* 50 (1961), pp. 327-42

1962

14   'The Ascension of Our Lord: The Mystery and its
        Significance', *Sermons for Sundays and Feasts*, ed P.J. Hamell,
        (Dublin 1962), pp. 215-22 (Reprint of No.9)

15   'The New Delhi Programme of the World Council of
        Churches II', *The Irish Theological Quarterly* 29 (1962), pp.
        52-67

16   'The Vatican Council: The Issues and the Intention', *The
        Irish Times* 23 January 1962, p.7

17   'Some Recent Ecumenical Literature', *The Irish Theological
        Quarterly* 29 (1962), pp. 248-58

18   'The Vatican Council and the Ecumenical Situation Today,
        The Irish Ecclesiastical Record 98 (1962), pp. 28-42

19   'The World Council of Churches' Recent Paris Meeting',
        The Irish Times 3, 4 September 1962.

1963

20   (ed.), *Praying for Unity. A Handbook of Studies, Meditations
        and Prayers.* (The Furrow Trust 1963), pp. 240. Editor's
        'Introduction' pp. 24-31

21   'Catholics and the Council', *Praying for Unity* (= No. 20),
        pp. 104-16.

22   'The Nature of the Church: Common Ground between
        Catholics and Protestants', *Doctrine and Life* 13 (1963),
        pp. 15-25

23   'An Octave of Prayer', *The Furrow* 14 (1963), pp. 49-54

24   'Common Ground between Catholics and Protestants',
        Guide 178 (May 1973). pp. 8-13. (= Reprint of No. 22)

25   'Ecumenism and Mariology: The Contribution of
        Catholics', *The Furrow* 14(1963), pp. 212-24

26   'Ecumenism and Mariology: The Contribution of
      Protestants', *The Furrow* 14(1963), pp. 349-60

27   'The Montreal Ecumenical Conference', *The Irish Press* 13
      July 1973, p.8

28   'The Second Vatican Council', *Biblical Theology* 13 (October
      1963), pp. 52-9

29   'A Pre-Tridentine Theology of Tradition. Thomas Netter of
      Walden (+1430)', *The Heythrop Journal* 4(1963), pp. 348-66

30   'Praying for the Catholic Church', *The Clergy Review* 48
      (1963), pp. 739-50. (=Reprint of No. 21)

1964

31   'Ecumenism and Conversion', *The Irish Theological
      Quarterly* 31(1964), pp. 132-49

32   'Presbyterians in Council. The Reformed Churches Four
      Hundred Years After', *Studies* 53(1964), pp. 286-304

33   'Hoping with Hope. The Vatican Council's Decree on
      Ecumenism', *The Irish Times*, 30 November 1964, p.6

1965

34   'Presbyterians in Council. The Reformed Churches Four
      Hundred Years After', *Biblical Theology* 15(March 1965),
      pp. 1-14. (=Reprint of No. 32)

35   'Conditional Baptism', *The Furrow* 16 (1965), pp. 87-92

36   'Joint Worship', *The Furrow* 16(1965), pp. 233-9

37   'The Five Per Cent', *The Furrow* 16(1965), pp. 370-4

38   'Presbyterians and Repentance', *The Furrow* 16(1965), pp.
      493-5

39   'The Churches' Industrial Council', *The Furrow* 16(1965),
      pp. 625-8

40   'Non-Sectarianism or Christian Co-operation?', *The Furrow*
      16(1965), pp. 770-2

1966

41   (ed.), *Church and Eucharist*, (Dublin and Melbourne 1966),
      pp. 298. Editor's 'Introduction', pp. 11-27

42   'The Church in Protestant Theology. Some Reflections on
      the Fourth Book of Calvin's *Institutes*', *The Meaning of the
      Church*. [Papers of the Maynooth Union Summer School
      1965] (Dublin and Melbourne 1966), pp. 110-43

43   'The Ecumenism Decree: Facts and Reflections', *The Irish
      Ecclesiastical Record* 105(1966), pp. 12-26

44   'The Greenhills Conference', *The Furrow* 17(1966), pp. 124-7

45   'Dialogue at Local Level', *The Furrow* 17(1966), pp. 246-8

46   'Mixed Marriages', *The Furrow* 17(1966), pp. 279-87

47   'The Third Glenstal Ecumenical Conference', *The Furrow* 17
      (1966), pp. 517-9

48   'Clerical Students' Convention', *The Furrow* 17(1966), pp.
      649-51

49   'The Church in Protestant Theology. Some Reflections on
      the Fourth Book of Calvin's Institutes', *Biblical Theology* 16
      (October 1966), pp. 1-15. (=Reprint of No. 42)

50   'Non Anglicani sed Angli?', *The Furrow* 17(1966), 781-6

51   'The Message of World Methodism', *The Irish Times* 29
      August 1966.

1967

52   'Penance: Sacrament of Reconciliation', *Sin and Repentance*
      [Papers of the Maynooth Union Summer School 1966], ed.
      Denis O'Callaghan, (Dublin and Sydney 1967), pp. 109-26

53   'Penance: Sacrament of Reconciliation', *The Furrow* 18
      (1967), pp. 67-80 (=Reprint of No. 52)

54   'What can Catholics learn from the Infant Baptism
      Controversy?' *Concilium* 4(April 1967) pp. 9-12. (=*The
      Sacraments. An Ecumenical Dilemna. Concilium* Vol. 24 (ed.),
      Hans Küng, (New York 1967), pp. 16-23)

55   'The Ecumenical Spirit', *The Capuchin Annual*, 34(1967), pp.
      251-8

56   'The Problem of Original Sin', *The Clergy Review* 52(1967),
      pp. 770-86

1968

57   (ed.), *Ecumenical Studies: Baptism and Marriage*, (Dublin
     1968), pp. 240. Editor's 'Preface', pp. 9-22

58   (ed.), *John Wesley's Letter to a Roman Catholic*. (London-
     Belfast 1968), pp. 64. Editor's 'Preface', pp. 7-10;
     'Introduction', pp. 22-47

59   'The Problem of Baptism', *Ecumenical Studies: Baptism and
     Marriage*, pp. 23-60. (= No. 57)

60   'Christ and Divorce', *Ecumenical Studies: Baptism and
     Marriage*, pp. 220-40 (= No. 57)

61   'Mixed Marriages: The Canonical Form', *The Furrow* 19
     (1968), pp. 94-7 (=extract from Editor's Preface in No. 57)

62   (ed.), *John Wesley's Brev Till en Romersk Katolik*. Nya
     Bokforlags Aktiebolaget, Stockholm, 1968, pp. 72
     (=Swedish translation of No. 58)

63   'Church and World', *The Capuchin Annual* 35(1968), pp. 107-20

64   'Belief and Trust', *Doctrine and Life* 18(1968), pp. 461-4

1969

65   *Theology of Ecumenism* [Theology Today No. 9] (Cork 1969).

66   'Mixed Marriages: The Lund Principle', *One in Christ* 5
     (1969), pp. 96-102

67   'George Tyrrell: Some Post-Vatican II Impressions', *The
     Heythrop Journal* 10(1969), pp. 243-55

68   'The Sacrament of Unity: Intercommunion and some
     Forgotten Truths', *The Way* 9(1969), pp. 107-17

69   'The Practice of Ecumenism', *Hibernia* (31 Jan-13 Feb
     1969), p.6

1970

70   *Teologia dell' Ecumenismo* (Catania, Edizioni Paolini,
     1970), pp. 135 (=Italian Edition of No. 64)

71   (ed.), *Irish Anglicanism 1869-1969*. (Dublin 1970), pp. xi +
     236. Editor's 'Preface' pp. vii-xi

72   'The Picture', *Irish Anglicanism 1869-1969* (= No. 70), pp. 211-27

73   'Bibliography of Ecumenism', *The Irish Theological Quarterly* 37(1970), pp. 327-52

74   'Ecumenism: What and Why?,' *The Furrow* 21(1970), pp. 416-27

75   'Irish Ecumenism: Courtship to Engagement', *The Irish Press* 2 February, p. 11

76   'Papal Power a Hundred Years After', *The Church of Ireland Magazine*, (5 April 1970), pp. 1-5

1971

77   *L'Oecumenisme.* (Quebec, 1971), pp. 93 (= French edition of No. 64)

78   *Teología del Ecumenismo* (Mexico, 1971), pp. 127 (Spanish edition of No. 64)

79   'Christian Unity', *Intercom. A Bulletin of the Catholic Communications Institute of Ireland*, January 1971, p. 12

80   'The Irish School of Ecumenics', *One in Christ* 7(1971), pp. 66-9

81   'The Irish School of Ecumenics', *The Month* 3(1971), pp. 147-8
82   'Eucharistic Agreement', *The Sunday Press*, 19 September 1971.

1972

83   'The Irish School of Ecumenics', *The Capuchin Annual* 39(1972), pp. 77-80

84   'The Anglican-Roman Catholic Agreed Statement on Eucharistic Doctrine: A Comment', *The Furrow* 23 (1972), pp. 23-6

1973

85   'Interchurch Marriage', *One in Christ* 9(1973), pp. 35-42

86.   'Eucharist: Means and Expressions of Unity', *One in Christ* 9(1973), pp. 270-83

87   'Ecumenism and Common Worship', *One in Christ* 9(1973), pp. 354-63

88   'The Irish School of Ecumenics', *Intercom. A Bulletin of the Catholic Communications Institute of Ireland*, September 1973, p.6

89   'First Impressions: from Canterbury to Jerusalem?', *The Irish Times* 13 December 1973, p.7

1975

90   (ed.), 'Report on the International Consultation on Mixed Marriage, Dublin, 2-6 September 1974', *One in Christ* 11 (1975), pp. 88-96; *The Furrow* 26(1975), pp. 126-31; *Doctrine and Life* 25(1975), pp. 156-64; *Theology* 78(1975), pp. 75-82.

91   (ed.), *Beyond Tolerance: The Challenge of Mixed Marriage.* (London, 1975), pp. xi + 193. Editor's 'Introduction', ix-xi

1976

92   'New Directory on Ecumenism', *The Furrow* 27(1976), pp. 491-3

93   'Salvation Today and Wesley Today', *The Place of Wesley in the Christian Tradition*, (ed.), Kenneth E. Rowe (Metuchen, 1976), pp. 94-116

1977

94   'Ireland's Ecumenics School', *The Word*, January 1977, pp. 11-14

1978

95   'Baptism in Ecumenical Perspective', *One in Christ* 14 (1978), pp.106-23

96   'Ecumenism, Ecumenical Theology and Ecumenics', *Irish Theological Quarterly* 45(1978), pp. 132-9

97   'Berkeley and Methodism: A New Letter', *Berkeley Newsletter*, Trinity College, Dublin No. 2 (November 1978), pp. 1-2

1979

98   'The Scandal of Disunity', *The Furrow* 30(1979), pp. 40-4

99   'Baptism in Ecumenical Perspective', *Foundations. A Baptist Journal of Theology and History* 22(1979), pp. 218-32 (Reprint of No. 95)

1980

100   'A Decade of Ecumenism', *Doctrine and Life* 30(1980), pp.
       21-7

101   'Human Rights Within the Church', *The Furrow* 31
       (1980), pp. 44-6

1981

102   'Christian Spring in China', *The Tablet*, 23 May 1981, pp.
       493-5.

103   'An Ecumenist on Mount Athos', *The Irish Times Weekend
       Supplement*, January 1981, p. 11

1983

104   'Christian Unity by 2000?', *One in Christ* 19 (January
       1983), pp. 2-13

105   'Two Decades of Ecumenism', *Doctrine and Life*, (September
       1983), pp. 399-414

106   'George Tyrrell: Some post-ARCIC Impressions', *One in
       Christ* 19/3 (1983), pp. 250-4

1984

107   'Peace-Making in Lent', *Doctrine and Life*, (March 1984,) pp.
       132-6

108   'Reconciliation in Northern Ireland: The Contribution of
       Ecumenism', *Studies* 73 (Winter 1984), pp. 300-8

1985

109   '20 Years after Vatican II: Ecumenism: Time for the
       Breakthrough', *The Month*, (April 1985), pp. 126-8

1986

110   'The Eucharist in the Columbanus Community', *Religious
       Life Review*, 25 (March-April 1986), pp. 90-9

111   'The Spirit of Forgiveness', *Pace* 18/1 (Spring 1986), pp. 9-10

112   'Ecumenism and Politics', *The Newman Review*, (Spring 1986), pp. 37-40

1987

113   'Reconciliation in Northern Ireland', *The Furrow* 38 (January 1987), pp. 9-16

114   'I Thirst: A Good Friday Meditation', *Religious Life Review* 26(March-April 1987), pp. 85-9

115   'Reconciliation in Northern Ireland: The Contribution of the Churches', *Reconciliation in Northern Ireland* [Papers of the Social Study Conference 1986], pp. 69-78

116   'Northern Ireland: A Challenge to Theology', *Northern Ireland A Challenge to Theology*, Centre for Theology and Public Issues, University of Edinburgh [Occasional Papers No.12], pp. 20-8

1989

117   'Goings and Comings', *Search* 12/2 (Winter 1989), pp. 53-7

1991

118   'Ecumenism: The Forgotten Dimensions', *The Month* (Sept-Oct 1991), pp 453-5

119   'Ecumenists: Missionaries with a Difference', *AMDG* 1991, pp. 53-4

1992

120   'The Way Forward', *Pace* 24/1 (Summer 1992), pp.19-21

121   'Jesuits and the Protestants Today', *Studies* (Summer 1992), pp. 203-11

122   'George Otto Simms, (1910-1991), *Studies* (Summer 1992), pp. 212-6

123   'Trinity College Dublin 1592-1992: Reflections of a Jesuit Ecumenist', *Studies*, (Winter 1992), pp. 399-407

The Contributors

JOSÉ MÍGUEZ BONINO is Professor of Theology, Instituto Estudios Teologicos, Buenos Aires.

JOHN A. BOSSY is Professor of History, University of York.

ROBIN BOYD is a former Director, Irish School of Ecumenics.

EMILIO CASTRO was, until January 1993, General Secretary, World Council of Churches.

GABRIEL DALY is a lecturer in theology, Trinity College, Dublin.

R. F. G. HOLMES is Principal, Union Theological College, Belfast.

PATRICK KELLY is an historian and Dean of Arts (Humanities), Trinity College, Dublin.

JOHN D'ARCY MAY is a lecturer in theology, Irish School of Ecumenics.

CHRISTOPHER O'DONNELL is a lecturer in theology, Milltown Institute, Dublin.

OLIVER RAFFERTY is a research student at Christ Church, Oxford.

FRANKLIN SHERMAN is Director, Institute for Jewish Christian Understanding, Muhlenberg College, Pennsylvania.

FRANK SULLIVAN is Professor of Theology, Gregorian University, Rome.

MARY TANNER is Secretary, Board for Mission and Unity, General Synod of the Church of England.

GEOFFREY WAINWRIGHT is Professor of Systematic Theology, Duke University, North Carolina.

EDWARD YARNOLD is a research lecturer in theology, Oxford University, and tutor at Campion Hall, Oxford.